THE
HOLE Is MORE than
the SUM of the PUTTS

Ultimate Golf Quotations

COMPILED BY COLIN M. JARMAN

CB
CONTEMPORARY BOOKS

Library of Congress Cataloging-in-Publication Data

The hole is more than the sum of the putts : ultimate golf quotations
/ complied by Colin M. Jarman.
p.   cm.
Includes index.
ISBN 0-8092-2683-9
1. Golf—Quotations, maxims, etc.   2. Golf—Humor.
I. Jarman, Colin, 1958–   .
GV967.H53   1999
796.352—dc21   98-41997
                                          CIP

Interior design by Impressions Book & Journal Services
Interior illustrations by Dan Krovatin

Published by Contemporary Books
A division of NTC/Contemporary Publishing Group, Inc.
4255 West Touhy Avenue, Lincolnwood (Chicago), Illinois
60646-1975 U.S.A.
Copyright © 1999 by Colin M. Jarman
Printed in the United States of America
International Standard Book Number: 0-8092-2683-9
99 00 01 02 03 04 LB 18 17 16 15 14 13 12 11 10 9 8 7 6 5 4 3 2 1

To anyone who has struggled, uncomplaining, round a golf course in my company ... searching beyond the call of duty for my lost golf balls (for there have been many). I thank you all, and please ask you to remember that ...

**Golf is a game in which rabbits
can aspire to be Tigers. Grrrr!**

Colin M. Jarman

CONTENTS

The sport's best medium is not television, radio, or the eye.
Even more than baseball, it's the sport of *words*.
Thomas Boswell

The humor of golf is a divine comedy in the deepest sense.
Like all sources of laughter it lies in contrast and paradox;
in the thought of otherwise grave men gravely devoting
hours and money to a technique which so often they,
apparently alone, do not know they can never master.
The solemnity of their eternal failure is vastly comic.
The perpetualness of their hope is nobly humorous.
R. C. Robertson-Glasgow

It is necessary to invent quotes more and more
these days because professional golfers are gradually losing
the power of speech. Already adverbs have been eliminated
entirely from their vocabulary. "I hit the ball super
but putted just horrible."
Peter Dobereiner

AUTHOR'S
FOUR-WOOD

Giving this book the title of "Ultimate" is a surefire guarantee that someone somewhere will scream, "He hasn't included what Arnie said about Jack, or that one about Sam Snead's hat, or ..." Just as there are an infinite number of ways to play any hole in golf, so there is an almost limitless supply of quotes about golf. This Ultimate Volume attempts to bring together as representative a collection of as much golfing verbalization as I can cram into this many pages. Just as a golfer is restricted to fourteen clubs in the bag, I am restricted to ten chapters.

To carry on the analogy, just as every golfer can choose from a wide selection of golfing brands and makes, I have also had a choice in how to fill the pages of this book. Since the underlying theme is humor, the result is a reflection of my personal taste and judgment. To me, humor can be an off-the-cuff quip, as subtle as a Lee Trevino chip shot, or a devastating one-liner with the side-splitting strike power of a John Daly tee shot. Within these pages you will find humorous quotes that are the playing equivalent of a Sarazen four-wood, a Mickelson lob-wedge, a Player bunker shot, a Palmer hitch-and-rip, even a Ballesteros hook and the Armour yips.

DEM JONES

Will the real R. Jones please stand up?

In researching this book to bring the reader the widest selection of golf quotations, I have had trouble in, literally, keeping up with the Joneses. And it seems so have a number of other sources. Coming across the name R. Jones is the bane of every golf quote collector. At my last count, there are six men who lay claim to that title (and there are probably more I have yet to stumble across):

Robert Tyre Jones Jr. a.k.a. Bobby Jones, Robert Tyre Jones Jr. II, Robert Tyre Jones Jr. III, Robert Trent Jones, and Robert Trent Jones Jr., not to forget Rees Jones.

So, if during the course of this book, I have erroneously ascribed a quote to the wrong R. Jones, I extend my sincere apologies now. All I can offer in return is the following thought, for those as confused as I:

The Tyre Jones is connected to the Bobby Jones, but the Bobby Jones is not connected to the Trent Jones, and the Trent Jones is not connected to the Rees Jones...
Dem Jones, dem Jones, dem R. Jones...

IN THE BEGINNING…

**The game of golf was not invented;
it happened.**
John Morgan, Golf (1976)

Golf was invented a billion years ago! Don't you remember it?
Old Scottish saying

Remember, this game was invented by the same people who
think good music comes from bagpipes.
Sign at a Chicagoland golf course

When that pre-historic Dutchman—or was he a Dane?—
carried his kolb or club over to Leith in a smack laden with
ankers of Schiedam, he little dreamt that he was draining the
life-blood of his land and sprinkling its life-giving drops over
the links of North Britain. The wildest dreams never forecast
the numbers or the prowess of the stalwart men and lissome
girls who now honor that Dutchman's memory and drive the
wild erratic guttie over the shining reaches by the sea.
W. F. Collier (1890)

Back in the misty distance of the Middle Ages, two anonymous Scotsmen (or possibly Dutchmen) got together one quiet Saturday morning, and one said to the other, "Tell you what, Angus (or possibly Hans), why don't we make some clubs and balls and belt them about the countryside, down by the beach? Since I am bigger and stronger than you, I'll give you two up a side for a five-shilling (or possibly guilders) Nassau, plus skins and automatic presses."

    Peter Dobereiner, Golf World *(1977)*

Golf may have been invented by Scottish shepherds with too much time on their hands about a thousand years ago, but it's been an American game ever since Bobby Jones crossed the big water in the 1920s and showed everybody how to play.

    Glen Waggoner, Divots, Shanks, Gimmes, Mulligans ... *(1993)*

If you believe in reincarnation, I was probably a Scotsman 250 years ago.

    Lee Trevino

Golf was named by drunken Scots after listening to barking dogs.

    Jim Bishop (1970)

People have been playing golf for over three hundred years longer than they've been playing the piano.

    Charles Price

In answer to the question "When did golf begin?"—Arnold Palmer invented it about eight years ago in a little town outside Pittsburgh.

    Frank Hannigan, USPGA Journal *(1964)*

I've never understood why so many countries want to claim credit for inventing golf. I can tell you the Irish have always denied all knowledge of anything like that.

    David Feherty

GENERAL
(A–Z)

ADVICE

Golf, more than most games, has a
number of clichés, often successfully
disguised as "tips." Watch out!
Kathy Whitworth

The first thing I learned was to swing hard and never mind
where it went.
Jack Nicklaus

Take it easily and lazily, because the golf ball isn't going to
run away from you while you're swinging.
Sam Snead, How to Play Golf *(1946)*

Be decisive. A wrong decision is generally less disastrous than
indecision.
Bernhard Langer

Keep on hitting it straight until the wee ball goes in the hole.
>   *James Braid*

Play each shot as if it's the first shot you're ever going to play. The tournament starts on the next shot you play.
>   *Greg Norman*

A golf ball is like a clock. Always hit it at 6 o'clock and make it go toward 12 o'clock. Just be sure you're in the same time zone.
>   *Chi Chi Rodriguez*

If you need a par, go for a birdie, because if you don't get the birdie, you should hopefully get the par.
>   *Nick Faldo*

Golf tips are like aspirin. One may do you good, but if you swallow the whole bottle, you will be lucky to survive.
>   *Harvey Penick*

Play the shot you can play the best, not the shot that would look the best if you could pull it off.
>   *Harvey Penick,* The Game for a Lifetime *(1996)*

One thing that's always available on a golf course is advice. If you play like I do, you think everybody knows something you don't know. If I see a bird fly over, I think he's going to tell me something.
>   *Buddy Hackett*

One of the best lessons in golf is to take what you can get.
>   *Jim Litke*

When I started having problems with my game, I got hundreds of letters offering me various remedies. One guy even sent me videos of war films to remind me how great it is to be British.

Sandy Lyle

Some of the things I didn't have to be taught as a rookie traveling pro were to keep close count of my nickels and dimes, stay away from whiskey, and never concede a putt.

Sam Snead, The Education of a Golfer *(1962)*

Never concede a chip shot.

Henry Beard, A Duffer's Dictionary *(1987)*

Never try to keep more than three hundred separate thoughts in your mind during your swing.

Henry Beard, Mulligan's Laws *(1994)*

Never wash your ball on the tee of a water hole.

Henry Beard, Mulligan's Laws *(1994)*

Never break your putter and your driver in the same round, or you're dead.

Tommy Bolt

Anytime you get the urge to golf, instead take eighteen minutes and beat your head against a good solid wall. This is guaranteed to duplicate to a tee the physical and emotional beating you would have suffered playing a round of golf. If eighteen minutes aren't enough, go for twenty-seven or thirty-six ... whatever feels right.

Mark Oman

Don't play too much golf. Two rounds a day are plenty.
> *Harry Vardon*

People are always telling me I should do one thing or another. I should change my grip or shorten my swing. I should practice more and goof around less. I shouldn't smile on Sunday—I should—I shouldn't—I should—I shouldn't. Frankly, I don't know why they worry. It's my life ... and I don't worry.
> *Fred Couples*

Telegram advice to Arnold Palmer—I understand you have a weight problem. As you know, I have kept my weight exactly the same for years. I will be glad to send you my diet.
> *Jackie Gleason*

Two pieces of advice given to Lanny Wadkins—
1. Always have your clubs with you when you go to play.
2. And take different routes to your bank because someone may be following you.
> *Claude Harmon*

Imagine the ball has little legs, and chop them off.
> *Henry Cotton*

Go play golf. Go to the golf course. Hit the ball. Find the ball. Repeat until the ball is in the hole. Have fun. The End.
> *Chuck Hogan*

Advice given to Nick Faldo—What you have to do is shoot the lowest score.
> *Ben Hogan*

Learn the fundamentals of the game and stick to them. Band-Aid remedies never last.
> *Jack Nicklaus*

Tee the ball high. Years of experience have shown me that air offers less resistance to dirt.

Jack Nicklaus (1977)

First, hit the ball. Second, find out where it went.

Tom Watson

I play off 18 and a guy who's off 17 starts telling me how to pronate my wrists, and how to address the ball, and whether I'm getting through it fast enough. That tends to piss me off.

Peter Cook

ANTI-GOLF

Golf is typical capitalist lunacy of upper-class Edwardian England.
George Bernard Shaw

One hundred years of experience had demonstrated that the game is temporary insanity practiced in a pasture.

Dave Kindred

Golf is cow-pasture pool.

O. K. Bavard

Playing golf is like chasing a quinine pill around a cow pasture.

Sir Winston Churchill

Golf is an ineffectual attempt to direct an uncontrollable sphere into an inaccessible hole with instruments ill-adapted to the purpose.

Sir Winston Churchill

Golf is hockey at the halt.
> *Arthur Marshall (1985)*

Golf is just the old-fashioned pool hall moved outdoors, but with no chairs around the walls.
> *Will Rogers*

I regard golf as an expensive way of playing marbles.
> *G. K. Chesterton*

Golf is the most useless outdoor game ever devised to waste time and try the spirit of man.
> *Westbrook Pegler*

All I've got against it is that it takes you so far from the club-house.
> *Eric Linklater,* Poet's Pub

What earthly good is golf? Life is stern and life is earnest. We live in a practical age. All around us we see foreign competition making itself unpleasant. And we spend our time playing golf! What do we get out of it? Is golf any use? That's what I'm asking you. Can you name me a single case where devotion to this pestilential pastime has done a man any practical good?
> *P. G. Wodehouse,* The Clicking of Cuthbert *(1922)*

By the time you get dressed, drive out there, play eighteen holes, and come home, you've blown seven hours. There are better things you can do with your time.
> *Richard M. Nixon*

I am a golfer. I have played for twenty years, but I have recently made a discovery. I hate it!

> *Rex Beach in* A New Way to Better Golf *(1932)*

Soccer is a simpleminded game for simple people; golf is merely an expensive way of leaving home.

> *Michael Parkinson,* Bats in the Pavilion *(1977)*

There are now more golf clubs in the world than Gideon Bibles, more golf balls than missionaries, and if every golfer in the world, male and female, were laid end to end, I, for one, would leave them there.

> *Michael Parkinson*

Golf is a game of such monumental stupidity that anyone with a brain more active than a cantaloupe has difficulty gearing down to its demands.

> *Peter Andrews*

Tell me honestly: Do you know anyone who truly likes to play golf? Oh, I suppose there are some people who derive pleasure from golf just as there are certain kinds of individuals who enjoy being snapped in the rib cage with knotted towels.

> *Peter Andrews*

Golf seems to me an arduous way to go for a walk; I'd prefer to take the dogs out.

> *Princess Anne of England*

On being asked if she would follow her father Greg and take up golf—No way! Golf's too boring.

> *Morgan-Leigh Norman*

APPEARANCE

There is no shape, no size of body, no
awkwardness nor ungainliness which puts
good golf beyond reach. There are good
golfers with spectacles, with one eye, with
one leg, even with one arm. In golf,
while there is life, there is hope.

Sir Walter Simpson

If you took me away from the golf tour, I'd be just another
pretty face, but I'd like to see Bo Derek after eighteen holes
in 100-degree weather. Those cornrows and beads would be
history.

Jan Stephenson (1982)

I like golf because you can be really terrible at it and still not
look much dorkier than anybody else.

Dave Barry

My goal is to play seventy-two holes someday without changing expression.

Jack Renner

On signing a $60,000 clothes deal with a Japanese company—
They like me in Japan. I'm small, yet I can hit the ball three
hundred yards.

Bernhard Langer (1985)

It doesn't bother me what ball I use, what color trousers I
wear, or what I ate the night before. How can that sort of
stuff have any effect on your game?

Greg Norman (1984)

On playing with Calvin Peete and Lee Trevino in the U.S. Open—Those nice white folks looked down the eighteenth fairway from the clubhouse windows and thought we were some kind of civil rights march stomping towards them. Or maybe they thought we had come to steal their hubcaps.

    Chi Chi Rodriguez

Golfers find it a very trying matter to turn at the waist, more particularly if they have a lot of waist to turn.

    Harry Vardon

I can't hit the ball more than two hundred yards. I have no butt. You need a butt if you're going to hit a golf ball.

    Dennis Quaid

AUTO-MOTIVE

**My car absolutely will not run
unless my golf clubs are in the trunk.**
Bruce Berlet (1984)

The difference between learning to play golf and learning to drive a car is that in golf you never hit anything.

    Anonymous

While in his early forties—I'm like a 1967 Cadillac. I've changed the engine twice, rolled back the odometer, and replaced the transmission. But now all the tires are going flat; it's time to put it in the junkyard.

    Lee Trevino

Reason for selling a Mercedes-Benz won in a tournament—It doesn't fit through the Wendy's drive-in.
> *Scott Hoch*

I have got a Ford Pantera, a Porsche Carrera, two BMWs, a Mercedes roadster, a De Tomaso Mangusta, another Porsche, another Mercedes, a station wagon, and a Jeep. I guess I'm a nut about cars. I've also got a one-iron. And if I ever broke that little one-iron, that'd be the death in the family.
> *Johnny Miller (1976)*

Resolve this thought in your mind ... Arnold Palmer might be the greatest golfer in the world, but he probably doesn't know a carburetor from a tailpipe.
> *Dan Jenkins,* Golf Digest *(1979)*

After driving two balls into a nearby parking lot—Well, that's full. Let's see if I can park this baby someplace else.
> *JoAnne Carner*

BETTING

**Gambling is part of the game.
It always has been and it always will be.**
Paul Azinger

The second worst thing in the world is betting on a golf game and losing. The worst is not betting at all.
> *Anonymous*

Never bet with anyone you meet on the first tee who has a deep suntan, a one-iron in his bag, and squinty eyes.

Dave Marr

A man's true colors will surface quicker in a five-dollar Nassau than in any other form of peacetime diversion I can name.

Grantland Rice

If golf is basically a test of nerve, a two-dollar Nassau is essentially a concentration aid.

Tom Callahan

The more competent a player, the smaller the stake that contents him. It is only when you get down into the submerged tenth of the golfing world that you find the big gambling.

P. G. Wodehouse

They play for big bucks at private clubs, too, but there's a difference. They can afford to lose.

Hale Irwin (1984)

BUYING POWER

**You can't go into a shop
and buy a good game of golf.**
Sam Snead

To Henry Ford II—You can buy a country, but you can't buy a golf swing. It's not on the shelf.

Gene Sarazen

Never buy a putter until you've had a chance to throw it.
Henry Beard, Mulligan's Laws *(1993)*

The grip: Get a firm grip on your credit cards; otherwise you will have to buy all the drinks and lunch. Rich guys never pay for shit.
Dan Jenkins

On what he might spend his prize money from winning the 1968 U.S. Open—I may buy the Alamo and give it back to Mexico.
Lee Trevino

[After seeing the Alamo, Trevino quickly changed his mind: "I'm not going to buy this place; it doesn't even have any inside plumbing!"]

Guys from Texas and Florida usually are good wind players. Californians? We're good at buying Mercedes and ordering dinner at expensive restaurants.
Gary McCord (1984)

COACHING

Tutorage under a competent instructor is worth much more than the slight remuneration you will pay him.
Sam Snead

I've never been to a coach in my life. When I find one who can beat me, then I'll listen.
Lee Trevino

There has been criticism that some professional golfers do not know how to teach. In defense of my competent colleagues in professional golf, I must point out that many pupils don't know how to take a lesson.

Tommy Armour

I like teaching people how to play the game properly. It's very rewarding to see instant improvement. I just wish I could teach myself sometimes, but that's harder.

Sandy Lyle

When I look back on my career, I was really lucky. I learned to play from Byron Nelson and Ben Hogan, which is like learning to paint from Michelangelo and Leonardo. How's it get better than that?

Ken Venturi

The practice ground is an evil place. It's full of so-called coaches waiting to pounce. You can see them waiting to dish out their mumbo jumbo. To hell with coaches.

Ernie Els

DIVORCE

After he had won the Million Dollar Challenge in South Africa—I asked my wife if she wanted a Versace dress, diamonds, or pearls as a present, and she said, "No!" When I asked her what she did want, she said a divorce, but I told her I wasn't intending to spend that much.

Nick Faldo (1995)

What you have when you play twenty Senior events and
make about fifteen regular tour stops is divorce.
  Miller Barber

The newspapers tell us that in America women seek divorces
because their husbands go off and play golf without them. The
crying need of English womanhood is some redress against the
husbands who force their wives to play golf with them.
  A. P. Herbert, The Man About Town *(1923)*

*After she divorced and later remarried her golfing husband
Bill*—We took a mulligan.
  Cheryl Kratzert (1981)

On his trusty putter—It's a marriage. If I had to choose
between my wife and my putter ... well, I'd miss her.
  Gary Player

DRUGS

**Our guess is that the inventor of
scopolamine, the truth-forcing drug,
grew weary of listening to golf scores.**
Colorado Springs Gazette

*After the announcement that Japan's S. Maruyama was avail-
able in the British Open Press Center*—What? Marijuana available for the press? I know the R&A are making some changes,
but this is ridiculous.
  Anonymous photographer (1998)

Golf is the equivalent of crack for middle-aged white men.
Mike Barnicle, columnist

A nonchemical hallucinogen, golf breaks down the human
body into components so strangely elongated and so tenu-
ously linked, yet with anxious little bunches of hypercon-
sciousness and undue effort bulging here and there, along
with rotating blind patches and a sort of cartilaginous eupho-
ria—golf so transforms one's somatic sense, in short, that
truth itself seems about to break through the exacerbated
and, as it were, debunked fabric of mundane reality.
John Updike

When Jack Nicklaus told me I was playing Seve Ballesteros
[in the Ryder Cup singles], I took so many pills that I was
glad they didn't have drug tests for golfers.
Fuzzy Zoeller (1983)

The chances of the PGA Tour developing a drug problem are
about the same as Gary Player and Tom Watson sharing a
cabin on the *Love Boat*.
Deane Beman (1974)

To what degree are you able to absorb the anxiety and pressure of this thing called the PGA Tour? They have pills that
can save you from absorbing radioactive isotopes. Perhaps
they can develop a pill to protect us from the radioactivity of
the tour.
Mac O'Grady, Sports Illustrated *(1984)*

After receiving treatment for an on-course snakebite—I'm so full
of dope that if you stand around me with a headache ... it'd
go away.
David Feherty (1992)

DYING FOR A GAME

**Golf is not a funeral,
though both can be very sad affairs.**
Bernard Darwin

Old golfers never die ... they simply lose their drive.
Anonymous

Old golfers never die ... they simply putter away.
Anonymous

Old golfers don't die ... we just lose our distance.
Ralph Gudahl

Old golfers never die ... they merely lose their grip.
Colin M. Jarman (1999)

Old golfers never die ... they become USGA officials.
Colin M. Jarman (1999)

Old caddies never die ... they just have irons in other fires.
Colin M. Jarman (1999)

Old greenskeepers never die ... they merely go to seed.
Colin M. Jarman (1999)

Every round I play, I shorten my life by two years.
Tommy Nakajima

After lightning had postponed play in the 1983 Masters—We don't want to get anybody killed. Of course, if we could pick which ones, it might be a different story.

   Hord Hardin (1983)

After being hit by lightning—My whole life flashed before me. I couldn't believe I had been that bad.

   Lee Trevino

Nothing compares to the thrill of hitting golf shots. That's it. That's all I want to do. I don't care about major titles. I don't care about publicity. I don't care if anybody remembers me or not. When I die, they can throw me in a pine box and forget me.

   Dave Hill (1970)

You can, legally, possibly hit and kill a fellow golfer with a ball, and there will not be a lot of trouble because the other golfers will refuse to stop and be witnesses because they will want to keep playing.

   Dave Barry

On learning that a radio station had reported his death—If that's true, I'm the first dead man to make six double bogeys on the back nine on the day of his funeral.

   Victor Mature (1982)

Sometimes I think the only way the Spanish people will recognize me is if I win the Grand Slam and then drop dead on the eighteenth green.

   Seve Ballesteros

After winning the Bobby Jones Award—I thought you had to be dead to win that.
   JoAnne Carner (1982)

EDUCATION

On his decision to leave college early—A college degree is not going to help you sink those two-footers.
   Johnny Miller

I didn't need to finish college to know what golf was all about. All you need to know is to hit the ball, find it, and hit it again until it disappears into the hole in the ground.
   Fuzzy Zoeller

The University of Houston, better known as the "University of Golf," where the gag goes, the entrance requirements are: a 64 on an accredited course and a sound short game.
   Jim Murray, The Best of Jim Murray *(1965)*

EXCLUSIVITY

There are clubs exclusively for the Jews and clubs where a Jew could only gain admittance if he arrived on the doorstep with Moshe Dayan at his side supported by a regiment of Israeli paratroopers.
   Michael Parkinson, Times *(London)*

I was twenty-five, and had spent my youth in a cloistered precinct of the middle class where golf was a rumored something, like champagne breakfasts and divorce, that the rich did.

John Updike, Golf Digest *(1984)*

On the pre–Tiger Woods fact that only two black pros were among the 239 PGA players —Professional golf is white. Lilywhite. White as freshly driven snow. White as Wonder bread. White as Cypress Point and Augusta National and Pine Valley and 99 $^{44}/_{100}$ percent of the other private golf clubs in America. White as a gallon of vanilla ice cream topped with a pinch of chocolate sprinkles.

Glen Waggoner, Divots, Shanks, Gimmes, Mulligans ... *(1993)*

EXERCISE

**That does look like very good exercise—
but what is the little ball for?**
Ulysses S. Grant

Golf is essentially an exercise in masochism conducted out of doors. . . . It is, at bottom, an elaborate and addictive rite calculated to drive them crazy for hours on end and send them straight to the whiskey bottle after that.

Paul O'Neil, Life *(1962)*

The biggest liar in the world is the golfer who claims that he plays the game merely for exercise.
> *Tommy Bolt*

Golf is a wonderful exercise. You can stand on your feet for hours, watching somebody else putt.
> *Will Rogers*

Golf is not just exercise; it is an adventure, a romance, a Shakespeare play in which disaster and comedy are intertwined and you have to live the consequences of each action.
> *Harold Segall*

Exercise? I get it on a golf course. When I see my friends collapse, I run for the paramedics.
> *Red Skelton*

FAIRWAY TO HEAVEN

Golf ... I came to regard as a holy exercise.
Alistair Cooke, Six Men *(1977)*

Golf is the Lord's punishment for man's sins.
> *James Reston*

God must have been a 2-handicapper from Augusta.
> *Dan Jenkins*

God won't stop me entering the kingdom of heaven just because I play sport on a Sunday.
  Gary Player

I'm gambling that when we get into the next life, Saint Peter will look at us and ask, "Golfer?" And when we nod, he will step aside and say, "Go right in; you've suffered enough." One warning, if you do go in and the first thing you see is a par 3 surrounded by water, it ain't heaven.
  Jim Murray

If you call on God to improve the results of a shot while it is still in motion, you are using "an outside agency" and subject to appropriate penalties under the rules of golf.
  Henry Longhurst

On Michael Bonallack's lofted drive during the 1971 British Open—Don't catch it, Lord! It's two strokes.
  Lee Trevino

On how to play through a lightning storm—Hold up a one-iron and walk. Not even God can hit a one-iron.
  Lee Trevino

If I'm on the course and lightning starts, I get inside fast. If God wants to play through, let him.
  Bob Hope

After a hailstorm fell in Texas—The next time the Almighty plays my course, I wish He would fix His ball marks on my greens.
  Jack Marin (1973)

I just hope I don't have to explain all the times I've used His name in vain when I get up there.

Bob Hope

God listens to me everywhere—except on the golf course.

Billy Graham

The determining bulk of Scottish people had heard of Golf, as they had heard of God, and often regarded the two of equal importance.

G. K. Chesterton

On a tournament-winning burst of five birdies in the final nine holes—God knew I couldn't putt, so He put me close to the hole.

Barbara Burrow

On his putting success—All I can do is start it. The Lord handles it from there.

Jimmy Demaret

If God had intended a round of golf to take more than three hours, He would not have invented Sunday lunch.

Jimmy Hill

Golf may be played on Sunday, not being a game within the view of the law, but being a form of moral effort.

Stephen Leacock, Other Fancies

Try to remember that a person may be a most indifferent golfer, and yet be a good Christian gentleman, and in some respects worthy of your esteem.

    Horace G. Hutchinson, Hints on the Game of Golf *(1886)*

After missing another short putt—So, it's me again, huh, Lord!? Why don't you just come down here and we'll play. And bring that kid of yours. I'll play you best ball.

    Tommy Bolt

No just and merciful God would demand as the price of salvation that we all learn to hit a one-iron.

    Charles P. Pierce

Statisticians estimate that crime among good golfers is lower than in any class of the community except possibly bishops.

    P. G. Wodehouse

Golf courses are the best places to observe ministers because none of them are above cheating a bit.

    John D. Rockefeller Sr.

But since I cannot play at golf
Unless I swear a wee,
I'll give it up. "What golf?" they cried.
Nae, mon—the ministry.

    Scottish rhyme

Only religious ceremonies proceed with more respect than the major golf tournaments in this country.

    Jimmy Cannon, Nobody Asked Me, But... *(1978)*

If you think of the Garden of Eden as a golf course, then the snake becomes a two-iron, and the apple a golf ball. It would explain a lot.

Glen Waggoner

Any golfer can be devout on a rainy Sunday.

Anonymous

FAMILY TIES

**A golf club is the extension of one's home;
the selection of members is purely a domestic
matter.**
W. G. L. Folkard

Everybody in my family is talented. My father, my mother, my brother, my sister Mary. She shot J. R. Gosh! I had to win the Amateur.

Nathaniel Crosby (1981)

The average suburbanite either putters around the house or the golf course.

Anonymous

I found a sponsor for my first year as a professional. But since then, I have also found a wife, a child, and a mortgage.

David Curry (1989)

His handicap was down to 12. But these things are not all. A golfer needs a loving wife, to whom he can describe the day's play through the long evenings.

P. G. Wodehouse

FOOD

**A man must be fed to play golf.
It is ill going golfing on an empty interior.**
Horace G. Hutchinson

I'd probably be the fat lady in a circus right now if it hadn't been for golf. It kept me on the course and out of the refrigerator.

Kathy Whitworth (1982)

The golfer finds that turkey day
Is not all that enticing.
Although I've put my clubs away,
It's one more chance for slicing.

Dick Emmons

I've heard the winner of the Masters hosts the dinner. If I ever won it, there would be no suits, no ties, and McDonald's.

John Daly

I'm not saying my golf game went bad, but if I grew tomatoes, they'd come up sliced.

Miller Barber

Hitting a golf ball correctly is the most sophisticated and complicated maneuver in all of sport, with the possible exception of eating a hot dog at a ball game without getting mustard on your shirt.

Ray Fitzgerald, Golf Digest *(1981)*

I'm a hot-dog pro. That's when someone in the gallery looks at his pairing sheet and says, "Here comes Joe Baloney, Sam Sausage, and Chi Chi Rodriguez. Let's go get a hot dog."

Chi Chi Rodriguez (1964)

After Nabisco withdrew its tour sponsorship—I just hope we can still get Oreos and Fig Newtons at the turn.

Paul Azinger

On taking vitamin supplements—I take a lot of Bs and Cs.... And I take bonemeal. That's for when I play like a dog.

Mary Dwyer (1981)

I've got a different idea about tempo. The key is a big, big breakfast—lots of pancakes, sausages, and eggs. I get all that breakfast in me, and I get real slowed down, and that helps me have a slower and smoother tempo.

Tim Herron (1996)

On his choice of carrying peanut butter sandwiches—Did you ever smell your golf bag after you carried a tuna sandwich around in the hot sun?

Al Geiberger (1978)

FRIENDS & ENEMIES

**The friends you make on the golf course
are the friends you make for life.**
Jessica Valentine

I play with friends, but we don't play friendly games.
Ben Hogan

The pat on the back, the arm around the shoulder, the praise
for what was done right, and the sympathetic nod for what
wasn't are as much a part of golf as life itself.
Gerald Ford

I guess there is nothing that will get your mind off everything
like golf will. I have never been depressed enough to take up
the game, but they say you get so sore at yourself that you
forget to hate your enemies.
Will Rogers

Remember they were friends. For years they had shared each
other's sorrows, joys, and golf balls, and sliced into the same
bunkers.
P. G. Wodehouse, A Woman Is Only a Woman *(1919)*

I wouldn't hurt a chicken crossing the road, but if I got a
man in trouble on a golf course, I'd kick the hell out of him.
I don't care if he's my best friend.
Sam Snead (1972)

I've seen lifelong friends drift apart over golf just because one could play better, but the other counted better.
Stephen Leacock

It's easy to be liked if you are 100th on the money list. You may have to worry about making ends meet, but everyone loves you.
Amy Alcott (1984)

FURRY CREATURES?
(NOT THE CLUB-COVER VARIETY)

The game is like a horse:
if you take your eye off it, it'll jump
back and kick your shins for you.
Byron Nelson

On the lack of caddies in post-WWI Britain—I expect to see dogs used universally in the future. With a dog as your caddie, there is no one to hear you swear and no one to make fun of your play.
Anonymous Labrador owner (1914)

There are two things not long for this world—dogs that chase cars and pro golfers who chip for pars.
Lee Trevino

[Also quoted as: "... putt for pars."]

Dogs on a golf course, like education, the death penalty, contraception, and women wearing trousers in the dining room, is an issue that divides.

"Laddie" Lucas

Dividing the swing into its parts is like dissecting a cat. You'll have blood and guts and bones all over the place. But, you won't have a cat.

Ernest Jones

I am so tense at times that I can hear the bees farting.

Mick O'Loughlin (1938)

On his first impressions of the U.S. Tour—I saw a coyote and a roadrunner, and I half expected to see Bugs Bunny.

David Feherty

His reason for a twenty-yard drive during the European Open at Sunningdale—Just as I was starting my downswing, a worm popped up right behind my ball, and I tried my best to miss it. That's why I hit the shot I did.

Greg Norman

Refuting alligator-wrestling rumors—The alligator was nothing big. I just saw a little five-foot alligator once near a water hole in Florida and flipped it over by its tail. That's easy. But the guy I was playing with made it sound like I wrestled with it.

Andy Bean (1978)

On the Sawgrass alligator—We call him Mr. Sawgrass, or sometimes Sir. But like everyone else here, he doesn't spend a great deal of time on the fairways.

Jim Blanks (1977)

Once when I was golfing in Georgia, I hooked a ball into the swamp. I went in after it and found an alligator wearing a shirt with a picture of a little golfer on it.

Buddy Hackett, Golf and Other Lies *(1968)*

*On the waterlogged conditions at La Costa—*Can we duck hunt off the eighteenth green?

Dave Stockton (1993)

Any golfer whose ball hits a seagull shall be said to have scored a "birdie."

Frank Muir

*Before losing the 1991 U.S. Senior Open play-off to Jack Nicklaus—*It's the big bear against the little mouse from Puerto Rico.

Chi Chi Rodriguez

GAMES WITHOUT FRONTIERS

All games are silly, but golf, if you look at it dispassionately, goes to extremes.
Peter Alliss

Golf is the only "sport" where the object is to play as little as possible.

Charles G. McLoughlin

Golf is the most straightforward, honest competition in the world. There are no substitutes allowed; the game doesn't require a lot of officials. In a goldfish bowl it tests your physical and mental skills, your patience, and your perseverance, and you play in all conditions. You get lousy breaks, and good breaks, and you have to cope. It is almost life.

Deane Beman (1987)

"Golf," he replied, "was much too serious a matter to be called a sport."

John Pearson, James Bond: The Authorized Biography *(1973)*

On being a role model for young black athletes—I'd like to show them that you don't have to get banged up on a football field or be 7′3″ to make a living.

Calvin Peete

If you play a bad hand at bridge, people will snap at you and call you names and never invite you to their homes again. But if you dub at golf, you only arouse a storm of friendly laughter.

Dr. W. Beran Wolfe

That was always the plan. Tennis at twenty-five, skiing at thirty-five, and golf at fifty. I waited so late to take up golf because I wanted to feel the swing and the arc and feel the calmness inside. One minute it's all fear and loathing, but hit a couple of good shots and you're on top of the world. I've gone crazy over this game.

Jack Nicholson, Golf *magazine*

Golfers are the greatest worriers in the world of sports. In fast-action sports, like football, baseball, or tennis, there is little time to worry, compared to the time a golfer has on his hands between shots.

Billy Casper Jr.

In a team sport, you can go out and make your own breaks. You can make a tackle. You can jump up and block Julius Erving's shot. Sometimes it is hard. I can't go out and jump on Jack Nicklaus's back.

Andy North

Ask any athlete who has thrown a block, sunk a free throw, hit a curveball, and tried to play golf. Nine times out of ten, they'll tell you that nothing in sports is as scary as a seven-foot putt you have to make.

Dick Schaap

Golf is an invitation to hit further than anyone could ever hit a baseball and not have to run afterwards.

Nike advertisement (1996)

I'd do better if the ball were two feet off the ground and moving.

Stan Musial

Golf is the only sport where the ball doesn't move until you have hit it.

Ted Williams

To Ted Williams—If you hit a "foul ball" in golf, you have to go and play it.

Sam Snead

There are some fellows who can hit .300 in baseball every year, but you would never trade one of them for Mantle, who might hit the ball out of the park anytime he comes up. It's the same in golf. The consistent guys will make a good living, but they're not going to play the great rounds that make you remember them.

Mike Souchak

I like golf because when somebody tells the gallery to be quiet, they get quiet. Try that in baseball, and they get louder.

Mark McGwire

Golf tournaments are lonely. In baseball there's eight other guys to keep me company.

Walter Hagen

In baseball you hit your home run over the right-field fence, the left-field fence, the center-field fence. Nobody cares. In golf everything has got to be right over second base.

Ken Harrelson

Too bad there aren't any water hazards in baseball like there are in golf. We could lose all the balls and go home.

Lon Simmons (1981)

Baseball may be a game of inches, as they say, but golf is a game of millimeters.

Arnold Palmer

Baseball reveals character; golf exposes it.

Ernie Banks

The golf swing is among the most stressful and unnatural acts in sport, short of cheering for the Yankees.
> *Brad Faxon*

On how, as a baseball pitcher, he copes with a bad golf game—I tell myself that Jack Nicklaus probably has a lousy curveball.
> *Bob Walk*

Big-league baseball players are the worst. They swing with power, don't ask for advice, and invariably hit to all fields.
> *Tommy Bolt*

Baseball players quit playing and they take up golf. Football players quit, take up golf. What are we [golfers] supposed to take up when we quit?
> *George Archer*

If you drop the pass in football, or miss the shot in basket-ball, or strike out in baseball, everybody knows it. If you hit a bad shot in golf, you can always claim you know a shortcut.
> *Bob Hope*

In other games you get another chance. In baseball you get three cracks at it; in tennis you lose only one point. But in golf the loss of one shot has been responsible for the loss of heart.
> *Tommy Armour*

On the off-season golfing success of NFL *players*—They ought to be good. They play more golf than we do.
> *Fuzzy Zoeller*

It's a lot easier hitting a quarterback than a little white ball.
> *Charles "Bubba" Smith*

Golf lacks something for me. It would be better if once in a while someone came up from behind and tackled you just as you were hitting the ball.

Harold "Red" Grange

During the 1982 U.S. Open—I shot a Red Grange today ... 77. Somebody should have shot me. I looked like I needed a white cane.

Tom Watson

After a friend conceded a one-foot putt—Thanks, but you really shouldn't have done that. When I coached football and got down to the one-foot line, nobody ever said it was good.

Jess Neely

In football, some coaches have stated, "When you throw a pass, three things can happen: two of them are bad." In golf, there is no limit.

Marino Parascenzo

Basketball coaches who shoot par in the summer are the guys I want on my schedule in the winter.

Abe Lemons

The big difference in golf is that the course always shoots par.... In golf, I can go one-on-one with the golf course, but there's no defense for a bad shot.

Michael Jordan (1997)

Most of my dreams have come true, so when I get older—twenty-eight, twenty-nine, thirty—I don't want to be doing *young* man's things. I want to kick back and start playing golf.

Shaquille O'Neal (1998)

The worst thing about getting fired by the 76ers was having enough time to work on my golf game ... and finding out how bad it was.

Doug Moe

It's so ridiculous to see a golfer with a one-foot putt and everybody saying "ssshhh!" and not moving a muscle. Then we allow nineteen-year-old kids to face a game-deciding free throw with 17,000 people yelling.

Al McGuire

There's more tension in golf than in boxing because golfers bring it on themselves. It's silly, really, because it's not as if the golf ball is going to jump up and belt you on the whiskers, is it?

Henry Cooper

Golfers can survive slumps better than boxers. If [boxers] have a bad streak, they get knocked on their cans.

Tom Watson

Golf is like tennis. The game doesn't really start until the serve gets in.

Peter Thomson

Tennis players don't have to play in pro-ams. Can you imagine what John McEnroe and Ivan Lendl would say if they were asked to play a quick five-setter with a few of the guys from the local club the day before Wimbledon?

David Feherty

One point on which all golfers can immediately agree is that, whatever else golf may be, it is not a game. How much simpler life would be if it were just a game, like tennis.

> *Peter Dobereiner,* The Glorious World of Golf *(1973)*

I prefer golf to tennis; all tennis courts look alike.

> *Brad Dillman*

The difference between golf and tennis is that tennis is murder—you just want to kill the other player. Golf is suicide—you just want to kill yourself.

> *Anonymous*

In tennis, you seldom have a chance, once things get going, to get shaky. You're too busy running around like a racehorse. But in golf—hell, it makes me nervous just to talk about it. That little white ball just sits there. A man can beat himself before he ever swings at it.

> *Ellsworth Vines*

I am the Ilie Nastase of golf. If golf didn't have a player like me, it would be a dreary sport.

> *Tom Weiskopf*

Golf is a game of space, and America is a spacious land.... This largeness of scale, the epic earthworks that carve a winding green firmament beneath a firmament of cloudy blue, is one of the powerful charms that strikes a newcomer to golf, and that continues to entrance the duffer heavy with years. The tennis court is a cage by comparison, and the football field a mirthless gridiron.

> *John Updike*

If you use the decathlon as a test of athletic ability, I guess I was the world's best athlete in '76 when I won the Olympic Decathlon, but when I stand at a tee, I'm just another guy who can't hit straight.

    Bruce Jenner

One of the advantages of bowling over golf is you seldom lose a bowling ball.

    Don Carter

Like pool, golf is primarily a game of position. The professional pool player never takes one shot at a time. He organizes a series of shots in his mind to sink all the balls on the table. The key is to get a good "leave," or an ideal position for the next shot.

    Robert Trent Jones Jr.

Golf is a game that must always be uncertain. I don't believe that anyone will ever master it to the extent that several have mastered billiards or chess. If someone should do so, I think he would give it up—but that is a danger most of us would be willing to risk.

    Bobby Jones

Golf is the loneliest of games ... not excluding postal chess.

    Peter Dobereiner

It isn't really a game; it's an art. If it were a game, played at unreflective speed, such as hockey, you would use one club only. Most golfers carry fourteen for the same reason that a painter's easel can accommodate fourteen or more brushes: they are not too many for the delicate, varied, and agonizedly solitary and introspective making of strokes.

    Peter Black

Golf is the easiest sport to look foolish at. I mean, if I bat against Roger Clemens, I'll look foolish. But if I bat against someone of my equal ability, I might not look so bad. In golf, though, it looks so simple, and then you have to hit this stationary ball.

Wayne Gretzky, Golf Digest *(1998)*

In so many English sports, something flying or running has to be killed or injured; golf calls for no drop of blood from any living creature.

Henry Leach

Playing polo is like trying to play golf during an earthquake.

Sylvester Stallone (1990)

On his soccer career which included a number of major league teams—I've had more clubs than Arnold Palmer.

Tommy Mulroy (1982)

My golf game's gone off so much that when I went fishing a couple of weeks ago, my first cast missed the lake.

Ben Crenshaw (1977)

If you give a man a fish, he will eat for today.
If you teach him to fish, he'll understand why some people think golf is exciting.

The Angler's Credo

Golf is a game to be played between cricket and death.

Colin Ingleby-McKenzie

GOLF

Here's to the man with club in hand
Here's to the king of bogey land;
Here's to the clubs with outlandish names
And here's to *golf,* the game of games!
The Father Gander Golf Book *(1909)*

In prehistoric times, cavemen had a custom of beating the ground with clubs and uttering spine-chilling cries. Anthropologists call this a form of primitive self-expression. When modern men go through the same ritual, they call it "golf."
Herbert V. Prochnow

The fascinations of golf can only be learned by experience. It is difficult to explain them. It has its humorous and its serious side. It can be begun as soon as you can walk, and once begun it is continued as long as you can see.
Henry E. Howland, Scribner's *magazine (1895)*

Playing golf is a privilege, not a sentence.
Harvey Penick

This game is so elusive. You try to maintain the peaks and level up the valleys.
Tom Watson (1979)

In a gin'ral way, all I can say about it is it's a kind iv game iv ball that ye play with ye'er own worst inimy, which is ye'ersilf.
Finley Peter Dunne

I couldn't tell you exactly what I like about golf. Just when you think you've got it mastered, it lets you know you haven't. I'm just crazy enough to do it.
Clint Eastwood

My ball is in a bunch of fern,
A jolly place to be;
An angry man is close astern—
He waves his club at me.
Well, let him wave—the sky is blue;
Go on, old ball, we are but two—
We may be down in three,
Or nine—or ten—or twenty-five—
It matters not; to be alive
Is good enough for me.
A. P. Herbert, "Mullion," from Mild and Bitter *(1936)*

I would rather play golf and break even, than work hard and come out ahead.
Mike Donald

Undulation is the soul of golf.
H. N. Wethered

On a golf course, unlike films, when you are good and ready, you hit it. And when you have made a mess of it, there is absolutely nobody to blame but yourself, your own greed, and your own stupidity. To me it has a pure practical, quasi-religious quality about it. Ultimate total responsibility.
Guy Hamilton, James Bond film director (1973)

What other four hours' activity can chasten a magnate with so rich a variety of disappointments, or unman a lothario with so many rebuffed desires?
John Updike

The more you play it, the less you know about it.
> *Patty Berg (1937)*

That was the trouble with golf, I thought. Only a golfer could ever understand why anyone would play the stupid, f***ing game.
> *Dan Jenkins,* Dead Solid Perfect *(1974)*

GOLF IS . . .

Golf is to me what his Sabine farm was to the poet Horace—a solace and an inspiration.
> *Ramsay Macdonald*

Golf is like a grindstone: whether it grinds you down or polishes you up depends on what you're made of.
> *English saying*

Golf is a lot of walking . . . broken up by disappointment and bad arithmetic.
> *Anonymous*

Golf is life. If you can't take golf, you can't take life.
> *Anonymous*

They say golf is like life, but don't believe them. Golf is much more complicated than that.
> *Gardner Dickinson*

Golf is used by people of every color, race, creed, and temperament, in every climate. No recreation, apart from the simple contests of the river and field, has been so universal since the world began. There is no freemasonry like the freemasonry of golf. Our happy game has wound a bright cordon round the world, and so does she play her part in the great evolution of general contentment.

Henry Leach

Golf is an open exhibition of overwhelming ambition, courage deflated by stupidity, skill soured by a whiff of arrogance. These humiliations are the essence of golf.

Alistair Cooke

Golf is a puzzle without an answer.

Gary Player

Golf is sixty or seventy contestants over two hundred acres doing unpredictable things at improbable times. It's an eighteen-ring circus without a ringmaster.

Nick Seitz

GOLF IS A GAME . . .

Golf is a game of endless predicaments.
Chi Chi Rodriguez

Golf is the hardest game in the world. There's no way you can ever get it. Just when you think you do, the game jumps up and puts you into your place.

Ben Crenshaw

Golf is a fascinating game. It has taken me forty years to discover that I can't play it.
 Edward Ray

Golf is assuredly a mystifying game. Even the best golfers cannot step onto the first tee with any assurance as to what they are going to do.
 W. Timothy Gallwey

Golf ... is not a particularly natural game. Like sword-swallowing, it has to be learned.
 Brian Swarbrick, A Duffer's Guide to Bogey Golf *(1973)*

Golf is, in part, a game; but only in part. It is also in part a religion, a fever, a vice, a mirage, a frenzy, a fear, an abscess, a joy, a thrill, a pest, a disease, an uplift, a brooding, a melancholy, a dream of yesterday, and a hope for tomorrow.
 New York Tribune *(1916)*

Golf is a game with the soul of a 1956 Rotarian.
 Bill Mandel

Golf is a game even the masters don't master.
 John Updike

Golf is a game in which a ball (one and a half inches in diameter) is placed on a ball (eight thousand miles in diameter). The object being to hit the small ball ... but not the larger.
 John Cunningham

Golf is a game that is measured in yards, but the difference between a hit and a miss is calipered in millimeters.
 Tony Lema

Golf is a game of days. And I can beat anyone on my day.
  Fuzzy Zoeller

Golf is a game of motion and rhythm, not of position and mechanics.
  Martin Hall

Golf is a better game played downhill.
  Jack Nicklaus

Golf is the one game I know which becomes more and more difficult the longer one plays it.
  Bobby Jones

Golf is not a game you can rush. For every stroke you try to force out of her, she is going to extract two strokes in return.
  Dave Hill, Teed Off *(1977)*

HANDICAPS

**I never lied about my handicap.
I just let my opponents talk themselves into a
trap.**
Bobby Riggs, Court Hustler *(1973)*

H is for *Handicap*, sweeter than candy,
A cap that, when needed, comes in very handi.
  Richard Armour, Golf Is a Four-Letter Word *(1962)*

Handicap: A device for collective bargaining on the first tee.
Anonymous

Handicap: An allocation of strokes on one or more holes that permits two golfers of very different ability to do equally poorly on the same course.
Henry Beard, A Duffer's Dictionary *(1987)*

It is as easy to lower your handicap as it is to reduce your hat size.
Henry Beard, Mulligan's Laws *(1994)*

Real golfers have two handicaps: one for bragging and one for betting.
Anonymous

Wouldn't it be great if we all had a handicap we could actually play to?
Mike Purkey, Golf *magazine (1995)*

One of the troubles with a very high handicap is that the owner is either looked upon as a poor golfer or a possible cheat.
George Plimpton, The Bogey Man *(1968)*

Nothing goes down slower than a golf handicap.
Bobby Nichols, Never Say Never *(1965)*

As a broad general rule, the Scots and the Irish tend to nourish handicaps that are higher than their levels of skill; the English tend to brag about handicaps of single figures while being unable to break 90.
Peter Dobereiner

If just some of the principles that keep players out of trouble in their day-to-day affairs were applied to their golf game, their handicaps would drop drastically.

Greg Norman

If I only had taken up golf earlier and devoted my whole time to it instead of fooling about writing stories and things, I might have got my handicap down to under 18.

P. G. Wodehouse, The Golf Omnibus *(1973)*

HANDS

*Words of inspiration for Seve Ballesteros before he won the 1979 British Open—*You have the hands, now play with your heart.

Roberto de Vicenzo [translated from the Spanish]

All good players have good hands. And I'm afraid you have to be born with them.

Dave Stockton

I have stubby hands with short fingers. Actually my wife, Barbara, has stronger hands than mine from doing the dishes.

Jack Nicklaus

*When his daughter offered to do the dishes at home—*No, Nancy, those hands are meant for golf, not dishes.

Domingo Lopez

Wrists: In golfers, the swollen joint that connects a sore hand to an aching elbow and a painful shoulder.
    Henry Beard, A Duffer's Dictionary *(1987)*

God made what is called the lifeline in the right palm of a human being for one special reason … It fits perfectly against the left thumb in a good golf grip.
    Harvey Penick, And If You Play Golf, You're My Friend *(1993)*

God must watch over left-handers, because nobody else does.
    Furman Bisher, Atlanta Journal *(1984)*

On being asked to name the best left-handed golfer he'd ever seen—Never saw one worth a damn.
    Harry Vardon

Being left-handed is a big advantage. No one knows enough about your swing to mess you up with advice.
    Bob Charles (1973)

If God wanted you to putt cross-handed, he would have made your left arm longer.
    Lee Trevino

The cross-handed grip is used principally by left-handed golfers who have purchased right-handed clubs by mistake (or vice versa) and is too special for discussion here.
    Rex Lardner, Out of the Bunker and into the Trees *(1960)*

HEAD'S-UP PLAY?

**If everybody could learn to hold
his head still, there wouldn't be any golfers
around still trying to break 100.**
Arnold Palmer

If only I kept my eye on the ball,
Looking downward as does the pro there,
I might not see where it was going, at all,
But there might be a chance it would go there.
Richard Armour, Golf Is a Four-Letter Word *(1962)*

There's only two things in the world you gotta do with your
head down: golf and praying.
Lee Trevino

I never did see the sense in keeping my head down. The only
reason I play golf is to see where the ball goes.
Charles Price, Golfer-at-Large *(1982)*

In golf, you keep your head down and follow through. In the
vice presidency, you keep your head up and follow through.
It's a big difference.
Dan Quayle

The reason the pro tells you to keep your head down is so
you can't see him laughing.
Phyllis Diller

Nobody ever looked up and saw a good shot.
> *Don Herold,* Love That Golf *(1952)*

When you look up and cause an awful shot, you will always look down again at exactly the moment you ought to start watching the ball if you ever want to see it again.
> *Henry Beard*

Looking up is the biggest alibi ever invented to explain a terrible shot. By the time you look up, you've already made the mistake that caused the bad shot.
> *Harvey Penick,* Little Red Book *(1992)*

I played Civil War golf: I went out in 61 and came back in 65.
> *Henny Youngman*

Ferdinand Magellan went round the world in 1512 ... which isn't too many strokes when you consider the distance.
> *Joe Laurie Jr.*

IDIOTIC IDIOM

Golf is just a game and an idiotic one at that.
Mark Calcavecchia

Golf is a funny game. It's done much for health, and at the same time has ruined people by robbing them of their peace of mind. Look at me: I'm the healthiest idiot in the world.
> *Bob Hope*

The trouble with me is I think too much. I always said you have to be dumb to play good golf.

JoAnne Carner

Excessive golfing dwarfs the intellect. Nor is this to be wondered at when we consider that the more fatuously vacant the mind is, the better for play. It has been observed that absolute idiots play the steadiest.

Sir Walter Simpson, The Art of Golf *(1887)*

Next to the idiotic, the dull, unimaginative mind is the best for golf.

Sir Walter Simpson, The Art of Golf *(1887)*

On Greg Norman's proposed World Tour—I'm not smart enough to figure out if it's good for the game or not.

Fred Couples (1995)

INJURY

**The only way to get hurt
playing golf is to get struck by lightning.**
Ted Williams

It is ridiculous to suggest, as some people do, that golf is a dangerous game. I myself have only been struck three times this season.

W. T. Linskill (1900)

Everyone gets wounded in a game of golf. The trick is not to bleed.

Peter Dobereiner, London Observer *(1967)*

My injured elbow feels great. It must be the two hundred autographs I'm signing warming it up.

Nick Faldo (1998)

Save the cry of "Fore!" may not always come in time and that there are golfers whose rapturous practice swing is always liable to catch the unsuspecting the mother and father of an uppercut, golfers are not obviously exposed to physical danger.

Norman Mair

KID'S STUFF

Golf: a game in which you claim the privileges of age, and retain the playthings of childhood.

Dr. Samuel Johnson

On her husband Billy's sponsors and their eleven children—He'll represent several clothing firms as usual. I just wish one of them was Pampers.

Shirley Casper (1977)

I can't believe the actions of some of our top pros. They should have side jobs modeling for Pampers.
Fuzzy Zoeller

There's a little boy in all of us. The trick is knowing how to let that child come out.
Mac O'Grady

Golf appeals to the idiot in us and the child. Just how child-like golfers become is proven by their frequent inability to count past five.
John Updike

Golf, like the measles, should be caught young, for, if postponed to riper years, the results may be serious.
P. G. Wodehouse, A Mixed Threesome

On when to start teaching his children to play—When they have an attention span that they can take instruction: I've always defined that as when they can play three holes without chasing a frog, and that's about an hour.
Jack Nicklaus

When you're fourteen, fifteen, sixteen, that's the best time of all. You're always out on the golf course with your buddies trying to beat the sunset.
Andy North (1998)

I was so small as a kid, I got started in golf as a ball marker.
Chi Chi Rodriguez

LADIES' TEASE

**Constitutionally and physically
women are unfitted for golf. The first
women's championship will be the last. They
are bound to fall out and quarrel on the
slightest, or no, provocation.**

Horace G. Hutchinson (1893)

Golf to my mind is a game for the ladies to enjoy. I think that when it becomes a job, they have to want to win very badly, and as a result, they can become tough, even bitchy.

    Henry Cotton

Look like a woman, but play like a man.

    Jan Stephenson

If a woman can walk, she can play golf.

    Louise Suggs

Ladies' links should be laid out on the model, though on a smaller scale, of the "long round"; containing some short putting holes, some longer holes, admitting of a drive or two of 70–80 yards, and a few suitable hazards. We venture to suggest 70–80 yards as the average limit of a drive advisedly: not because we doubt a lady's power to make a longer drive, but because that cannot well be done without raising the club above the shoulder. The posture and gestures requisite for a full swing are not particularly graceful when the player is clad in female dress.

    Lord Wellwood, Golf

There are many things that hold a woman back in golf that are not common to the other popular sports—tennis and swimming. I know of no tennis clubs that bar women, and there are no restrictions at all on the use of the ocean.

Glenna Collett-Vare (1928)

"After all, golf is only a game," said Millicent.
Women say these things without thinking. It does not mean that there is a kink in their character. They simply don't realize what they are saying.

P. G. Wodehouse, The Clicking of Cuthbert *(1922)*

Golf humanizes women, humbles their haughty natures, tends, in short, to knock out of their systems a certain modicum of the superciliousness, that swank, which makes wooing a tough proposition for the diffident male.

P. G. Wodehouse

If I had my way, no man guilty of golf would be eligible to hold any office of trust or profit under these United States, and all female golfers would be shipped to the white-slave corrals of the Argentine.

Henry L. Mencken

Let us examine the proposition that women golfers are people. It requires an effort to adjust to this idea, for ever since the beheading of the first woman golfer, Mary, Queen of Scots, the golf world has openly regretted that the practice didn't start a trend.

Peter Dobereiner

When a woman swings the club, it sounds "whooooooosh, plop!" A good man player sounds "whizz, tok!" If you take a hard-boiled egg, remove the shell, and hurl it against a wall, you approximate the sound of a woman golfer's shot. A man's impact is harsher, crisper—more like a .22 caliber pistol being discharged in the next room.

> *Peter Dobereiner,* For the Love of Golf

Three things there are as unfathomable as they are fascinating to the masculine mind: metaphysics, golf, and the feminine heart.

> *Arnold Haultain (1908)*

Golf is a diabolical contrivance, but it is not so devilish as the woman scorned for a driving range.

> *Milton Gross,* Eighteen Holes in My Head *(1959)*

A pretty girl will always have the toughest time learning to play golf, because every man wants to give her lessons.

> *Harvey Penick*

After playing in the Australian Skins Game against three male opponents—It's just a one-off thing, a fun thing. There's no place for women on the men's tour, just like there's no place for men on the women's tour.

> *Laura Davies (1996)*

Time can run backwards if there's a woman on the course.

> *Henry Beard,* Mulligan's Laws *(1994)*

Aware of their long life expectancy, they play slowly, hunt for a ball for twenty minutes, and permutate their scores the way they figure out who has to pay for what after lunch at Schrafft's.

> *Rex Lardner,* Out of the Bunker and into the Trees *(1960)*

Women are handicapped by having boobs.
   Ben Wright, CBS TV (1995)

Golf is like an eighteen-year-old girl with big boobs. You
know it's wrong, but you can't keep away from her.
   Val Doonican

The reason I don't play golf is because I was a caddie when I
was thirteen. Women never gave up a ball that was lost somewhere in the trees and thicket and down through the poison
ivy. It was during one of these searches that I vowed to the
Lord above that if I ever earned enough money, I would
never set foot on a course again.
   Art Buchwald

There are two things that guys on tour do not like: playing in
the wind and me dating their sisters.
   Gary McCord

LEADING THE PACK

**The slums of Chicago are full
of first-round leaders.**
Jim Colbert

On leading the 1964 British Open—Class, someone once said,
is "the ability to undergo pressure with grace." So, what did I
do? I just did what comes naturally ... I vomited.
   Charles Price, Golfer-at-Large (1982)

I turn mean with a six-stroke lead. I'm not happy with a two-shot win. I want more. I want to demoralize them.

> *Johnny Miller*

On his intestinal fortitude while leading a tournament—My butterflies are still going strong. I just hope they are flying in formation.

> *Larry Mize*

On the advantage of leading a tournament rather than being a stroke back—Would you rather be broke or have money in the bank?

> *Ben Hogan*

It's always hard to sleep when you've got a big early lead. You just lie there and smile at the ceiling all night.

> *Dave Stockton*

LOSING

**I don't remember much about
the tournaments I lose.**
Jack Nicklaus (1987)

On being asked if losing was a disaster—It is, when it's a lovely spring afternoon and you don't have anything else planned.

> *Jack Nicklaus,* New York Times *(1978)*

No one remembers who came second.

> *Walter Hagen*

I am absolutely delighted to have come second. Who cares about winning when you can be second? I love being runner-up.

Tom Weiskopf (1978)

Win and they carry you to the clubhouse on their shoulders. Lose and you pay the caddie in the dark.

Gene Sarazen

Never have so many spent so much to sit in relative comfort to brag about their failures.

Keith Jackson

It is hard to enjoy a thrashing, but every good man is tested in the crucible of humiliation. Unfortunately in golf there are more times like this than others.

Chip Beck (1989)

Show me a man who is a good loser, and I'll show you a man who is playing golf with his boss.

Nebraska Smoke-Eater

Show me a good loser, and I'll show you a seldom winner.

Sam Snead

Golf is a game of getting used to failure.

David Duval (1997)

Once a golfing champion allows himself to suspect that playing a superb round is not the be-all and end-all of life, he is lost.

Anonymous

On being asked if his 1966 U.S. Open play-off loss was similar to two previous play-off losses in '62 and '63—Pretty similar ... I lost all three!

> *Arnold Palmer (1966)*

On relinquishing a halfway lead in the 1954 Masters as an amateur—I'm almost delighted I lost. I might have turned pro otherwise.

> *Billy Joe Patton*

On losing a six-stroke lead in the 1996 Masters—I'm disappointed, but I'm not going to run around like Dennis Rodman and head-butt somebody.

> *Greg Norman*

On finishing second in the 1983 U.S. Open, after lying 115th following her first round—I did something by climbing over 113 golfers. The only trouble is there were 114 ahead of me.

> *JoAnne Carner*

I'm a good loser. I've had more practice at it than anyone else.

> *David Feherty*

LUCKY CHARM

The mark of a champion is the ability to make the most of good luck and the best of the bad.

> *Anonymous*

The fourth hole found him four down, and one had the feeling that he was lucky not to be five.

> *P. G. Wodehouse,* Excelsior *(1950)*

On the golf course, a man may be *the dogged victim of inexorable fate*[*], be struck down by an appalling stroke of tragedy, become the hero of unbelievable melodrama or the clown in a side-splitting comedy. Any of these within a few hours, and all without having to bury a corpse or repair a tangled personality.

    Bobby Jones, The World of Golf

[*Title of a Dan Jenkins book: The Dogged Victims of Inexorable Fate*]*

There is a widely held belief among golfers who finish second in tournaments that they are tragic victims and have been swindled by the law firm of Destiny, Fate & Luck.

    Dan Jenkins, Fairways and Greens *(1994)*

The fundamental problem with golf is that every so often, no matter how lacking you may be in the essential virtues required of a steady player, the odds are that one day you will hit the ball straight, hard, and out of sight. This is the essential frustration of this excruciating sport. For, when you've done it once, you make the fundamental error of asking yourself why you can't do this all the time. The answer to this question is simple: the first time was a fluke.

    Colin Bowles

I do not remember having met a golfer who did not consider himself on the whole a remarkably unlucky one.

    Horace G. Hutchinson, Hints on the Game of Golf *(1886)*

However unlucky you may be, it really is not fair to expect your adversary's grief for your undeserved misfortune to be as poignant as your own.

    Horace G. Hutchinson, Hints on the Game of Golf *(1886)*

You get either the youngest caddie or the oldest golf cart—
and neither works.

Richard Haskell (1982)

The trouble with this game is that they say the good breaks
and bad breaks even up. What they don't tell you is that they
don't even up right away. You might go two or three years
and all you get is bad break, bad break, bad break. That gets
annoying in a hurry.

Johnny Miller (1984)

Golf is the strangest game in the world. It involves a lot of
luck. And when your ball starts rattling in the trees, then it's
all luck.

Rex Caldwell, San Francisco Chronicle *(1983)*

And thus, with self-deception bland,
We mourn the fours that should have been,
Forgetting, on the other hand,
The luck that helped us through the green;
Calmly accepting as our due
The four-hole which we fluked in two.

Thomas Risk, "The Golfer's Discontent,"
from The Lyric of the Links

Golf is not a fair game. It's a rude game.

Fuzzy Zoeller

Golf, especially championship golf, isn't supposed to be any
fun, was never meant to be fair, and never will make any
sense.

Charles Price

A golf match is a test of your skill against your opponent's luck.

    Henry Beard, Mulligan's Laws *(1993)*

Golf is the cruelest of sports, and like life, it's unfair. It's a harlot. A trollop. It leads you on. It never lives up to promises. It's not a sport; it's bondage. An obsession. A boulevard of broken dreams. It plays with men. And runs off with the butcher.

    Jim Murray

In the United States, I am lucky. In Europe, I am good.

    Seve Ballesteros

MARRIAGE

**Shall the married man play golf?
This admits of no argument. Certainly.
Of all the plagues to a woman in the
house is a man during the day.**
Dr. Proudfoot (1890)

Selecting a putting stroke is like selecting a wife. To each his own.

    Ben Hogan

I've always had a wife—golf. No man should have more than one.

    Freddie McCleod

There are plenty of golfers in this country who take almost an eternity to select a club, and in the United States a number of first-class performers take just as long to make a selection as they do to choose a wife ... and sometimes they make the wrong choice in each case.

   Dai Rees, On Golf *(1959)*

In case you don't know very much about the game of golf, a good one-iron shot is about as easy to come by as an understanding wife.

   Dan Jenkins

"A bad wife'll strap a terminal hook on you," Donny said once. "You can just start walking left every time you swing a club."

   Dan Jenkins, Dead Solid Perfect *(1974)*

Many men are more faithful to their golf partners than to their wives and have stuck with them longer.

   John Updike

I think the press made a grave mistake in calling Arnold, Jack, and myself "the Big Three." I think "the Big Three" were Winnie Palmer, Barbara Nicklaus, and Vivienne Player.

   Gary Player

Jack Nicklaus has done a number of very smart things in his life, but the smartest thing he ever did was marry Barbara.

   Herb Graffis

I am delighted with my score, and I won't beat my wife tonight.

   Jack Nicklaus (1989)

It is sometimes said that only when he stands at the altar on his wedding day does a man experience quite the same sensation of impending doom as he feels each week on the first tee of a Sunday morning.

Norman Mair, Of Games and Golf

Cartoon caption of a man missing a very short putt—First it was my marriage. Now the magic has gone out of my putter.

W. A. Vanselow, Golf Digest

The only thing I ever asked of Joan was that if she was angry with me, please don't say anything until after my round. The game was difficult enough without trying to play after arguing with my wife.

Paul Runyan

Marjorie decided to take up golf, and the captain's paradise I had lived in for a decade fell apart like Johnny Miller's long-iron game.

Peter Andrews, "Scenes from a Marriage," in the New York Times

I've avoided playing thirty-six holes in one day in a tournament for more than five years. The only time I would usually consider playing more than eighteen is when my wife Claudia insists that I give her a lesson.

Lee Trevino

They say, "Trevino is wondering whether to play a five- or a six-iron to the green." When, all the time, I'm gazing at some broad in the third row of the gallery, wondering where my wife is.

Lee Trevino

The tee, the start of youth, the game our life,
The ball when fairly bunkered, man and wife.
>   *Patric Dickinson*, A Round of Golf Courses *(1951)*

Golf is undertaken mostly by husbands and wives over nine holes on Friday evenings or Sunday afternoons, when nothing better is scheduled, often with results so discordant, they make Ralph and Alice Kramden sound positively blissful by contrast.
>   *Nick Seitz*

We were happily married for eight months. Unfortunately, we were married for four and a half years.
>   *Nick Faldo*

MEDICAL OPINION

Golf is an ideal diversion, but a ruinous disease.
>   *Bertie Forbes*

Golf increases the blood pressure, ruins the disposition, spoils the digestion, induces neurasthenia, hurts the eyes, calluses the hands, ties kinks in the nervous system, debauches the morals, drives men to drink or homicide, breaks up the family, turns the ductless glands into internal warts, corrodes the pneumogastric nerve, breaks off the edges of the vertebrae, induces spinal meningitis and progressive mendacity, and starts angina pectoris.
>   *Dr. A. S. Lamb (circa 1900)*

[Apart from all that, golf is good for you!]

Golf is probably some kind of mental disorder like gambling or women or politics.
>   *Dan Jenkins,* Dead Solid Perfect *(1974)*

Golf has probably kept more people sane than psychiatrists have.
>   *Harvey Penick*

Golf is a game where guts, stick-to-it-iveness, and blind devotion will get you nothing but an ulcer.
>   *Tommy Bolt*

Golf is neither a microcosm of nor a metaphor for life. It is a sport, a bloodless sport, if you don't count ulcers.
>   *Dick Schaap*

I don't trust doctors. They are like golfers. Every one has a different answer to your problem.
>   *Seve Ballesteros*

In golf, as in medicine—the best way to get out of trouble is to avoid it.
>   *Richard Gordon,* Dr. Gordon's Casebook *(1982)*

Pinky Kerr is on th' decline but refuses t' consult a doctor fer fear he'll tell him t' play golf.
>   *"Kin" Hubbard,* New Sayings by Abe Martin *(1917)*

Doctors and mind experts go round explaining that it's perfectly OK to explode on the course because it releases your built-up tensions. They don't tell you, though, how you can rave like a wild beast and break 90.
>   *Sam Snead,* The Education of a Golfer *(1962)*

We all have stupid genes in us, and golf brings out those stupid genes.
>   *John Madden,* All Madden *(1996)*

On learning he was allergic to grass—It could be worse: I could be allergic to beer.

   Greg Norman

Pain and suffering are inevitable in our lives, but misery is an option.

   Chip Beck

After beating Walter Hagen in a challenge match despite poor health—A sick appendix is not as difficult to deal with as a five-foot putt.

   Gene Sarazen (1922)

After a bad round in the 1974 Hawaiian Open—About the only thing left for me is acupuncture ... in the brain.

   George Archer

Why his new "replacement" body parts might affect his Senior status—My knee's only a few months old, my back is only seventeen, and I recently got a new hip. I might be too young now.

   George Archer (1996)

MONEY MATTERS

**We tournament golfers are much overrated.
We get paid too much.**
   Tom Watson

If golf is a rich man's sport, why are there so many poor players?

   Anonymous

I've always argued that we ought to play right down the middle of Saigon if the price is right.

Frank Beard (1970)

On being leading money-winner of the tour without a tournament victory—I can't win anything but money.

Frank Beard

In those days [the 1930s] the money was the main thing, the only thing I played for. Championships were something to grow old with.

Byron Nelson

Nineteen-forty, when I won six of nine tournaments, including the Masters, was my big year. I was even able to hang on to enough money so that I needed only a small loan for the cab fare home.

Jimmy Demaret (1954)

I'm third in earnings and first in spending.

Tony Lema (1965)

If a great golf swing put you high on the money list, there'd be some of us who would be broke.

Raymond Floyd

On rumors of his leaving college and turning pro—They are saying millions. I don't really know what a million is going to do for me. I've always played around with a couple of thousand for tuition and books and food.

Matt Kuchar (1998)

What happened to all my dough? I spent it! It cost an absolute fortune to live the life of Riley. I don't regret a single penny.

Tony Jacklin (1993)

After winning $6,000 at the 1967 U.S. Open—Did I ever win that much money before? I never saw that much money before.

    Lee Trevino

I plan to win so much money this year, my caddie's gonna finish in the Top Twenty money-winners.

    Lee Trevino

After undergoing surgery—I missed a bunch of tournaments, but considering all the hospital insurance I carry, I figure I wound up leading money-winner.

    Lee Trevino (1977)

I'm working as hard as I can to get my life and cash to run out at the same time. If I can just die after lunch on Tuesday, everything would be perfect.

    Doug Sanders

The money is completely unimportant ... once you have won enough of it.

    Johnny Miller

On achieving £1 million in career earnings—Where did it all go?

    David Feherty (1991)

On approaching the $1 million mark in career earnings—The problem is that I'm already two million in spending.

    Chi Chi Rodriguez

I owe everything to golf. Where else could a guy with an IQ like mine make this much money?

    Hubert Green (1981)

If backing a Broadway play is the worst investment in the world, sponsoring a golf pro surely ranks a strong second.
>   *Mark Mulvoy and Art Spander,*
>   The Passion and the Challenge *(1977)*

The name of the game is to get the ball in the hole and pick up the check. It's a nice feeling.
>   *Sam Snead*

I like the thought of playing for money instead of silverware. I never did like to polish.
>   *Patty Sheehan*

On the $110,000 appearance money at the 1995 Dubai Classic— To an oil prince it's emir pittance.
>   *John Walters,* Sports Illustrated

*After his £200,000 check for winning the British Open was lost—*The first one was delivered to an address four blocks away. Somebody must have thought it was his lucky day.
>   *Tom Lehman (1996)*

*Explaining his coaching fees: $140 for thirteen lessons and $1,000 for one lesson—*If you expect a miracle, you should expect to pay for one.
>   *Derek Hardy*

If you are in the Top Twenty on Sunday, a birdie will make you twice what a bogey will cost you.
>   *Mark Brooks*

On his first tour win in a dozen years—For two or three days after I won, I kept calling the phone number where you can get your bank balance, and I listened to it over and over again.

> *Leonard Thompson*

NAKED TRUTH

> **Gowf is a way o' makin' a man go naked. I would say tha' nowhere does a man go so naked as he does before a discernin' eye dressed for gowf.**
> *Michael Murphy,* Golf in the Kingdom *(1976)*

Golf is more fun than walking naked in a strange place, but not much.

> *Buddy Hackett*

On the pressures of competition golf—You know you can't hide. It's like walking down the fairway naked.

> *Hale Irwin*

I had always expected that trying to play golf in the company of big-time pros and a gallery would be something like walking naked into choir practice.

> *Dan Jenkins,* The Dogged Victims of Inexorable Fate *(1970)*

On a naked streaker that appeared during the 1985 British Open at Sandwich—You can't really tell whether that's a man or a woman.

> *Sandy Lyle*

On tackling the same streaker—There is one statistical category on the tour in which I will always be number one, and that is Leading Tackler. I have one, and everybody else is second with none.

> Peter Jacobsen

Jack Lemmon once told me that, to be an actor, you had to be willing to walk out on stage, take off all your clothes slowly, and take two full turns so everybody can see exactly what you've got. I think playing golf—especially being in contention on the last day—is like that.

> Peter Jacobsen (1995)

NATIONAL TRAITS

**Golf is too slow a game for Canada.
We would go to sleep over it.**
John B. McLenan (1891)

I like going there for the golf. America's one vast golf course today.

> Edward, Duke of Windsor

Golf combines two favorite American pastimes: taking long walks and hitting things with sticks.

> P. J. O'Rourke, Modern Manners (1983)

On why Australia produces so many great golfers—Meat pies, good beer ... and plenty of sunshine.

> Wayne Grady (1990)

In Britain, you skip the ball, hop it, hump it, run it, hit
under it, on top of it and then hope for the right bounce.
>   *Doug Sanders,* Sports Illustrated *(1984)*

In Britain, there's a will to win. In America, there's a need
to win.
>   *Glynn Tiernan,* New York Times *(1988)*

Golf is a thoroughly national game. It is as Scotch as haggis,
cock-a-leekie, high cheekbones, or rowanberry jam.
>   *Andrew Lang*

You have to play golf in Scotland. What else is there to do
there? Wear a skirt?
>   *George Low*

Scotsman: The only player not trying to hit the ball out of
sight.
>   *Anonymous*

On Irish greens—Certainly they are the greenest, which is
hardly surprising in a country where housewives habitually
peep out of their cottage windows and observe that it is a
beautiful day for hanging the washing out to rinse.
>   *Peter Dobereiner,* The Glorious World of Golf *(1973)*

I had a reputation for being tough. You had to be when you
were Italian.
>   *Gene Sarazen*

I've played in Japan. Is that near Asia?
>   *Fred Couples*

I love it here in the United States. In Japan, I have no privacy. In the States, I can have a hole in my jeans and nobody will notice it.

Ayako Okamoto

NATURAL WONDER

As you walk down the fairway of life, you must smell the roses, for you only get to play one round.
Ben Hogan

Echoing Hogan's words, after winning the 1991 British Open— The only thing I regret is that I had no time to smell the roses.

Ian Baker-Finch

Spring was designed like an old set of MacGregor irons ... to rejuvenate the soul.

Deane Beman

It was a morning when all nature shouted, "Fore!" The breeze, as it blew gently up from the valley, seemed to bring a message of hope and cheer, whispering of chip shots holed and brassies landing squarely on the meat.

P. G. Wodehouse, The Heart of a Goof *(1923)*

If golf has a defect, it is that it prevents a man being a whole-hearted lover of nature. Where the layman sees waving grass and romantic rectangles of undergrowth, your golfer beholds nothing but a nasty patch of rough from which he must divert his ball.

P. G. Wodehouse

Oh, golf is for smellin' heather and cut grass and walkin' fast across the countryside and feelin' the wind and watchin' the sun go down and seein' yer friends hit good shots and hittin' some yerself. It's love and it's feelin' the splendor o' this good world.

Michael Murphy, Golf in the Kingdom *(1976)*

When I first look at designing a hole, I consider what Mother Nature has already created on that property, and then I try to mold a golf hole that fits naturally into what there is. . . . I guess you could say that Mother Nature is a co-designer of each of my courses.

Jack Nicklaus

Golf has some drawbacks. It is possible, by too much of it, to destroy the mind. . . . For the golfer, Nature loses her significance. Larks, the casts of worms, the buzzing of bees, and even children are hateful. . . . Rain comes to be regarded solely in its relation to the putting greens; the daisy is detested, botanical specimens are but hazards, twigs break clubs. Winds cease to be east, south, west, or north. They are ahead, behind, sideways. And the sky is dark according to the state of the game.

Sir Walter Simpson, The Art of Golf *(1887)*

NINETEENTH HOLE

**Golfing excellence goes hand in hand
with alcohol, as many an Open and
Amateur champion has shown.**
Henry Longhurst

N is for *Nineteenth,* the hole that's the best
And the reason some golfers play all of the rest.
Richard Armour, Golf Is a Four-Letter Word *(1962)*

Nineteenth hole: The only hole on which golfers do not
complain about the number of shots they took.
Henry Beard, A Duffer's Dictionary *(1987)*

The first eighteen holes give a golf club its reason to exist;
the nineteenth gives it the money.
Robinson Murray

I like to say I was born on the nineteenth hole, the only one
I ever parred.
George Low Jr.

What the nineteenth hole proves beyond a shadow of a
doubt is that the Scots invented the game solely in order to
sell their national beverage in large quantities.
Milton Gross

We borrowed golf from Scotland as we borrowed whiskey.
Not because it's Scottish, but because it is good.
Horace G. Hutchinson

Unlike the other Scotch game of whiskey drinking, excess in it is not injurious to the health.

Sir Walter Simpson, The Art of Golf *(1887)*

Scotland is a peculiar land that is the birthplace of golf and sport salmon fishing, a fact which may explain why it is also the birthplace of whiskey.

Henry Beard, An Angler's Dictionary *(1983)*

Where I play, the greens break toward the bar.

George Gobel

The first time I played the Masters I was so nervous, I drank a bottle of rum before I teed off. I shot the happiest 83 of my life.

Chi Chi Rodriguez

Indeed, few sights are more odious on the golf course than a sauntering beered-up foursome obviously having a good time.

John Updike, New York Times Book Review *(1973)*

The terrible paradox in the world of golf is that when you're playing well, you get late tee times. So, you can get drunk the night before because you've got all morning to sleep it off.

Frank Beard

Watching a golf tournament is different from attending other sports arenas. For one thing, the drunks are spread out in a larger area.

Don Wade

I have never led the tour in money winnings, but I have many times in alcohol consumption.

Fuzzy Zoeller

During the 1984 PGA Championship —The way I hit the ball today, I need to go to the range. Instead, I think I'll go to the bar.

    Fuzzy Zoeller

I'll always remember the day I broke 90. I had a few beers in the clubhouse and was so excited, I forgot to play the back nine.

    Bruce Lansky

If you foozle with your cleek,
And your putts are let's say—weak.
If your drives, for all to see,
Do not always leave the tee.
And to slice them is a habit,
If, in short, you're a rabbit.
Do not put your clubs away
Drink a Guinness every day.

    Guinness advertisement

On the refusal of the waiters at Royal St. George's to serve drinks to professionals Walter Hagen and Gene Sarazen—You ought to stop this nonsense, or I'll take the Royal away from St. George's.

    Prince Edward [VIII] of England

If you drink, don't drive. Don't even putt.

    Dean Martin

Golf is a drinking game. Whether you play good or bad, "Hey, let's have a beer and forget about it."

    John Daly (1997)

Wire sent to his hotel after winning the Canadian Open—Fill
the bathtub with champagne.
  Walter Hagen

W. C. Fields was fond of playing the Bel-Air Course [in Los
Angeles] sideways with his pal Oliver Hardy. He liked being
in the trees where he could drink without scandalizing the
natives.
  Jim Murray

If I died ... it meant I couldn't play golf. No way was I giving up golf, so I gave up drinking.
  Bob Hope

A fifth at night ... a 68 in the morning.
  Walter Hagen

My handicap is that I don't have a big enough beer cooler for
the back of my golf cart.
  Rick D'Amico (1983)

OFF ONE'S GAME

**Sometimes I drive well, sometimes
I pitch and chip well, sometimes I putt well,
but they don't always work together well.**
  Jack Nicklaus (1986)

When I left the golf course after a round this year, a lady told
me my biorhythms were off. I told her my golf game was off.
  Jack Nicklaus

My game is so bad that the flags ought to be at half-staff.
> *Al Malesta,* San Francisco Examiner *(1982)*

"I'm off my game," the golfer said
And shook his locks in woe;
"My putter never lays me dead,
My drives will never go;
Howe'er I swing, howe'er I stand,
Results are still the same,
I'm in the but, I'm in the sand—
I'm off my game!"
> *Andrew Lang,* Off My Game

*On a poor performance the week after winning the 1989
European Open*—Yesterday I was walking on water. Today I
needed someone to show me how to get out of it.
> *Andrew Murray*

On missing her first halfway cut in twenty-six years—It's a little
odd checking on flights out of town on Friday.
> *JoAnne Carner (1995)*

On missing the cut at the 1992 Cannes Open—I keep thinking
that I might go out and play like Jack Nicklaus, but instead,
it's more like Jacques Tati.
> *David Feherty (1992)*

On missing several cuts during the 1997 season—Last year, I
didn't work much on weekends. I was a little like a banker.
> *Chip Beck (1998)*

I think golf is the hardest sport to play. One day you're up on
Cloud Nine, and the next day you couldn't scratch a whale's
belly.
> *Sam Snead (1984)*

OLDEST SWINGERS IN TOWN

**To that man, age brought only
golf instead of wisdom.**
George Bernard Shaw

Years ago we discovered the exact point, the dead center of
middle age. It occurs when you are too young to take up
golf, and too old to rush the net.

Franklin P. Adams, Nods and Becks *(1944)*

To a much younger opponent—My God! I've got socks older
than you!

Lee Trevino (1980)

Golf is like driving a car: as you get older, you get more
careful.

Sam Snead

The only good thing about the old days is talking about
them.

Bill Melhorn, Golf Secrets Exposed *(1984)*

When you are too old to chase other things, you can always
chase golf balls.

Anonymous

The older you get, the stronger the wind gets ... and it's
always in your face.

Jack Nicklaus

The older you get, the longer you used to be.
Chi Chi Rodriguez

When you get up there in years, the fairways get longer and the holes get smaller.
Bobby Locke

You know you're getting old when you start watching golf on TV and enjoying it.
Larry Miller

After carding an opening-round 67 in the 1989 Masters—It shows me there is still a spark in the fire. I've only got to throw a log on it.
Lee Trevino

On the three things that "go" when a golfer gets old—His nerve, his memory … and I can't remember the third thing.
Lee Trevino

Golf has robbed old age of its regrets, for it can be played from the cradle to the grave.
Gustav Kobbé

Any game where a man sixty can beat a man thirty ain't no game.
Burt Shotten

On his sixty-ninth birthday—That's the easiest 69 I ever made.
Ben Hogan

I'll shoot my age if I have to live to be 105.
Bob Hope

Some of these legends have been around golf a long time. When they mention a good grip, they're talking about their dentures.

Bob Hope

In thirty years we're going to be in our nineties. We're going to play three-hole tournaments for $900,000, and the one who remembers his score wins.

Bob Brue

At our age there's also the matter of confidence. It's a little like sex—one bad performance, and you begin to wonder.

Julius Boros (1975)

OPPOSITES ATTRACT

Most golfers prepare for disaster.
A good golfer prepares for success.
Bob Toski

Reverse every natural instinct you have and do just the opposite of what you are inclined to do, and you will probably come very close to having a perfect golf swing.

Ben Hogan

First you teach a golfer to hook the ball by using his hands and arms properly. Then you teach him to take the hook away by using his body and legs properly.

Harvey Penick

You must work very hard to become a natural golfer.

Gary Player

If there was one thing I have learned during my years as a professional, it is that the only thing constant about golf is its inconstancy.

Jack Nicklaus

There's no better game in the world when you are in good company, and no worse game when you are in bad company.

Tommy Bolt

Make the hard ones look easy and the easy ones look hard.

Walter Hagen

It is better to miss the shot a hundred times in the right way than to play it successfully in the wrong.

H. J. Whigham, The Common Sense of Golf *(1910)*

Golf is an invitation to play well and know it's going to end; to play poorly and think it's never going to end.

Nike advertisement (1996)

I never rooted against an opponent, but I never rooted for him either.

Arnold Palmer

How often have we seen a round go from an episode of *The Three Stooges* to the agonies of *King Lear*—perhaps in the space of one hole?! I will never forget a friend who declared after his tee shot that he wanted to kill himself but, when the hole was finished, said with total sincerity that he had never been so happy in his entire life. No other game is capable of evoking a person's total commitment.

Michael Murphy

On his victory walk to the 18th green at the 1984 U.S. Open—
That walk was the warmest feeling and the coldest streak
down my back of my life.
   Fuzzy Zoeller

*After carding a 74 in the opening round of the 1955 San Antonio
Open at Brackenridge Park—*I don't want anyone to know I've
been here. No one should come.
*After shooting a 63 in the second round—*Man, I've never seen
a golf course improve so much overnight!
   Jimmy Demaret

PARCENTAGE GOLF

**Golf is 20 percent talent and
80 percent management.**
Ben Hogan

The game of golf is 90 percent mental and 10 percent mental.
   Henry Beard, Mulligan's Laws *(1994)*

Golf is 20 percent mechanics and technique. The other 80
percent is philosophy, humor, tragedy, romance, melodrama,
companionship, camaraderie, cussedness, and conversation.
   Grantland Rice

Fifty percent of the fairways we play on today are better than
90 percent of the greens we played thirty years ago.
   Jim Ferrier

Golf is 90 percent inspiration and 10 percent perspiration.
Johnny Miller

Ninety percent of golf is played from the head up.
Deacon Palmer

On the average, a maximum of 4.097 percent of the time
associated with a round of golf is spent whacking the golf
ball with a golf club.
Geoff Howson

PERFECTION

**Golf is not, on the whole, a game for realists.
By its exactitudes of measurement it invites
the attention of perfectionists.**
Heywood Broun

Man, I crawled on that shot like an eight-wheel rig rollin'
down Interstate 35. Just wore it out. And the minute the ball
started for that flagstick, I knew the war was over and it was
time to call in the boats and piss on the Admiral.
Dan Jenkins, Dead Solid Perfect *(1974)*

It may have been the greatest four-wood anyone ever hit. It
was so much on the flag that I had to lean sideways to follow
the flight of the ball.
Gary Player

A perfectly straight shot with a big club is a fluke.
    Jack Nicklaus

The perfect round of golf has never been played. It's eighteen
holes in one. I almost dreamt it once, but I lipped out at
eighteen. I was mad as hell.
    Ben Hogan

*[Also quoted as: "I dreamed one night that I had seventeen holes in
one and one 2, and when I woke up, I was so goddamn mad."]*

Once in a while a seven-iron rips off the club face with the
pleasant tearing sound, as if pulling a zipper in space, and
falls toward the hole like a raindrop down a well.
    John Updike, New York Times Book Review *(1973)*

What other sport holds out hope of improvement to a
man or woman over fifty? ... For a duffer ... the room for
improvement is so vast that three lifetimes could be spent
roaming the fairways carving away at it, convinced that perfection lies just over the next rise.
    John Updike (1982)

This is the substance of our Plot—
For those who play the Perfect Shot,
There are ten thousand who do not.
    Grantland Rice, Dedicated to the Duffer

Let a pro hit 999 of 1,000 shots perfect, and he curses the
golfing gods because of one unfortunate shot.
Let an amateur hit 999 of 1,000 shots poorly but hit one perfectly, and he exalts the game.
    Mac O'Grady

After winning the 1993 British Open—In my entire career I have never gone round a golf course and never mishit a shot. Every drive was perfect, every iron was perfect. I was in awe of myself.
Greg Norman

POLITICALLY SPEAKING

Golf in the interest of good health and good manners. It promotes self-restraint and affords a chance to play the man and act the gentleman.
William H. Taft

Golf is a game kings and presidents play when they get tired of running countries.
Charles Price

Golf, in my opinion, is a game for deposed Latin American dictators in plaid pants; it allows them to putter away their exile until God's extradition.
John Leonard, New York Times *(1982)*

Rail-splitting produced an immortal president in Abraham Lincoln, but golf, with 29,000 courses, hasn't produced even an A-Number-1 congressman.
Will Rogers

The difference between golf and government is that in golf you can't improve your lie.
George Deukmejian

It is true that my predecessor did not object as I do to pictures of my golf skill in action. But neither, on the other hand, did he ever bean a Secret Service man.

   John F. Kennedy

One lesson you'd better learn if you want to be in politics is that you never go out on a golf course and beat the president.

   Lyndon B. Johnson

For an American of a certain age, cultural outlook, and political inclination, a love of golf is more than faintly embarrassing. Is there any sound more evocative of greedy Republican smugness than the sound of golf spikes on brick?

   David Owen

[And Democrat smugness sounds like soft spikes on turf?]

The only difference I was aware of between Democrats and Republicans was that Republicans seemed to have lower handicaps and more sets of clubs, while Democrats like to bet more … and pay off quicker.

   Dan Jenkins, Dead Solid Perfect *(1974)*

On why he refused to run for governor of Pennsylvania in the 1960s—I might have ended up in the White House.

   Arnold Palmer

I attribute the insane arrogance of the later Roman emperors almost entirely to the fact that, never having played golf, they never knew that strange chastening humility which is engendered by a topped chip shot. If Cleopatra had been ousted in the first round of the Ladies' Singles, we should have heard a lot less of her proud imperiousness.

   P. G. Wodehouse

THE PRESS

**Golf is gaining so enormously in popularity,
and so many now take an interest in the matches
of good, and especially of professional players,
that it would be a boon to a very large number of
readers if reports of matches could be made more
life-like, showing appreciation of the real turning
points of the game and confining themselves less
exclusively to a dry chronicling of details.**

Horace G. Hutchinson (1890)

To a group of journalists—You like to moan that none of us
today can compare with the old guys—Jones, Hogan,
Nelson. I guess it's true of golf writers, too. Now, that
Grantland Rice—boy, he could really get it done.

Tom Kite

If someone dropped an atom bomb on the sixth hole,
the press would wait for a golfer to come in and tell them
about it.

Ben Hogan

During a tedious postround press conference—Someday a deaf
mute will win a golf tournament, and you guys won't be able
to write a story.

Ben Hogan

On seeing his picture in a New York newspaper—How can they
have my picture? I ain't never been to New York!

Sam Snead

Looking back today, I can think of no surer way to find yourself a golf writer in your fifties than to think you were Ben Hogan in your twenties.

Charles Price, Golfer-at-Large *(1982)*

After winning his third British Open—I'd like to thank the media from the heart of my bottom.

Nick Faldo (1992)

On an overweight reporter who fell into a deep bunker during the 1997 British Open—Instead of getting out in two, it took two to get him out.

Mark Rolfing, abc tv

After a clicking camera put him off his swing—What's the penalty for killing a photographer ... one stroke or two?

Davis Love III

READING MATTER

Human nature is so funny, it is a thousand pities that neither Aristotle nor Shakespeare was a golfer.
Horace G. Hutchinson

The smaller the ball used in the sport, the better the book. There are superb books about golf, very good books about baseball, not very many good books about basketball, and no good books on beach balls.

George Plimpton

I am not happy with my own game. Maybe I should read my own book.

Ian Woosnam (1989)

To improve my golf, I once read one of those great, involved books on positive thinking. I gave up when I heard the author had committed suicide.

Nick Job (1982)

On some proposed golf book titles—The first one is called *How to Get the Most Distance Out of Your Shanks,* and the other is *How to Take the Correct Stance on Your Fourth Putt.*

Lee Trevino

Duffers who consistently shank their balls are urged to buy and study *Shanks—No Thanks* by R. K. Hoffman, or in extreme cases, M. S. Howard's excellent *Tennis for Beginners.*

Henry Beard, A Duffer's Dictionary *(1987)*

The nice thing about these golf books is that they usually cancel each other out. One book tells you to keep your eye on the ball; the next says not to bother. Personally, in the crowd I play with, a better idea is to keep your eye on your partner.

Jim Murray

The entire handbook can be reduced to three rules.
One: You do not touch your ball from the time you tee it up to the moment you pick it out of the hole.
Two: Don't bend over when you are in the rough.
Three: When you are in the woods, keep clapping your hands.

Charles Price, Esquire

More instruction material on how to hit a middle iron is written in America during any six-month period than has been written about thoracic surgery since doctors stopped working out of the back rooms of barbershops.

Peter Andrews, Golf Digest *(1984)*

It has been estimated that more golf poetry exists in Scotland than heather.

Dan Jenkins (1970)

On his 1960 book Golf Is My Game—It took me two years to write, and I threw away three times the amount that was used. Maybe I should have stopped writing sooner.

Bobby Jones

To me, golf is an inexhaustible subject. I cannot imagine that anyone might ever write every word that needs to be written about the golf swing.

Bobby Jones

On how he kept calm before winning his first major—I like cowboy-and-Indian books. During the 1979 British Open, I read until I forgot my worries and started worrying about the Indians instead.

Seve Ballesteros

SCIENCE

The game is not so easy as it seems. In the first place, the terrible inertia of the ball must be overcome.
Lord Wellwood

Golf is a science, the study of a lifetime, in which you can exhaust yourself but never your subject.

David Forgan

Those who think in terms of golf being a science have unfortunately tried to part from each other the arms, head, shoulders, body, hips, and legs. They turn a golfer into a worm cut into bits, with each part wriggling in every which way direction—this is "paralysis by analysis."

    Ernest Jones

Anyone who hopes to reduce putting—or any other department of the game, for that matter—to an exact science is in for a serious disappointment and will only suffer from the attempt.

    Bobby Jones

SECRETS

**I wish to emphasize that there are
no secrets to golf. The secret of success is
practice, constant but intelligent practice.**
Ernest Jones (1953)

The secret of golf is to turn three shots into two.

    Bobby Jones

I've discovered the great secret of golf. You can't play a really hot game unless you're so miserable that you don't worry over your shots. Look at the top-notchers. Have you ever seen a happy pro?

    P. G. Wodehouse, The Heart of a Goof *(1923)*

Secret disbelief in the enemy's play is useful.

    Sir Walter Simpson, The Art of Golf *(1887)*

Golf is a sport whose secret is to hit the ball hard, straight, and not too often.

Anonymous

I don't have any big secret about putting. Just hit at it. It's either going to miss or go in.

Ben Crenshaw (1984)

The secret of missing a tree is to aim straight at it.

Michael Green

Good-looking form is one of the secrets of good golf. Look beautiful, and you'll play beautiful. However, some old codgers with whom I play, play mighty ugly and beat the pants off me.

Don Herold

Golfers have analyzed the game in order to find the secret. There is no secret.

Henry Cotton

SELF-EXPRESSION

I think anybody, any businessman, any athlete who's successful has to be egocentric. I don't think there is a question about that. If you are going to try to be good at something, you can't let somebody else do it for you.

Jack Nicklaus

On one hole I'm like Arnold Palmer, and on the next like Lili Palmer.

Sean Connery

All men are created equal, and I am one shot better than the rest.

    Gene Sarazen

I'm a golfaholic. And all the counseling in the world wouldn't help me.

    Lee Trevino

After winning the 1988 Masters—Me a superstar? What's that? I still wash the dishes and drive my own car. I am a popular player, but people like Greg Norman and Seve Ballesteros are regarded as superstars. They are Hollywood. The nearest I'll get to flying a jet is a remote-controlled one.

    Sandy Lyle

After winning the 1989 Masters—We stopped off for gas in Hicksville, and they were saying, "Is it him? It is him, isn't it?" It was a nice feeling.

    Nick Faldo

The person I fear most in the last two rounds is myself.

    Tom Watson

I'm just a grown caddie studying golf.

    Harvey Penick, Little Red Book *(1992)*

My career started off slowly, then tapered off.

    Gary McCord

Perhaps if I dyed my hair peroxide blond and called myself the "Great White Tadpole" people would take more notice of me.

    Ian Woosnam

On comparing life on tour to his role as PGA *commissioner—*
When you spend your life hitting four-woods to greens when
other guys are hitting irons, you develop a pretty thick skin.
>   *Deane Beman*

The limit of my ambition is not to lose my balance on the
next backswing.
>   *Mark James*

"The man who hates golfers" is what they call me. They
couldn't be more wrong. I design holes that are fun to play.
>   *Robert Trent Jones*

On his relative obscurity on the European *tour—*My mum
hates to start searching for my name from the bottom of the
list each week.
>   *Andrew McGee*

I've done as much for golf as Truman Capote has for sumo
wrestling.
>   *Bob Hope*

SEX

What is there in life but golf and girls?
Jim Colbert (1977)

Golf is like sex. Trying your hardest is the worst thing you
can do.
>   *Rick Reilly,* Sports Illustrated *(1998)*

The only really unplayable lie I can think of is when you are supposed to be playing golf, and come home with lipstick on your collar.

Arnold Palmer

The pleasure derived from hitting the ball dead center on the club is comparable only to one or two other pleasures that come to mind at the moment.

Dinah Shore (1981)

It's the most humbling sport ever. It's like a lousy lover. It's like some guy who's never there when you need him. Every once in a while, he comes and makes you feel like heaven on earth. And then the moment you say, "I really need this," he's gone.

Dinah Shore

After winning the 1983 U.S. Women's Open—Maybe people will stop thinking of me only as a sex symbol and realize I can really play golf.

Jan Stephenson

I've had sex in a lot of places. I wouldn't want to have it in the bunker, because of the sand. I'd kind of like to have it on the green; it would be nice and soft.

Jan Stephenson, Playboy *(1983)*

I've always had three rules for playing well on tour: no push-ups, no swimming, and no sex after Wednesday.

Sam Snead (1977)

After a golfer has been out on the circuit for a while, he learns how to handle his dating so that it doesn't interfere with his golf. The first rule usually is no woman-chasing after Wednesday.

Tony Lema

Somebody asked me the other day about this Parkinson woman some of the members are supposed to be involved with. I told them that at my stage of life the greatest thrill a guy gets is sinking a forty-foot putt.

    Tip O'Neill (1981)

The golf swing is like sex. You can't be thinking about the mechanics of the act while you are performing.

    Dave Hill, Teed Off *(1977)*

Golf and sex are about the only things you can enjoy without being good at either.

    Jimmy Demaret

A good straight drive or a soft chip stiff to the pin gives him the bliss that used to come thinking of women, imagining if only you and she were alone on some desert island.

    John Updike

Playing golf is like going to a strip joint. After eighteen holes you're tired and most of your balls are missing.

    Tim Allen

On not having a steady girlfriend—That would be too much like playing the same golf course all the time!

    Seve Ballesteros

Golf is the most overtaught and least-learned human endeavor. If they taught sex the way they teach golf, the human race would have died out years ago.

    Jim Murray

Playing with your spouse on the golf course runs almost as great a marital risk as getting caught playing with someone else's anywhere else.

Peter Andrews

Golf and masturbation have at least one thing in common. Both are a lot more satisfying to do than they are to watch.

Anonymous

SINGING

To the amply bosomed opera singer Ernestine Schumann-Heink—My dear, did you ever stop to think what a lovely bunker you would make?

Walter Hagen

*On learning that he had been challenged to a match by the British Open champion—*Why, that would be like me challenging Bing Crosby to a singing contest, wouldn't it?

Ben Hogan

I never sing on a golf course—that would be too conspicuous. At golf, I only allow myself to whistle.

Bing Crosby (1976)

I do a lot of humming out on the course. I tend to stick with one song ... I shot a 66 to "Moon River."

Jack Nicklaus

TALK

Golferswhotalkfastswingfast.
Bob Toski, Golf Digest *(1982)*

The talking golfer is undeniably the most pronounced pest of our complex modern civilization … and the most difficult to deal with.
P. G. Wodehouse, The Salvation of George Mackintosh *(1920)*

Golfers talk a lot, and they talk very well as a rule. Out in the privacy of the course, invigorated by the sweet air and the spring of the turf, a man opens up. He speaks his mind candidly on almost any subject. Things strike him humorously, including himself.
Herbert Warren Wind, The Lure of Golf *(1954)*

Always fade a ball. You can't talk to a hook.
Dave Marr (1968)

You can talk to a fade, but a hook won't listen.
Lee Trevino

To Tony Jacklin, who refused to talk to him during a round—
You don't have to talk … just listen.
Lee Trevino

Talking to a golf ball won't do you any good. Unless you do it while your opponent is teeing off.
Bruce Lansky

Golf actually makes for international understanding, drawing men together as it does through their common sorrows. The standard alibis have been freely translated into every known language, including bad language.

> *Robinson Murray*

Golf is the Esperanto of sport. All over the world, golfers talk the same language—much of it nonsense and much unprintable—endure the same frustrations, discover the same infallible secrets of putting, share the same illusory joys.

> *Henry Longhurst,* Round in Sixty-Eight *(1953)*

English is difficult. I speak only Hong Kong golf English. When I go professional, I take teacher, say must speak English. Every day it is A, B, C, D; A, B, C, D. But no A, B, C, D in golf; only 1, 2, 3, 4, maybe 5. So I take another teacher.

> *Lu Liang Huan ["Mr. Lu"] (1971)*

On playing with Mr. Lu in the 1971 British Open—They put me out with a Chinaman to improve my English.

> *Roberto de Vicenzo*

I learn English from American pros, so that is why I speak so bad. I call it PGA English.

> *Roberto de Vicenzo*

I have talked to golf balls all my golfing life. I accept that a golf ball is inanimate; I understand that a golf ball does not have ears or a brain or even a nervous system. But it is, nonetheless, pleasing to see a golf ball pop right out of a bunker at the exact moment you've yelled, "Skip, golf ball, skip!" So, yes, I talk to golf balls; I admit to that. If I had to guess, I'd say we are talkers in the majority.

> *Michael Bamberger*

The only time I talk on a golf course is to my caddie. And then only to complain when he gives me the wrong club.
Seve Ballesteros

If you pick up a golfer and hold it close to your ear, like a conch shell, and listen—you will hear an alibi.
Fred Beck, 89 Years in a Sand Trap *(1965)*

I can't understand why people say Ben Hogan is so untalkative. He speaks to me on every green. He says, "You're away."
Jimmy Demaret

The hardest thing to learn about golf is keeping quiet about it.
George Houghton

It seems that the most reticent of men on other subjects no sooner takes to golf than eloquence descends on him.
John Hogben

Out of the mouths of America's most clean-cut group of athletes, except perhaps bowlers, comes a rich vein of slang that makes the hyped-up wild men of the NFL seem bland.
Thomas Boswell

Have you actually listened to golfers talking to each other? "Looked good starting out" … "Better direction than last time" … "Who's away?" It sounds like a visitor's day at a home for the criminally insane.
Peter Andrews

On a golfing partner—His drive has gone to pieces, largely through having more hinges in it than a sardine tin. But he could always play his iron shots, and his never-ending chatter must be worth at least two holes to his side.

> *James Agate,* Diary *(August 7, 1938)*

TELEVISION & RADIO

**I would rather play Hamlet on Broadway
with no rehearsal than play TV golf.**
Jack Lemmon

Reporting from the 1978 U.S. Open—Leader Tom Watson teed off this morning before large legions of links-loving loyalists. And that's pro golf as I see it.

> *H. G. Listiak,* KOY *Sports Radio*

If you want to take long walks, take long walks. If you want to hit things with sticks, hit things with sticks. But there's no excuse for combining the two and putting the results on television. Golf is not so much a sport as an insult to lawns.

> National Lampoon *(1979)*

The professional golf watcher never catches the action. I could write a volume on "Great Moments in Golf I Have Missed."

> *Peter Dobereiner,* The Glorious World of Golf *(1973)*

I don't like to watch golf on television because I can't stand people who whisper.

David Brenner (1977)

Watching golf on TV is one thing. Trying to watch a golf tournament in person is like trying to cover a war on foot.

Jay Cronley, Playboy *(1981)*

Watching the Masters on CBS is like attending church service. Announcers speak in hushed, pious tones, as if to convince us that something of great meaning and historical importance is taking place. What we are actually seeing is grown men hitting little balls with sticks.

Tom Gilmore, San Francisco Chronicle *(1984)*

We watch the Masters more than any tournament, to see the course, the scenery, and the almost always thrilling competition—not to hear the commentators. The Masters could be broadcast with Muzak as background.

Peter McCleery, Golf Digest *(1998)*

It's almost as if the American commentators were being paid by the word. I confess that when I hear of their salaries, I sometimes think they are.

Peter Alliss

On being asked if he watched golf on tv when he was young—
When I was growing up, they had just found radio.

Arnold Palmer

If you call personality the battle of Hollywood stars, then, yes, we do lack personality. But the personality of golf is good golf. If you want to see a comedian, you ought to tune in *Saturday Night Live.*

Tom Watson, The Sporting News *(1982)*

On the decline in golf's TV ratings—We have almost no controversy. Maybe I should get in a fistfight with Jack Nicklaus on the eighteenth green.
   Tom Watson

Anyone who likes golf on television would enjoy watching the grass grow on the greens.
   Andy Rooney

ABC [TV] = A Billion Commercials.
   Peter McCleery, Golf Digest *(1998)*

WEATHER

If there's nae wind, it's nae golf!
Old Scottish saying

Q. What are the three saddest words in golf?
A. December in Chicago
   iGOLF, golf Internet website

During the 1979 San Diego Open—I didn't realize how windy it was yesterday until I came out today and got a look at Tom Watson. The wind had blown fourteen freckles off Tom's face. Now, that's windy!
   Jerry McGee

I love rotten weather. The founders of the game accepted nature for what it gave or what it took away. Wind and rain are great challenges. They separate real golfers. Let the seas pound against the shore, let the rains pour.
   Tom Watson (1981)

On the windy conditions experienced at the British Open—In the United States, you play target golf, but over here the target moves. You can have the right club at the top of your swing and the wrong one at impact.

> *David Feherty*

On how to handle the wet and windy conditions experienced at the British Open—Just keep laughing and smiling.

> *Walter Hagen*

After a stormy round in the 1983 Women's Kemper Open—The wind was so strong, there were whitecaps in the porta-john.

> *Joyce Kazmierskis*

On the opening days of the 1998 Masters—The wind gusts approached 40 mph, which made the flagsticks resemble slender geezers bending over to look for their house slippers. Fortunately, the overnight rain had drenched the greens and slowed them down from their normal speed, which is that of an F-18.

> *Dan Jenkins,* Golf Digest *(1998)*

If the wind is in your face, you swing too hard just to get the ball through it; if the wind is at your back, you swing too hard just to see how far you can get the ball to go.

> *Henry Beard,* Mulligan's Laws *(1994)*

On Hurricane Bertha—You don't suppose Ely Callaway had anything to do with that?

> *Mike Purkey,* Golf *magazine (1996)*

On being told it was more than 100 degrees in the shade—Well, I'm glad we don't have to play in the shade.

> *Bobby Jones*

On being asked how hot it was on the course—It's as hot as my first watch.

    Fuzzy Zoeller

If the sun is up, why aren't you playing golf?

    Lee Trevino

After a bad day on the greens in the 1983 San Jose Classic—I think all that rain shrunk the cups.

    Juli Inkster

During a rain-affected game—You know, if this wasn't my living, I wouldn't do this if you paid me.

    Christy O'Connor Jr.

WINNING

The longer you play, the better chance the better player has of winning.
Jack Nicklaus

It's not whether you win or lose, but whether I win or lose.

    Sandy Lyle

I don't care what anybody says. The first tournament is not the hardest one to win. It's always the second one.

    John Daly

Winners are a different breed of cat. They have an inner drive and are willing to give of themselves whatever it takes to win.

    Byron Nelson

Second doesn't matter. Second is about as important as fifty-second. Winning is the reason you are playing.

Arnold Palmer

Before the Disney World Classic—I want to win here, stand on the eighteenth green, and say, "I'm going to the World Series!"

Larry Nelson

To be a champion, you have to find a way to get the ball in the cup on the last day.

Tom Watson

In order to win, you must play your best golf when you need it most, and play your sloppy stuff when you can afford it. I shall not attempt to explain how you achieve this happy timing.

Bobby Jones, Golf Is My Game *(1960)*

On being asked, before his final round, what he had to shoot to win the tournament—The rest of the field.

Roger Maltbie

After winning his first major at the 1992 PGA—I feel as if I've got a monkey off my back. In fact, I feel as if I've got a whole troop of monkeys off my back.

Nick Price

Every time you win a little prize of some kind, it stimulates you a little bit, if for no other reason than it's one time you didn't get your brains beat out at something.

Dave Marr (1975)

After her victory in the 1983 Orlando Classic—Winning is the greatest feeling. It's like walking barefoot in the mud.
> *Lynn Adams*

How can they beat me? I've been struck by lightning, had two back operations, and been divorced twice.
> *Lee Trevino*

After winning the 1977 U.S. Open—All of a sudden I am an expert on everything. Interviewers want your opinion on golf, foreign policy, and the price of peanuts.
> *Hubert Green*

Why he jumped in the lake after winning the Memphis Classic— I hadn't won in so long, I wanted to make sure this one soaked in.
> *Jerry Pate*

After winning the 1992 Volvo PGA Championship at Wentworth—By law, everybody ought to feel as great as I do now at least once in their life. I'd like to take on Superman for two rounds. If I felt any better, it would probably be illegal.
> *Tony Johnstone*

After winning the 1992 British Open—I am just a tired little petal.
> *Nick Faldo*

WORK

Work is the thing that interferes with golf.
Frank Dane

My worst day on the golf course still beats my best day in the office.
   John Hallsey (1984)

Never try to do business with someone who is having a bad game.
   William H. Davis

If you break 100, watch your golf. If you break 80, watch your business.
   Joey Adams

If your wife interferes with your golf, get a new wife.
If your business interferes with your golf, get a new business.
   Don Herold, Love That Golf *(1952)*

Your financial cost of playing golf can best be figured out when you realize if you were to devote the same time and energy to business instead of golf, you would be a millionaire in approximately six weeks.
   Buddy Hackett

When you talk turkey with a businessman, you must look squarely at him during the entire conversation. It's the same with putting.
   Gene Sarazen

The seasoned golfing salesman knows when to win, when to come out all even, and when to fall apart at the seams and absorb a valuable thrashing.

Herbert Warren Wind

Statistics indicate that, as a result of overwork, modern executives are dropping like flies on the nation's golf courses.

Ira Wallach

If I have any genius at all, it must be a genius for play! I love to play—I love fishing and hunting and trapshooting and Ping-Pong and chess and pool and billiards and driving a motorcar, and at times I love golf, when I can get the shots going somewhere near right. It seems I love almost any pursuit except work.

Bobby Jones

EQUIPMENT

ACCESSORIES

Golfing trophy: Merely proof of the putting.
Shelby Friedman

I have seen mink head covers, bamboo shafts, concave sand wedges, the twelve-wood, the seven-and-a-half-iron, floating balls, linoleum shoes, dome-shaped tees, distance measurers, girdles that keep your elbows together...and putters as ugly as Stillson wrenches. But the silliest thing I have ever seen in golf is the head cover that goes with the ball retriever.
Charles Price, Golf-at-Large *(1982)*

Golfers who carry ball retrievers are gatherers, not hunters.... Their dreams are no longer of conquest, but only of salvage.
David Owen, Golf Digest *(1998)*

Umbrella: The only long, stick-shaped object with a shaft and a handle routinely found in golf bags that is just as useless in getting the ball into the hole as a putter is.

Henry Beard, A Duffer's Dictionary *(1987)*

The best way to tell whether any golf gadget will help your game is to try to picture Freddie Couples using one.

Henry Beard, Mulligan's Laws *(1993)*

Old golf pros tend to do one of three things: they go on the Senior Tour or retire to the broadcast booth or become inventors of golf gimmicks guaranteed to shave ten strokes off your game.

Peter Jacobsen

On his therapeutic magnetic golf belt—You've just got to be careful walking past the refrigerator.

Jim Colbert (1996)

ANY OLD IRON

The niblick, with its heavy head of iron, is a capital club for knocking down solicitors.

Old English saying

Brassie: Traditional name for the two-wood, whose sole was at one time made of brass. The three-wood is sometimes referred to as a spoon, the four-wood as a baffie, the five-iron as a mashie, the seven-iron as a mashie-niblick, and the nine-iron as a niblick. Any club wrapped around a tree is a smashie. If a club is thrown into a water hazard, it is a splashie.

Henry Beard, A Duffer's Dictionary *(1987)*

"I killed him with my niblick," said Celia.
I nodded. If the thing was to be done at all, it was unquestionably a niblick shot.

   P. G. Wodehouse, The Salvation of George Mackintosh *(1920)*

George Mackintosh...a handsome, well-set-up man, with no vices except a tendency to use the mashie for shots which should have been made with the light iron.

   P. G. Wodehouse, The Salvation of George Mackintosh *(1920)*

If you hit a ball with a mashie, it will sometimes go farther than if you miss it with a driver.

   Ring Lardner

BALLS

Earth: God's golf ball.
   Captain Beefheart

The golf ball is white, dimpled like a bishop's knees, and is the size of small mandarin oranges or those huge pills which vets blow down the throats of constipated cart horses.

   Frank Muir

A golf ball can usually achieve four things. It can go left, right, high, or low...and, on occasion, it can go straight as well.

   Anonymous

Ball: A dimpled, rubber-covered, solid- or compressed-cored, high-compression sphere with a weight of 1.62 ounces and a diameter of 1.68 inches that will enter a cup 4.25 inches in diameter and 4.0 inches deep after an average of 3.87 putts.

Henry Beard, A Duffer's Dictionary *(1987)*

A ball will always come to rest halfway down a hill, unless there is sand or water at the bottom.

Henry Beard

A golf ball just sits there and defies you not to lose it.... Golf would be much easier if the ball moved a little and you were on skates.

Gary McCord, Golf for Dummies *(1996)*

That little white ball won't move until you hit it, and there's nothing you can do after it has gone.

Babe Zaharias

The beauty about golf is the ball doesn't know how big you are.

Claude Harmon

With glasses I can see ants on the ground, but for some reason the ball looks too big to go in the hole.

Dick Meyer (1982)

You can't lose an old golf ball.

John Willis, Willis' Rule of Golf *(1980)*

A golf ball simply cannot find the hole by itself. Even if it could, the ball would never do so willingly, after the hatred and hammering you've heaped on it to get it to the green.

Dick Brooks

Never, never, never, never, will I ever be able to force myself to hit a pink golf ball. After all, the line has to be drawn somewhere.

Peter Dobereiner (1982)

Spring is the season of balls: golf, tennis, base, and moth.

L. L. Levinson

For a while on the links we can lord it over our tiny solar system [the ball] and pretend we are God. No wonder then that we suffer so deeply when our planet goes astray.

Michael Murphy, Golf in the Kingdom

After a shot went astray—It hit a spectator...but the ball's OK.

Jerry Pate

Had the gutta-percha ball not been invented, it is likely enough that golf itself would now be in the catalog of virtually extinct games, only locally surviving, as stool-ball and knurr and spell.

Horace G. Hutchinson (1899)

I really do not see why we should allow the Haskell [ball] to come in. It should be slaughtered at the ports. The discovery of a ball that flies considerably further would be a menace to the game of golf. It would immediately make all our holes the wrong length.

Manchester Guardian *(1901)*

[Nice to see some things don't change...!]

On the new, ultradistance balls—What a farce is this business of length! Golf is surely the only game, either in the United States or Britain, whose whole character has been changed solely by so-called "improvements" in the instruments with which it is played. . . . I cannot believe that the parties concerned would alter the stands at Wimbledon, Forest Hills, Wembley, and Yankee Stadium simply to accommodate a new ball, which when struck in the same manner, happened to go further. I rather fancy they would tell the manufacturers what to do with their new ball.

    Henry Longhurst, Round in Sixty-Eight *(1953)*

Every ball maker all over the world, according at any rate to the advertisements, makes a ball which goes farther than everybody else's.

    Henry Longhurst (1966)

CART BLANCHE

Golf is great exercise, particularly climbing in and out of the carts.
Jack Berry

A golf cart is a two-wheeled bag-carrier that decreases the exercise value of playing eighteen holes of golf from about the level of two sets of doubles tennis to the equivalent of an hour and a half of shopping.

    Henry Beard, A Duffer's Dictionary *(1987)*

You know the old rule: He who have the fastest cart never have to play bad lie.
> *Mickey Mantle,* Esquire *magazine (1971)*

I've had a good day when I don't fall out of the cart.
> *Buddy Hackett*

The golf course being rather far,
I have an excuse to take the car.
And since the holes are far apart,
I have an excuse to use a cart.
But one thing has me still defeated—
You cannot hit the ball while seated.
> *Donna Evleth*

On learning that carts would be permitted on the Senior Tour—
They'd have to carry me out of here before they would get me in a golf cart.
> *Arnold Palmer (1985)*

*On his campaign to outlaw compulsory carts—*This is not such a call to arms as a call to legs. Arise, golfers of America, and insist on your rights. Realize the satisfactions of real golf. After all, you have nothing to lose but your excess poundage, your incipient heart attacks, and your extortionate cart fees.
> *Peter Dobereiner,* Golf Digest *(1991)*

*On Casey Martin's using a cart in the 1998 U.S. Open—*A lot of people will be watching, that's for sure. . . . It will be interesting to see how he drives the cart, where he parks it and all.
> *Ernie Els*

Cart paths at Pebble Beach! What next? Astroturf greens at St. Andrews?
> *Art Spander,* Golf Digest *(1977)*

CLUBS IN GENERAL

**Golf clubs aren't only tools.
They're totems. The game turns on illusions.**
Frank Hannigan

The trouble that most of us find with the modern matched set of clubs is that they don't really seem to know any more about the game than the old ones did!
  Robert Browning, A History of Golf *(1955)*

It doesn't matter what kind of club head is on one end of that shiny metal shaft if a fat head is on the other.
  Robinson Murray

They say some men are good putters or good chippers. Nonsense. The whole secret of golf is to choose the right club for the right shot.
  Gary Player (1974)

The only thing you should force in a golf swing is the club back into the bag.
  Byron Nelson

A professional will tell you the amount of flex you need in the shaft of your club. The more the flex, the more strength you will need to break the thing over your knee.
  Stephen Baker

Acquiring a new set of golf clubs is rather like getting married. The honeymoon is wonderful, but how things go after that depend on whether the courtship has properly tested the true compatibility of partners.
  Peter Dobereiner

IRONS IN THE FIRE

Headline above an article on the lob wedge—
All You Need Is Lob.
Golf *magazine (1996)*

You must have a good fluid swing to make that club pay off.
If I catch one of my amateur friends playing with a one-iron,
he had better be putting with it.
  Tommy Bolt, The Hole Truth *(1971)*

Actually, the only time I ever took out a one-iron was to kill
a tarantula. And I took a 7 to do that.
  Jim Murray

The one-iron is almost unplayable. You keep it in your bag
the way you keep a Dostoyevsky novel in your bookcase—
with the vague notion that you will try it someday. In the
meantime, it impresses your friends.
  Tom Scott and Geoffrey Cousins

No Instant Golfer can ever do anything with a two- or three-
iron but poke the fire.
  Jim Murray

*After hitting three consecutive shots into the water during the
1983 Sea Pines Heritage Classic—*I was stubborn. I knew the
four-iron was the right club.
  Ben Crenshaw

In golf, you're always thinking about how the course is playing, whether the greens are fast or slow, or whether the wind
is blowing or dying or shifting. All of a sudden, you say, "Aw!
Just give me a five-iron."
  Rex Caldwell, Golf *magazine (1983)*

You can't hit a good five-iron when you're thinking about a six-iron on the backswing.

  Charles Coody

I call my sand wedge my half-Nelson, because I can always strangle the opposition with it.

  Byron Nelson (1945)

PUTTERS

**I've gone through more putters
than Carter's has pills.**
Tom Watson

The putter, after all, is the one club in your bag no sane player has ever sliced a ball into the woods with, and it's the only club that after you hit with it, nobody looks at you funny when the ball only goes ten feet.

  Leslie Nielsen, Bad Golf: My Way *(1996)*

On lending Tiger Woods a putter during the 1998 British Open—That's my backup putter. I finished first, and Tiger finished one shot off. That's why it's my backup.

  Mark O'Meara

Too much is done with too little thought. It must be mind over putter.

  Horton Smith

If you can drive farther with a putter than a wood, then by all means do so.

  Michael Green

I may be the only golfer never to have broken a single putter, if you don't count the one I twisted into a loop and threw into a bush.

    Thomas Boswell, Golf Digest *(1980)*

I was always more of a breaker than a thrower—mostly putters. I broke so many of those, I probably became the world's foremost authority on how to putt without a putter.

    Tommy Bolt, How to Keep Your Temper
    on the Golf Course *(1969)*

Confidence builds with successive putts. The putter, then, is a club designed to hit the ball partway to the hole.

    Rex Lardner, Out of the Bunker and into the Trees *(1960)*

Happiness is a long walk with a putter.

    Greg Norman

The less said about the putter, the better. Here is an instrument of torture, designed by Tantalus and forged in the devil's own smithy.

    Tony Lema

One minute the sword [putter] is making you king; the next it is lacerating you.

    Mac O'Grady

Fred Couples is having problems. He may tie that putter onto the back of his car and drag it all the way to the next tournament.

    Lee Trevino (1985)

I call my putter "Sweet Charity" because it covers a multitude of sins from tee to green.

    Billy Casper

On long-handled putters—If you want to use it in the pole vault, fine. Nobody ever sank a putt of any length with a long putter unless the ball accidentally hit two coins and a spike mark.

> *Dan Jenkins,* Fairways and Greens *(1994)*

On refusing to use a long-handled putter—If I'm going to putt and miss, I want to look good doing it.

> *Chi Chi Rodriguez*

On not using a long-handled putter—I'd chip with a five-iron before I used one of these things.

> *Ben Crenshaw*

You can't let a putter think it is indispensable. I keep another one (named Number 2) in the car trunk. I switch at least once a year, just to prove to Betsy she can be switched.

> *Fuzzy Zoeller*

TECHNOLOGY

**Golfers used to be made on the golf courses.
Now they are made in machine shops.**
Donald Ross

Hickory golf was a game of manipulation and inspiration; steel golf is a game of precision and calculation.

> *Peter Dobereiner,* The Glorious World of Golf *(1973)*

[Pray tell, what of graphite and titanium?—distance and misdirection!]

Golf is doing great. Why change it? I mean, they're all arguing over square grooves and V-grooves and slick grooves and titanium shafts and graphite shafts and bamboo shafts and big grips and little grips. The human side still has to hit it. Believe me when I tell you this—it's not the arrows. It's the Indians.

Lee Trevino

In terms of optimum club-head speed, the length of the hosel and the apparent angle of the groove-to-punch mark declination, minus the reciprocal of the angle of the axis of the shaft as it relates to the heel, must under no circumstances exceed the distance in millimeters between the axis of the shaft or the neck or socket and the back of the heel. There. That ought to take care of my wife. I don't think she would read this anyway, but she'll definitely never get past that paragraph. We can speak freely now.

David Owen, My Usual Game: Adventures in Golf *(1995)*

Almost everything looks different when you reenter golf after a long layoff. Take the clubs. In most any golf shop I've entered, I've been able to find nothing but long rows of things that look like parts that have fallen off a DC-10.

Dan Jenkins, Golf Digest *(1990)*

I apologized to my wife for the fact that the PowerClout WideBody Launcher was so expensive. It cost $2,367, primarily because it is constructed of Flutorium-X, a rare metal found only in the volcanoes near Bali, and blended with the lining of killer whales.

Dan Jenkins, Fairways and Greens *(1994)*

This being the age of torque ratios, Bubble shafts, and club designs more complex than DNA sampling, it's no wonder guys on the tour... hit tee shots that go further than most people go on vacation.

Ron Green Jr., Golf *magazine (1996)*

Humongous Big Berthas with Star Wars shafts that have more kick points than a Bruce Lee movie.

Gary McCord, Golf Digest *(1997)*

WOODS

**For most amateurs the best wood
in the bag is the pencil.**
Chi Chi Rodriguez

On "personally humanizing" golf clubs—My own driver, incidentally, I see as a brawn, Irish sailor in a dirty sweatshirt who can perform prodigious feats when he is in the mood. Unfortunately, most of the time he is drunk.

Peter Dobereiner, Golf Digest *(1978)*

If there's a faster way to turn a Jekyll into a Hyde than by handing a man the driver, we don't know of it.

Lew Fishman

After using John Daly's Killer Whale driver—It was like swinging a scaffolding pole.

Ian Pyman

DRESS CODE

**Whoever plays with a ball and a club shall be
fined twenty shillings or their upper garment.**
The Magistrates of Brussels, Belgium (1360)

Baffling late-life discovery: Golfers wear those awful clothes
on purpose.
Herb Caen

"Play It as It Lies" is one of the fundamental dictates of golf.
The other one is "Wear It if It Clashes."
Henry Beard, Golfing *(1985)*

No golfer ever swung too slow. No golfer ever played too fast.
No golfer ever dressed too plainly.
Henry Beard, Mulligan's Laws *(1994)*

We should be allowed to wear shorts. God Almighty!
Women are allowed to wear them, and we've got better legs
than they do.
Greg Norman

Never play golf with a guy who wears shorts and anklets.
Unless you can beat him. It's a horrible thing...losing to
shorts and anklets.
Dan Jenkins, Golf Digest *(1997)*

It was the Thirties that gave us Jimmy Demaret's pink shoes
and polka-dot slacks—outfits that would make Doug Sanders
look like a Bond's window display.
Dan Jenkins, The Dogged Victims of Inexorable Fate *(1970)*

Those golfers who look as though they got dressed in the dark should be penalized two strokes each for offending the public eye.

Doug Sanders

Doug Sanders's outfit has been described as looking like the aftermath of a direct hit on a pizza factory.

Dave Marr (1983)

A dozen years later, at the 1995 World Matchplay, on David Duval's multi-colored shirt—It looks like a direct hit on a pizza factory.

Dave Marr, BBC TV

[To which, Marr's co-commentator Peter Alliss replied: "Mind you, if you saw Claudia Schiffer wearing it, you'd think it looked all right."]

Claude Harmon not only taught me most of what I know about the golf swing, he took me out of argyle socks.

Dave Marr

Now look here at all those baby-face mullets on the tour. They come out here dressed up in their Ben Hogan blues and grays. They ought to come to Old Tom and let him show 'em how to match their reds with their pinks and their fuchsias.

Tommy Bolt

During a heavy downpour at the Houston Open—Here I am ruining a $100 pair of shoes, a $110 cashmere sweater, and a $65 pair of slacks. Hell, I'm ruining more than I can win.

Tommy Bolt

Most unlikely people play golf, including people who are
blind, who have only one arm, or even no legs, and people
often wear bizarre clothes to the game. Other golfers don't
think them odd, for there are no rules of appearance or dress
at golf.

    Ian Fleming, Goldfinger *(1959)*

You can't call it a game. You don't run, you don't shoot, you
don't pass. All you have to do is buy some clothes that don't
match.

    Steve Sax

There is one thing in the world that is dumber than playing
golf. That is watching someone else play golf. What do you
actually see? Thirty-seven guys in polyester slacks squinting at
the sun. Doesn't that set your blood racing?

    Peter Andrews, Golf Digest

To a brightly dressed St. Andrews spectator—I say, are those
your old school colors or your own unfortunate choice?

    Bernard Darwin (1955)

On his high school days—I thought all the guys who played
golf were a bunch of sissies. They all wore pink sweaters.

    Larry Nelson

I'd give up golf if I didn't have so many sweaters.

    Bob Hope

On the potential distractions in the gallery—Shorts and a tight
sweater have caused more guys to bogey a hole than a bad
slice.

    Jim Murray (1968)

On female golfers and fashion—Just ask yourself how good
Nicklaus would be if he had to do his nails and put up his
hair every night before a tournament? Could he shoot 68 if
he was trying to make up his mind which dress to wear to
the party that night?

Jim Murray (1968)

Just because the weather is cold, there is no need to appear in
public like a sack of potatoes. All it needs is some thermal
underwear.

Sponsor's letter to women players (1981)

Trousers are now allowed to be worn by ladies on the course.
But they must be removed before entering the clubhouse.

Sign at an Irish golf club

I wish they would start talking about the quality of my golf,
not my wardrobe; print my score, not my measurements.

Craig Stadler

*After being asked the size of the "tight-fitting" green jacket pre-
sented to him upon winning the Masters*— I don't know, and
I'm not about to take it off and find out.

Craig Stadler (1982)

If a golfer gets superstitious, he'll go one way—down. Some
players may wear the same shirt for four straight days. No
wonder they don't attract much of a gallery.

Gary Player

Before the 1993 Ryder Cup—The only thing that scares me is
the Americans' dress sense.

Mark James

On golf in cold and windy Scotland—I can't swing the way I
want to with four sweaters and my pajamas and a rain jacket on.
  Lee Trevino

On a caddie's lack of dress sense—We are just praying we're
both still out here when Roy's pants come back in style.
  Lee Trevino

Golf is a game where white men can dress up as pimps and
get away with it.
  Robin Williams (1986)

Golf enables me to dress like an idiot.
  Huey Lewis

Golf is not a sport. Golf is men in ugly pants, walking.
  Rosie O'Donnell

There is one more important characteristic: it must have a
large and smooth area for advertising. That, above all, is the
purpose of golf hats.
  Peter Dobereiner (1982)

Can you imagine anything sillier than a man wearing
knickers? That's like putting Bermuda shorts on an alligator.
  Charles Price, Golf Digest *(1983)*

*On being asked to wear a number on his back during
competition*—For that kind of money, I'd wear a skirt.
  Jimmy Demaret

Mere dregs of the golfing world who enter competitions for
the hell of the thing or because they know they look well in
sports clothes.
  P. G. Wodehouse, Feet of Clay *(1950)*

On his early sponsorship deals—My chief regret was that I hadn't signed up with a good Chinese laundry and a nation-wide we-pick-it-up-anywhere dry-cleaning service.
  Jack Nicklaus

I wish that someone would tell me:
a. why golfers only wear one glove, and
b. why no commentator in the history of the game has ever been heard to explain why.
  Mike Seabrook, A Good Walk Spoiled?

Golf—indeed all sport—retains an eye-lowered reverence, a religious solemnity, when the hushed talk gets round to Augusta's green jacket.
  Frank Keating

The Masters green jacket plays castanets with your knees.
  Chi Chi Rodriguez

SHOES

**Golf got complicated when I had to wear shoes
and begin thinking about what I was doing.**
  Sam Snead

You show me a player who swings out of his shoes, and I'll show you a player who isn't going to win enough to keep himself in a decent pair of shoes for long.
  Sam Snead

People who wear white shoes are either golfers or tourists.
  Jimmy Cannon

I even enjoy the mingled pleasure and discomfort of breaking in a new pair of golf shoes.

Arnold Palmer, My Game and Yours *(1963)*

On his new rubber-spiked shoes—I felt like Spiderman.

Fuzzy Zoeller (1984)

I come from a different era. I'm from the club era. I started out shining shoes, giving lessons, selling 10E shoes to some guy who wears 12C and making him like it.

Lee Trevino, USA Today *(1983)*

Never wear golf shoes to a dance.

Henry Beard, A Duffer's Dictionary *(1987)*

SHOT MAKING & TECHNIQUE

BAD SHOTS

**Golf is not a game of good shots;
it's a game of bad shots.**
Ben Hogan

One bad shot does not make a losing score.
Gay Brewer

It is possible to play golf, and in fact win, by hitting an awful
lot of bad shots if somehow you make up for them with
spectacular recoveries or fantastic putting.
Peter Thomson

I expect to make at least seven mistakes a round. Therefore,
when I make a bad shot, I don't worry about it; it's just one
of those seven.
Walter Hagen

Walter Hagen once said that every golfer can expect to have four[!!] bad shots in a round and when you do, just put them out of your mind. This, of course, is hard to do when you're not even off the first tee when you've had them.

Jim Murray

Arnold Palmer, after hitting a tee shot behind a tree: Well, you're always writing about Ben Hogan. What would Hogan do in a situation like this?
Jim Murray: He wouldn't be in a situation like this!

I am the world's foremost master at the topped shot. Not everyone can learn to play this delicate little line drive around the green with finesse.

Jim Murray, The Sporting World of Jim Murray *(1968)*

Topping the ball is a problem that usually afflicts only beginning golfers, and it is quickly left behind once a player has learned to master the hook, the slice, the shank, and the airball.

Henry Beard, A Duffer's Dictionary *(1987)*

It is not a crime to play a bad shot, and the player may yet be a good husband and father and a true Christian gentleman.

Bernard Darwin

No man has mastered golf until he realizes that his good shots are accidents and his bad shots are good exercise.

Eugene R. Black

To his caddies—When I make a bad shot, your job is to take the blame.

Seve Ballesteros

Your bad days at golf are not at all serious to your fellow players. If anything, each of your bad shots builds the other fellow's ego.

James Gallagher

One thing that will help you keep your calm while playing golf is to remember that nobody gives a damn about your bad golf...but you.

Don Herold

On a bad shot in the Dubai Desert Classic—That was a Shiite effort.

David Feherty

Good golf isn't a matter of hitting great shots. It's finding a way to make your bad ones not so bad. If I hadn't learned to do that, you'd still be thinking that "Trevino" was Italian.

Lee Trevino (1979)

If you hit a bad shot, just tell yourself it is great to be alive, relaxing, and walking around a beautiful golf course. The next shot will be better.

Al Geiberger

The purgatory of my inane inefficiencies with a golf club spells doom for the flight of the ball.

Gary McCord, Just a Range Ball in a Box of Titleists *(1997)*

You need a fantastic memory in this game to remember the great shots, and a very short memory to forget the bad ones.

Gary McCord (1984)

Any golfer serious enough about his game to want to break 120 must learn to stop worrying about the last ten or twenty missed strokes.

Stephen Baker, How to Play Golf in the Low 120s *(1962)*

There are three types of bad shots in golf: those that cost you a half stroke, those that cost you a full stroke, and those that cost you two strokes. Only stupidity costs you more than two strokes.

Bob Toski (1983)

I'm usually like a yo-yo out there. I play good and then I play bad and then I play good.

Juli Inkster

I've quit worrying about poor shots. I just tell myself, "Relax, Bozo. If you can't have fun, you shouldn't be out here."

Patty Sheehan

Even if you hit forty bad shots, you should still keep trying. The other fellow might hit forty-one.

Gary Player

As soon as Bond had hit the shot, he knew it wouldn't do. The difference between a good golf shot and a bad one is the same as the difference between a beautiful woman and a plain one—a matter of millimeters.

Ian Fleming, Goldfinger *(1959)*

A golfer rarely needs to hit a spectacular shot unless the one that precedes it was pretty bad.

Harvey Penick, And If You Play Golf, You're My Friend *(1993)*

It is a law of nature that everybody plays a hole badly when going through.
Bernard Darwin (1934)

Don't let the bad shots get to you. Don't let yourself become angry. The true scramblers are thick-skinned. And they always beat the whiners.
Paul Runyan (1977)

As of this writing, there are approximately 2,450 reasons why a person hits a rotten golf shot, and more are being discovered every day.
Jay Cronley, Playboy *(1981)*

Like all Saturday foursomes, it is in difficulties. One of the patients is zigzagging about the fairway like a liner pursued by submarines.
P. G. Wodehouse, On Golf *(1973)*

DRIVING AMBITION

**A good drive enables you to play
the rest of the hole.**
Anonymous

My goal this year is basically to find the fairways.
Lauri Peterson

All those who drive thirty yards suppose themselves to be great putters.
Sir Walter Simpson, The Art of Golf *(1887)*

There is no such thing as a golfer uninterested in his driving. The really strong player seems to value his least; but this is merely because so many of his shots are good that they do not surprise him. Let it, however, be suggested that some other is a longer driver than he, and the mask of apathy will at once fall from his face, his tongue will be loosened, and he proceeds to boast.

Sir Walter Simpson, The Art of Golf *(1887)*

I would much rather be hitting the driver and a nine-iron out of the rough than hitting a driver and a four-iron out of the fairway.

Jack Nicklaus (1983)

A long drive is good for the ego.

Arnold Palmer, My Game and Yours *(1963)*

I don't stand there and wiggle the club like Arnold Palmer and them cats. I walk up and hit it about 350 yards. I figure I could drive longer if I ran up and hit it.

Muhammad Ali (1973)

Golfers are very fond of insisting, and with great justice, that the game is not won by the driver. It is the short game—the approaching and putting—that wins the match. Nevertheless, despite the truth of this, if there were no driving, there would be very little golf.

Horace G. Hutchinson, Hints on the Game of Golf *(1886)*

On being paired with power-drivers Ian Woosnam and John Daly during the 1993 British Open—I may be paired with them, but I'm unlikely to be actually playing alongside them. In fact, there's a danger they might decide to call me through, thinking that I'm part of the match behind.

David Feherty

I got as much fun as the next man from whaling the ball as hard as I could and catching it squarely on the button. But from sad experience I learned not to try this in a round that meant anything.

Bobby Jones

There are no short hitters on the tour anymore—just long and unbelievably long.

Sam Snead (1984)

On his eternal search for distance off the tee—I never win a match. I spend my golfing life out-of-bounds. I never even count my strokes. I know that I can never beat anyone who "putts" along down the middle. All the same, I get more fun out of my golf than any other man I know when I am hitting my drives.

P. G. Wodehouse

On her powerful drives—I just hitch up my girdle and let 'er fly.

Mildred "Babe" Zaharias

I only hit the ball 220 yards off the tee, but I can always find it.

Bonnie Lauer (1977)

I hit a 341-yard drive in Hawaii once...it was downhill, downwind, down everything.

Laura Davies

I once hit a drive 500 yards...on a par 3. I had a three-wood coming back.

Chi Chi Rodriguez

Recalling a play-off tee shot that cost him the 1989 British Open at Troon—People still tell me I was stupid to take a driver and knock my ball into that bunker. Well, even I didn't think I could reach it, even I didn't realize how pumped up I was.

Greg Norman

You know what they say about big hitters . . . the woods are full of them.

Jimmy Demaret

I'm hitting the woods just great, but I'm having a terrible time getting out of them.

Harry Tofcano

When I first came out on tour, I swung all out on every tee shot. My drives finished so far off line, my pants were grass-stained at the knees.

Fuzzy Zoeller

After all three of his four-ball partners drove into the woods— What's over there? A nudist colony?

Lee Trevino (1970)

Some may hit the ball for miles, but they are not the winners; they just lose their ball.

Lee Trevino

The most dangerous thing I can do is drive to the bank. I've got a bad swing, a bad stance, and a bad grip, but my banker loves me.

Lee Trevino

*To his wayward playing partner—*Obviously a deer on the fairway has seen you tee off before and knows that the safest place to be when you play is right down the middle.

Jackie Gleason

*On the benefits of accuracy over distance—*Airmail without zip code will never find its target.

Bob Toski

On his extra distance off the tee—I can airmail the golf ball, but sometimes I don't put the right address on it.
Jim Dent

Don't you just hate it when you don't know who is going to show up on the first tee...you or your evil, hacking, three-putting twin?
Mike Purkey, Golf *magazine (1996)*

Most of us cannot let go and let the genie out of the lamp. We know he's in there, hidden in our bones and muscles, because he does come out now and then. When he does, we wind up asking him for ten yards more on the drives, and he goes back in.
John Updike

No matter how short the par 3, the drive is never a gimme.
Henry Beard, Mulligan's Laws *(1994)*

GRIPPING STUFF

**He folded her in his arms...
using the interlocking grip.**
P. G. Wodehouse

If a player doesn't have a good grip, he has two chances—slim and none.
Gene Sarazen

If some players took a fork to their mouths the way they take the club back, they'd starve to death.
Sam Snead

Too many golfers grip the club at address like they were trying to choke a prairie coyote to death.

    Curt Wilson (1970)

If you have a bad grip, you don't want a good swing.

    Harvey Penick

A bad grip has ruined more golf games than Ladies' Day.

    Lee Trevino

Relax? How can anybody relax and play golf? You have to grip the club, don't you?

    Ben Hogan

A weak left hand? That's all right—I take checks with the other one.

    Bobby Locke

You can fake about anything, but a bad grip will follow you to the grave.

    Gary McCord, Golf for Dummies *(1996)*

I've been squeezing the club so hard, the cow is screaming.

    J. C. Snead

I kept hanging on to my clubs like I hang on to the steering wheel of one of my race cars, and that is the worst possible thing I could do.

    Nigel Mansell (1988)

Golfers don't fist fight. They cuss a bit. But they wouldn't punch anything or anybody. They might hurt their hands and have to change their grip.

    Dan Jenkins, Dead Solid Perfect *(1974)*

HOLE IN ONE

**What's the most difficult shot?
I find it to be the hole in one.**
Groucho Marx

It has been estimated that a golfer's chances of making a hole in one are much greater than the probability that he will read the rules of the game.
Herb Graffis

Man blames fate for other accidents but feels personally responsible for a hole in one.
Martha Beckman

There are two reasons for making a hole in one: the first is that it is immensely labor-saving.
H. I. Phillips

In making a hole in one, I stand with the feet fairly wide apart and the weight evenly distributed on both heels. I use the interlocking grip, a three-quarters swing, a thirty-five cent ball, and the regulation prayer. I generally wear light underwear, as there is nothing that will upset a stroke more than an itch that comes from a woolen or hair-lined undershirt at the moment of the upswing, and prefer socks that are smart without being vulgar.
H. I. Phillips

On betting $10 on and making a hole in one, after being told it was a 100,000-to-1 chance—The trick is to know when that one time is about to happen.
Walter Hagen

After making a hole in one at the U.S. Open—Let's see if we can make back-to-back eagles.

> *Sandy Lyle*

After ignoring his caddie's insistent choice of a six-iron and before acing the fourteenth in the Nike Monterey Open with a five-iron—You just carry the bag, and I'll hit the shots.

> *David Toms (1995)*

On prize money awarded for holes in one—It occurred to me at once, if it happened to me, I should take the matter to court and claim that a hole in one was not a matter of skill, since no golfer in recorded history has ever made one on purpose, but rather an act of God—or, if you like, the result of a lottery or game of chance, and therefore not taxable.

> *Henry Longhurst*

[Lottery winnings in the U.K. are not taxable, but hole-in-one prizes are.]

In Japan, player who scores hole in one while leading tournament always lose. It's proven jinx.

> *Ayako Okamoto (1984)*

If I ever make a hole in one,
A thrill that I've never known,
I won't be believed and I'll have no fun,
For I'm sure to be playing alone.

> *Richard Armour,* Golf Is a Four-Letter Word *(1962)*

A distinguished professor of pathology, who recently holed out in one at the fourth at Walton Heath, thus opening the round 4371444, asks whether he is the only man in history to have started a round of golf with his own telephone number.

> *Henry Longhurst*

HOOKS & SLICES

**Anyone slicing the ball has reached
the top of his game. The harder he hits
the ball, the more it will slice.**
Jack Burke Sr.

Hook: The addiction of 50 percent of all golfers.
Slice: The weakness of the other half.
Jim Bishop (1970)

I hate a hook. It nauseates me. I could vomit. It's like a rattlesnake in your pocket.
Ben Hogan

I took up golf as something to do when a wet field made cricket unplayable, but soon I was playing when the sun shone as well. I gave it up soon after I married. I claimed it was a supreme sacrifice, but the development of a cancerous slice probably had more to do with it.
Michael Hobbs, Golf for the Connoisseur

Letter to Golf Digest—I applaud your article on how to fix your slice or hook. I would be the first to rid myself of the slice I possess, but I've grown fond of it, as it's the only consistent shot I have.
Frank Fisher of Salt Lake City (1997)

When a pro hits it left to right, it's called a fade.
When an amateur hits it left to right, it's called a slice.
Peter Jacobsen

Playing golf is a little like carving a turkey: it helps if you have your slice under control.
Bob Orben

A 5 with a slice will always beat a 6 by Arnold Palmer.
  Jesse Brown

Practice tee: The place where golfers go to convert a nasty hook into a wicked slice.
  Henry Beard, A Duffer's Dictionary *(1987)*

This golfer has a wicked slice
And quite a follow-through.
That's why his partner, who stood too close,
Is on the green in two.
  Richard Armour, Golf Is a Four-Letter Word *(1962)*

Lorena Bobbitt: A nasty slice.
  Gary McCord (1994)

MISSES

**This is a game of misses. The guy
who misses the best is going to win.**
  Ben Hogan

*On how he four-putted on the sixteenth during the 1988
Masters*—I miss, I miss, I miss, I make!
  Seve Ballesteros

Real golfers don't miss putts—they get robbed!
  Anonymous

Tap-in: A putt short enough to be missed one-handed.
  Henry Beard, A Duffer's Dictionary *(1987)*

Missing a short putt doesn't mean that I have to hit my next drive out-of-bounds.
> *Tony Lema*

Hagen said that no one remembers who finished second. But they still ask me if I ever think about that putt I missed to win the 1970 Open at St. Andrews. I tell them that sometimes it doesn't cross my mind for a full five minutes.
> *Doug Sanders*

On how he carded a 13 during the 1961 U.S. Open—Easy, I missed a twenty-footer for a 12.
> *Arnold Palmer*

The least thing upsets him on the links. He misses short putts because of the uproar of the butterflies in the adjoining field.
> *P. G. Wodehouse,* The Clicking of Cuthbert *(1922)*

The average expert player—if he is lucky—hits six, eight, or ten real shots in a round. The rest are good misses.
> *Tommy Armour*

No doubt the public knows less about the inside intricacies of first-class golf than any other sport. It seems to be their particular delight to watch a famous golfer miss a shot and then hold him up to ridicule.
> *Tommy Armour*

Every year I played, I discovered more and more ways to miss shots, obscure and yet more important mistakes I had never dreamed of making.
> *Bobby Jones*

I am the 747 of golf. One look at the target and I'm gone. Miss 'em quick. That's always been my theme song.
Moe Norman

Golf is not a game of great shots. It's a game of most accurate misses. The people who win make the smallest mistakes.
Gene Littler

MOON SHOT

On seeing the moon through a telescope—
Faith, sir. She's terrible full o' bunkers.
Old Tom Morris

*On his six-iron moon shot—*There we go! Miles and miles and miles!!
Alan Shepard (1971)

*During the shot—*It looks like a slice to me, Al.
Ed Mitchel

*After the shot—*I said a few unprintable words under my breath and called it a mulligan.
Alan Shepard

[He also explained: "Because of the cumbersome suit I was wearing, I couldn't make a very good pivot on the swing. And I had to hit the ball with just one hand."]

*Alan Shepard prepared to blast his way out of a bunker—*10-9-8-7-6-5-4-3-2-1!
Gleneagles' gallery

First golfer on the moon is he,
Yet mad enough to pop.
Because of the lack of gravity,
The poor lad's putt won't drop.
>   *Richard Armour,* Golf Is a Four-Letter Word *(1962)*

OVER PAR-TICULAR

What do I like about golf?
It's certainly not the low scores.
Huey Lewis

The invisible opponent whose tangible form is the card and
pencil; the toughest opponent of them all—Old Man Par.
>   *Bobby Jones*

Old Man Par may be a helluva player, good enough to earn
$100,000 a year on the PGA Tour, and win thirty-three U.S.
Open Championships, but I would like to get him in a dark
alley one night and club him to death with my mashie. I
would use a gun, except that I know my limitations when it
comes to shooting Par.
>   *Peter Dobereiner,* Golf Digest *(1980)*

In golf as in life, the attempt to do something in one stroke
but needs two is apt to result in taking three.
>   *Walter Camp*

It'll take three damn good shots to get up in two today.
>   *Old Scottish caddies' saying*

I was three over. One over a house, one over a patio, and one over a swimming pool.

    George Brett

After taking 12 at the final hole in the 1961 Los Angeles Open— Every cloud has a silver lining. Well, this will give the average duffer a bit of heart from here on in.

    Arnold Palmer

*After Jack Nicklaus shot an 83 in the British Open—*All my life I wanted to play like Jack Nicklaus, and now I do.

    Paul Harvey, ABC TV (1981)

*After he carded an 80 in the PGA Championship—*I don't know when I'm going to play again. I've had enough brain damage for August.

    Nick Faldo

After carding an 82 in defense of his British Open crown— I guess I'll hand in my card and have them review my handicap.

    Justin Leonard (1998)

A triple bogey is three strokes more than par, four strokes more than par is a quadruple bogey, five more than par is a quintuple, six is a sextuple, seven is a throwuple, eight is a blowuple, and nine is an ohshutuple.

    Henry Beard, Golfing (1985)

As every golfer knows, no one ever lost his mind over one shot. It is rather the gradual process of shot after shot watching your score go to tatters—knowing that you have found a different way to bogey each one.

    Thomas Boswell

I'm playing like Tarzan—but scoring like Jane.
   Chi Chi Rodriguez

My best score ever was 103, but I've only been playing fifteen
years.
   Alex Karras

After another high-scoring round—I thought winning the
Oscar would help my golf game. I guess some things will
never change.
   Jack Nicholson (1998)

Hush-a-bye, baby, pretty one, sleep;
Daddy's gone golfing to win the club sweep.
If he plays nicely (I hope that he will);
Mother will show him the dressmaker's bill.
Hush-a-bye, baby, safe in your cot;
Daddy's come home, and his temper is hot.
Cuddle down closer, baby of mine;
Daddy went round in a hundred and nine.
   Anonymous

PRACTICE MAKES PAR-FECT

Home, home on the range.

I take the revolutionary view that all this talk about the
virtues of practice, for the average club golfer, at any rate, is a
snare and delusion. "Practice makes perfect," they say. Of
course, it doesn't. For the vast majority of golfers it merely
consolidates imperfection.
   Henry Longhurst

It seems to me that we must practice a lot or not at all. The halfhearted, infrequent, casual practice spells just before a tournament usually serve only to confuse a player, by awakening him to the fact that he can hit the ball in a dozen different ways and still miss them.

Henry Cotton

Today you can drive up to the average country club practice area and see three dinosaurs for every golfer who's out there working on pitch-and-run shots.

Lee Trevino

I'm no good unless I hit over 300 balls a day. You may not see me at the tournament because I practice at a different course. I tell the guys I haven't picked up a stick in weeks, but that's a bunch of bull. I'd go nuts if I didn't hit balls.

Lee Trevino (1976)

Why waste good shots in practice when you might need them in a match?

Walter Hagen

It is good to practice at night. You hit the ball and listen. If you hear crack-crack-crack, you know you have hit the trees. Lost ball. But you hear nothing, you know you are in the middle of the fairway.

Costantino Rocca

Practice puts brains in your muscles.

Sam Snead

The click of a solid wood shot soaring far down the fairway is well worth all the hours of practice.
    Jimmy Demaret

Driving range: A place where golfers go to get all the good shots out of their systems.
    Henry Beard, A Duffer's Dictionary *(1987)*

Practice golf is like a boxer working on a punch bag. It doesn't hit back.
    Chi Chi Rodriguez

Undirected practice is worse than no practice. Too often you become careless and sloppy in your swing. You'd be better off staying home and beating the rugs.
    Gary Player

Swinging at daisies is like playing electric guitar with a tennis racket: if it were that easy, we could all be Jerry Garcia. The ball changes everything.
    Michael Bamberger

The teacher experiences no grave difficulty in having a student understand the importance of putting. Getting them to practice it is quite another matter.
    John Duncan Dunn

I prefer practicing alone to playing for nothing.
    Raymond Floyd

THE PUTTS OF THE EARTH

**The best way to putt is the way
you putt the best.**
Old golf saying

Driving is a game of free-swinging muscle control, while putting is something like performing eye surgery and using a bread knife for a scalpel.
    Tommy Bolt

Putting allows the touchy golfer two to four opportunities to blow a gasket in the short space of two to forty feet.
    Tommy Bolt

Natural golfers are bad golfers, but natural putters are good putters.
    Percy Boomer

Don't trust little putts until you've sunk 'em;
De mortuis nil nisi...is all bunkum.
    Bill Duncan

Putting is the absolute key to golf. It can erode the whole fabric. It's ruined my iron play for a long time now because I've been trying to push irons too near the pin to compensate; and once that starts, you start straining off the tee; and once that starts, you might as well stay at home and watch movies.
    Arnold Palmer (1979)

The game would be nothing without this troublesome business round the hole.
    Joyce Wethered

Close in golf usually means one more putt.
    Bob Murphy

A putt cannot go in the hole if it's short. I'd rather face a
four-footer coming back than leave the ball on the front lip.
    Tom Watson

The devoted golfer is an anguished soul who has learned a lot
about putting, just as an avalanche victim has learned a lot
about snow.
    Dan Jenkins, Sports Illustrated *(1962)*

Walter Travis, probably the greatest putter the game has
ever seen, always said that he visualized the putting stroke as
an attempt to drive an imaginary tack into the back of the
ball.
    Bobby Jones

On his caddie's advice on how to make a difficult putt—He told
me to keep the ball low.
    Chi Chi Rodriguez

Hitting a golf ball and putting have nothing in common.
They're two different games. You work all your life to perfect
a repeating swing that will get you to the greens, and then
you have to try to do something that is totally unrelated.
There shouldn't be any cups, just flagsticks. And the man
who hit the most fairways and greens and got closest to the
pins would be the tournament winner.
    Ben Hogan

*[Hogan is also quoted as saying: "There is no similarity between golf
and putting; they are two different games—one played in the air, and
the other on the ground."]*

Like other things essentially foolish in themselves, such as preaching, putting becomes attractive in proportion to the skill acquired in it.

Sir Walter Simpson, The Art of Golf *(1887)*

Nonchalant putts count the same as chalant putts.

Henry Beard, Mulligan's Laws *(1994)*

The golf game isn't over till the last putt drops.

Cary Middlecoff

ATTITUDE

Putting is a state of mind. I wish I had sixteen-year-old nerves to go with my fifty-nine-year-old swing.

Sam Snead

Putting is largely mental, and on this account becomes so difficult. The novice who has not back of him recollections of scores of missed putts a couple of feet or so from the hole is more apt to bring off a putt of this distance, especially on a keen green, than the other fellow. He is not troubled with any thought of being a yard or more away from a miss, and in blissful ignorance bangs away and holes.

Walter J. Travis (1900)

When a putter is waiting his turn to hole out a putt of one or two feet in length, on which the match hangs at the last hole, it is of vital importance that he think of nothing. At this supreme moment he ought to fill his mind with vacancy. He must not allow himself the consolations of religion.

Sir Walter Simpson, The Art of Golf *(1887)*

Putting is the least manly thing in golf, and, therefore, when a player gets older and he does not win as much, he blames it on his putting. He does not want to admit that his power may be leaving him.

Jack Nicklaus

The next time you see a good player stalking backward and forward on the green, do not be led away by the idea that he is especially painstaking, but rather pity him for a nervous individual who is putting off the evil moment as long as he possibly can.

Ted Ray

A golf player is someone who can drive seventy miles an hour in heavy traffic with perfect ease but blows up on a two-foot putt if somebody coughs.

Anonymous

Putting is clutch city. Usually my putting touch deserts me under pressure. From five feet in to the hole, you are in the throw-up zone.

Dave Hill

Everyone wants to be known as a great striker of the ball, for some reason. Nobody wants to be called a lucky, one-putting S.O.B., and nobody thinks he is.

Gary Player (1962)

Anyone can read a putt. It's not hard. Anybody can tell if a painting's crooked on the wall. Well, it's not that different from that.

Mike Clayton

I'd rather watch a cabbage grow than a man worrying his guts over a two-foot putt.
Michael Parkinson

Show me a man with both feet firmly planted on the ground, and I'll show you a man making a crucial putt on the eighteenth green.
Herm Albright

When I putt, my emotions collide like tectonic plates. It's left my memory circuits full of scars that won't heal.
Mac O'Grady

Very calm person make very good putt. Me try to be very calm. If I hear a bird sing, it's no good. Must think only of ball in hole. On the green, not bird and me. Only me. That makes very good putt.
Lu Liang Huan ["Mr. Lu"] (1971)

The ball doesn't care how positive you are thinking when you hit it with a putter moving *and* aimed in the wrong direction.
Dave Pelz

All I was seeking was that, on surveying a four-foot putt, a massive calm should automatically come over me instead of the impression that I was about to try to hit the ball with a live eel.
Henry Longhurst

Bad putting stems from thinking "how" instead of "where."
Jackie Burke Jr.

Love and putting are mysteries for the philosopher to solve. Both subjects are beyond golfers.
Tommy Armour

MAKING PUTTS

A man who can putt is a match for anyone.
  Willie Park

…but the man who can approach does not need to putt.
  J. H. Taylor

A good player who is a great putter is a match for any golfer.
A great hitter who cannot putt is a match for no one.
  Ben Sayers

If you could putt as straight as you drive, you would hole a
hell of a lot more putts.
  W. J. Cox

When the ball is down and the putter handed back to the
caddie, it is not well to say, "I couldn't have missed it."
Silence is best. The pallid cheek and trembling lip belie such
braggadocio.
  Sir Walter Simpson, The Art of Golf *(1887)*

The majority treat the hole as a place more difficult to get
into than it really is. Now, the fact is, that (from short distances) the hole is pretty big, and from all distances is capable
of catching a ball going at a fair pace. Many more putts
would go in if players credited holes with a little of that
catching power which they really possess.
  Sir Walter Simpson, The Art of Golf *(1887)*

On the final stroke that won him the 1931 British Open—I held
the putter in a vicelike grip, and from the moment I took it
back from the ball, I was blind and unconscious.
  Tommy Armour

After holing a difficult putt while she was pregnant—That putt was so good, I could feel the baby applaud.
   Donna Horton-White

The better you putt, the bolder you play.
   Don January

Every putt can go in, but I don't expect every putt to go in.
   Jane Blalock

There are no points for style when it comes to putting. It's getting the ball in the cup that counts.
   Brian Swarbrick

MULTIPLE PUTTS

On leaving putts short—I've never once seen the cup move towards the ball.
   Henry Longhurst (1983)

If you three-putt the first green, they'll never remember you. Three-putt the eighteenth, they'll never forget you.
   Walter Hagen

I just try to put it on the fairway, then the green, and not three-putt.
   Peter Thomson

Not only are three-putt greens probable, at times they are an achievement.
   Charley Pride

I have three-putted in forty countries.
   Fred Corcoran (1977)

Many golfers enjoy putting to such an extent that they take three or four putts to the green.

Grantland Rice

Real golfers don't cry when they line up their fourth putt.

Karen Hurwitz

Prayer never seems to work for me on the golf course. I think this has something to do with me being a terrible putter.

Billy Graham

A sliced or hooked drive has a certain grandeur, a clunked iron shot can be grimly chased down the fairway and struck again, and a foozled chip shot has its gentle comedy. But there is nothing funny or grand about an easy putt that declined to roll into the hole...especially when the match hinged on it.

John Updike, Golf Digest *(1994)*

The way I putted today, I must've been reading the greens in Spanish and putting them in English.

Homero Blancas (1970)

I putted like Joe Schmoe, and I'm not even sure Joe would appreciate that.

Arnold Palmer (1960)

I'm having putting troubles. It's not the putter; it's the puttee.

Frank Beard

Taking more than two putts to get down on a lightning-fast, steeply sloped green is no embarrassment unless you had to hit a wedge between the putts.

Henry Beard, Mulligan's Laws *(1994)*

I enjoy the "oohs" and "aahs" from the gallery when I hit my drives. But I'm getting pretty tired of he "aaws" and "uhhs" when I miss the putt.

John Daly

Bad putting is due more to the effect the green has upon the player than it has upon the action of the ball.

Bobby Jones

Mary had a little putt, she needed it for par.
Mary has a second putt...the first one went too far!

Margaret Kennard, Rhymes from the Rough *(1992)*

Money Putts

Even when times were good, I realized that my earning power as a golf professional depended on too many ifs and putts.

Gene Sarazen (1950)

Miss a putt for $2,000? Not likely!

Walter Hagen

Putts get real difficult the day they hand out the money.

Lee Trevino

The Long, the Short, and the Ball

Long putts travel on the wings of chance.

Bernard Darwin

Those longish second putts take a lot out of you even when you make 'em.

Cary Middlecoff

On a ninety-foot putt—Putting from that distance is a little like trying to touch a girl sitting on the far side of a couch. You can reach her, but you're not likely to accomplish much.

> Charles Price

When a golfer these days misses a forty-foot putt, he grimaces and agonizes like a cowboy struck in the heart by an Indian arrow.

> Ben Hogan (1975)

After missing a very long putt—I was on the dance floor, but I couldn't hear the band.

> Chi Chi Rodriguez

I sank a long and curling putt,
It's like I've seldom seen;
It would have helped my scoring but,
'Twas on the practice green.

> Richard Armour, Golf Is a Four-Letter Word (1962)

Long ago I learned that no putt is short enough to take for granted.

> Bobby Jones

On reaching forty years of age—I never used to miss anything inside ten feet. The last three or four years, I've been putting like other people. I've found out you can miss a putt. I didn't realize that people missed putts.

> Jack Nicklaus

Nowadays, of course, putts within six inches or so are frequently conceded, as being unmissable. Not with my grandmother; she would have stood over Arnold Palmer if he had been on the lip of the hole.

> George M. Fraser, McAuslan in the Rough (1974)

I once shot a wild elephant in Africa, thirty yards away and it didn't hit the ground until it was right at my feet. I wasn't a bit scared, but a four-foot putt scares me to death.

Sam Snead (1965)

You can always recover from a bad drive, but there's no recovering from a bad putt. It's missing six-inchers that causes us to break up our sticks.

Jimmy Demaret

DOWNHILL PUTTS

The three things I fear most in golf are lightning, Ben Hogan, and a downhill putt.

Sam Snead

After carding a 77 in the 1974 U.S. Open—I had some uphill putts...after each of my downhill putts.

Homero Blancas

The fellows today play too much golf. They burn themselves out. And on their tombstones it says, "Here lies a millionaire. The downhill putts got him."

Gene Sarazen (1970)

It's better to have a twenty-foot uphill putt than a six-foot downhill one.

Russell Claydon (1989)

YIPS ("Yes, I Putt Shakily")

The yips are that ghastly time when, with the first movement of the putter, the golfer blacks out, loses sight of the ball, and hasn't the remotest idea of what to do with the putter or, occasionally, that he is holding a putter at all.

> *Tommy Armour*

I have a hunch that the yips is a result of years of competitive strain, a sort of punch-nuttiness with the putter.

> *Tommy Armour*

Yips don't seize the victim during a practice round. It is a tournament disease.

> *Tommy Armour*

Can you name the "greatest" atomic-energy scientist? Yet, designing, engineering, and constructing an atomic bomb is simple compared to trying to teach a fellow how to stop shaking.

> *Tommy Armour (1952)*

There's no word for it; the Germans don't have a word for "yips."

> *Bernhard Langer*

I take encouragement from those rare days that I do not four-putt.

> *Bernhard Langer*

I've gotten rid of the yips four times, but they hang in there. You know those two-foot downhill putts with a break? I'd rather see a rattlesnake.

> *Sam Snead*

Like so many before him, he developed the yips, and watching him from three foot or so was like watching a man attempting to hole out with an electric eel.

Martin Johnson, Obsession

My hands were shaking. The only problem with that is that you never know which shake is going to hit the putt.

Patty Sheehan

I've got the yips...not with my putter, with my wedge.

Lionel Herbert (1970)

SHOT MAKING

Wind, hole design, and a hundred other factors in golf mean that you will never hit the same shot two times in a row.
Phil Mickelson

The hardest shot is the chip at ninety yards from the green where the ball has to be played against an oak tree, bounces back into a sand trap, hits a stone, bounces onto the green, and then rolls into the cup. That shot is so difficult, I have only made it once.

Zeppo Marx

My favorite shots are the practice swing and the conceded putt. The rest cannot be mastered.

Lord Robertson

I am still undecided as to which of these two is the hardest shot in golf for me: any unconceded putt, or the explosion shot off the first tee. Both have caused me more strokes than I care to write about.

Ring Lardner

On his delicate chip shots—Son, I can poop one into the water and it don't even splash.

Tommy Bolt

The good chip is like the good sand trap shot; it's your secret weapon. It allows you to whistle while you walk in the dark alleys of golf.

Tommy Bolt (1969)

The best-stroked putt in a lifetime does not bring the aesthetic satisfaction of a perfectly hit wood or iron shot. There is nothing to match the whoosh and soar, the almost magical flight of a beautifully hit drive or five-iron.

Al Barkow

If I had cleared the trees and drove the green, it would've been a great shot.

Sam Snead

A beautifully struck driver; a solid iron shot; a seventy-foot putt rolled right up to the cup—there are a lot of little victories in a round of golf.

David Duval (1997)

It's often necessary to hit a second shot to really appreciate the first one.

    Henry Beard

Thou giv'st me to the world's last hour
A golfer's fame divine;
I boast—thy gift—a Driver's power,
If I can Putt—'tis thine.

    Patric Dickinson, A Round of Golf Courses *(1951)*

When hitting wedge shots, I've a flair
That's turning my hair gray;
They stop, I swear, right next to where
The pin was...yesterday.

    Dick Emmons

I drove a ball into the air.
It fell to earth, I know not where.
But if I'd found it, I'll bet you,
I would have done that hole in two!

    Miles Bantock (1901)

There is the glorious sensation of making a true hit. This is not only true of the drive. There is a right or wrong way of hitting a yard putt. The right way is bliss, the wrong way purgatory. The pleasure of the long drive or second shot to the green gives as fine an emotion as is possible for any sinner to receive on earth.

    R. H. Lyttleton

Only a player himself knows which shots he's scared of hitting.

    Jack Nicklaus (1971)

On his play during the 1991 Masters—It's like putting furniture together. The parts are there, but the glue is still a little wet.
> Tom Watson

After her tee shot bounced off a tree and nestled in her bra—I'll take a two-shot penalty, but I'll be damned if I'm going to play the ball where it lies.
> Elaine Johnson (1992)

Your worst putt will be as close as your best chip.
> Arnold Palmer

They say I'm famous for my chip shots. Sure, when I hit 'em right, they land, just so, like a butterfly with sore feet.
> Lee Trevino

Just figure out a way to get it in the hole, no matter what it looks like.
> Lee Trevino

I've seen enough crazy shots to know they happen in the best of families.
> Lee Trevino

I can hit a nice banana. That's my instinct. When I get over the ball, I think of a dozen things and hit a nice banana.
> Wayne Gretzky (1998)

On the most important shot in golf—The next one.
> Ben Hogan

Oh, praises let us utter
To our most glorious King!
It fairly makes you stutter
To see him start his swing;
Success attend his putter!
And luck be with his drive!
And may he do each hole in two,
Although the bogey's five!
    P. G. Wodehouse, The Coming of Gowf *(1919)*

STANCE

**I always like to see a person stand up
to a golf ball as though he were perfectly
at home in its presence.**
Bobby Jones

Stance: The position in which one stands immediately before
clubbing an innocent tee to death.
    Tim Brooke-Taylor, Golf Bag *(1988)*

The golfer who stands at the ball as rigid as a statue usually
becomes a monumental failure.
    Dick Aultman

I have one fault when I play golf, I really admit it.
I find I'm too close to the ball—I mean after I hit it!
    Maurice Seitter

Addressing a golf ball would seem to be a simple matter; that is, to the uninitiated who cannot appreciate that a golf ball can hold more terrors than a spacious auditorium packed with people.

> *Bobby Jones*

SWING AND A MESS

A bad attitude is worse than a bad swing.
Payne Stewart

My golfing partner couldn't hit a tiled floor
with a bellyful of puke.
> *David Feherty*

I was swinging like a toilet door on a prawn trawler.
> *David Feherty (1993)*

My swing is no uglier than Arnold Palmer's, and it's the same ugly swing every time.
> *Nancy Lopez (1984)*

If I swung the gavel the way I swung the golf club, the nation would be in a helluva mess.
> *Thomas "Tip" O'Neil (1980)*

My golf swing is like ironing a shirt. You get one side smoothed out, turn it over and there is a big wrinkle on the other side. You iron that side, turn it over and there's another wrinkle.
> *Tom Watson (1987)*

My swing is so bad, I look like a caveman killing his lunch.
Lee Trevino

My backswing off the first tee had put him in mind of an elderly lady of dubious morals trying to struggle out of a dress too tight around the shoulders.
Patrick Campbell

He took a swing like a man with a wasp under his shirt and his pants on fire, trying to impale a butterfly on the end of a scythe.
Paul Gallico, Golf Is a Nice Friendly Game *(1942)*

It doesn't matter if you look like a beast before or after impact, as long as you look like a beauty at the moment of impact.
Seve Ballesteros

Comment after a partner's poor shot—Worse swing I ever heard.
Charlie Boswell [blind golfer]

SWING TIME

**A hit must be perfectly timed,
but a swing will time itself.**
Grantland Rice

The golf swing is like a suitcase into which we are trying to pack one too many items.
John Updike

Golf is an awkward set of bodily contortions designed to produce a graceful result.

    Tommy Armour

If you were asked to imagine what flavor of ice cream would describe your golf swing, I would like to hear you answer, "vanilla." The more simple your approach to the swing is, the better off you are. It's the simple things that last.

    Harvey Penick, And If You Play Golf, You're My Friend *(1993)*

On how he developed his golf swing—I dug it out of the ground.

    Ben Hogan

The ultimate judge of your swing is the flight of the ball.

    Ben Hogan

There is one essential only in every golf swing: the ball must be hit.

    Sir Walter Simpson, The Art of Golf *(1887)*

Let the club swing itself through. Help it on all you can, but do not you begin to hit with it. Let it do its work itself, and it will do it well. Interfere with it, and it will be quite adequately revenged.

    Horace G. Hutchinson, Hints on the Game of Golf *(1886)*

You've got to turn yourself into a material as soft as putty, and then just sort of slop the club head through. You'll hit much farther and with less effort.

    Johnny Miller

A golf swing is more than just a way of advancing the ball. It's a signature.

    Patty Sheehan

To get an elementary grasp of the game of golf, you must learn, by endless practice, a continuous and subtle series of highly unnatural movements, involving sixty-four muscles, that result in a seemingly "natural" swing, taking all of two seconds to begin and end.

    Alistair Cooke

You get rewarded at the bottom end of the club by what you do at the top end.

    Jerry Barber

Nobody swung a golf club too slowly.

    Bobby Simpson

Slow is long, fast is short.

    Don January

I don't think you're swinging too fast unless the wooden tee or a patch of grass near it catches fire, or the ball explodes, or the club hits your left shoulder before you consciously begin your downswing...or you start your backswing while the ball is still in the ball washer.

    Leslie Nielsen, Bad Golf: My Way *(1996)*

If you could have a golfer start his swing without a ball there, then suddenly inject the ball in front of the club in the middle of the downswing, he would probably hit the best shot of his life.

    Ken Venturi

The arc of your swing doesn't have a thing to do with the size of your heart.

    Carol Mann, Newsweek *(1981)*

You can be black or white, introvert or extrovert, male or female, but to my mind there are only two types of people in the world: golfers and non-golfers. Once bitten, it is akin to having your neck punctured in Transylvania—there is no known antidote. If the Prince of Darkness offered to turn a swing that resembles a man attempting to chop wood inside a telephone kiosk into a thing of awesome power and beauty, I think I would have to sign up and take my chance with the afterlife.

Martin Johnson, Obsession

Everybody has two swings: the one he uses during the last three holes of a tournament and the one he uses the rest of the time.

Tony Penna

To a pupil—Everybody has two swings…a beautiful practice swing and the choked-up one with which they hit the ball. So, it wouldn't do either of us a damned bit of good to look at your practice swing.

Ed Furgol

As far as swing and technique are concerned, I don't know diddly-squat. When I'm playing well, I don't even take aim.

Fred Couples

Golf swings are like snowflakes…there are no two exactly alike.

Peter Jacobsen

I still swing the way I used to, but these days when I look up, the ball is going in a different direction.

Lee Trevino

Golf is a game based not only on an intellectual understanding but also on sensitivity for the instrument. You can't bully your way to a good golf swing.

Jim Flick

Nothing has changed since cavemen days when some
Neanderthal in plaid pants first picked up a club and tried to
groove an inside-out path. We're all still looking for a repeating swing that works.

> *Glen Waggoner*

When I learned to play golf, I had to run from the
groundskeeper. He was always taking shots at me, and I had
to swing fast.

> *Chi Chi Rodriguez*

Learning to play or making a swing change is like running
twenty times with your head into a brick wall. After a while,
you sit back and say, "What am I doing this for?"

> *Gary McCord,* Golf Digest *(1996)*

A good golf swing is simply useless in any other human
pursuit.

> *Bernard Suits*

WHIFFS & BUTTS

The magical impotence of an utter whiff.

> *John Updike,* The New Yorker *(1979)*

Whiff: A stroke that completely missed the ball. The more
prevalent term for this type of shot is "Warm-up swing."

> *Henry Beard,* A Duffer's Dictionary *(1987)*

During the 1984 Senior Open—If you're stupid enough to
whiff, you should be smart enough to forget it.

> *Arnold Palmer*

BEHAVIOR & EMOTION

**Golf is a game that creates emotions
that sometimes cannot be sustained
with the club still in one's hand.**
Bobby Jones

AGGRESSION

**Golf is a nonviolent game,
played violently from within.**
Bob Toski

The club weighs less than a pound. The ball weighs less than
two ounces. We don't need to prepare for violence.
Bob Toski

The are several good ways to swing at a golf ball, but only
one good way to play golf... aggressively!
Greg Norman, Shark Attack

*In response to Seve Ballesteros's less than heartfelt "commisera-
tions" that he had volunteered to sit out the 1993 Ryder Cup singles—*Sorry I didn't get to kick your ass!
Lanny Wadkins

Hit 'em hard. They'll land somewhere.
Stewart Maiden (1919)

The right way to play golf is to go up and hit the bloody thing.

George Duncan

Just knock the hell out of it with your right hand.

Tommy Armour

I may go for it or I may not. It all depends on what I elect to do on my backswing.

Billy Joe Patton

Before the 1974 U.S. Open—I'm going for the flag today. I'm gonna be a firecracker out there. I'm gonna be so hot, they're gonna be playing on brown fairways tomorrow.

Chi Chi Rodriguez

You can't see inside guys, into their minds, or their stomachs. I'm aggressive, but because there are lots of guys out there with real fast swings, who hit the ball miles, they get called aggressive and I get called conservative. It just ain't so.

Tom Kite (1989)

ANGER

Golf always makes me so damned angry.
King George V of England

Show me someone who gets angry once in a while, and I'll show you a guy with a killer instinct. Show me a guy walking down the fairway smiling, and I'll show you a loser.

Lee Trevino (1983)

Golf cannot be played in anger, or in any mood of emotional excess. Half the golf balls struck by amateurs are hit, if not in rage, surely in bewilderment, or gloom, or in cynicism, or even hysterically. All of those emotional excesses must be contained by the professional, which is why balance is one of the essential ingredients of golf. Professionals invariably trudge phlegmatically around the course—whatever emotions are seething within—with the grim, yet placid and bored look of cowpokes, slack-bodied in their saddles, who have been tending the same herd for two months.
George Plimpton

It is better to smash your clubs than lose your temper.
Lord Balfour (1890)

Never smash a club over your opponent's head. You can't replace it under the fourteen-club rule.
H. Thomson

Last week I made a double bogey and didn't even get mad. Now, that's bad.
Jack Nicklaus (1977)

CHARACTER BUILDING

**I know of no recreation which is
a better character builder than golf.**
Tony Jacklin

A well-adjusted man is one who can play golf as if it were a game.
Anonymous

If there is larceny in a man, golf will bring it out.
Paul Gallico

Nothing dissects a man in public quite like golf.
Brent Musburger

Golf does strange things to other people, too. It makes liars
out of honest men, cheats out of altruists, cowards out of
brave men, and fools out of everybody.
Milton Gross

Indeed, the highest pleasure of golf may be that on the fairways and far from all the pressures of commerce and ratio-
nality, we can feel immortal for a few hours.
Colman McCarthy

It is one of the chief merits of golf, that non-success at the
game induces a certain amount of decent humility, which
keeps a man from pluming himself on any petty triumphs he
may achieve in other walks of life....Sudden success at golf
is like the sudden acquisition of wealth. It is apt to unsettle
and deteriorate the character.
P. G. Wodehouse

It's funny that everybody who used to call Curtis Strange the
hothead who was so hard on himself are now calling him a
great competitor. What's the difference?
Curtis Strange (1988)

CHOKING APART

We all choke. You just try to choke last.
Tom Watson

A lot of guys who have never choked have never been in the
position to do so.
Tom Watson

I wish they would come up with another word for it, because it has no similarity to having a piece of prime rib stuck in your throat. Now, that's choking.

Peter Jacobsen

The guy who chokes least wins the most.

Hubert Green

Golf is a choke game. Nobody ever shanked a three-iron because his opponent threw him a curveball or put too much topspin on the ball.

Mark Mulvoy

On his second-place finish to Bobby Jones in the 1953 U.S. Open—I was so tight you couldn't a drove flaxseed down my throat with a knot maul.

Sam Snead

On the pressures she faced during a tense final round in the lpga Championship—I was trying to smile, but I was choking so badly my lips stuck to my teeth.

JoAnne Carner

After his fourth Masters win in 1978—It's awfully hard to smile when you're choking to death.

Gary Player

On his four-stroke victory in the 1968 U.S. Open—I was trying to get so far ahead, I could choke and still win.

Lee Trevino

We all choke, and the man who says he doesn't choke is lying like hell...we all leak oil.

Lee Trevino (1980)

Choking is one aspect of golf that, from the start, came naturally to me. Given even a paper-thin opportunity to let my side down and destroy my own score, I will seize it. "It's all on you, partner!" is a surefire battlecry to swing extra hard and dribble the ball into the flowering weeds. The muttered hint, "Remember, you have a stroke here," freezes my joints like a blast from Siberia.

John Updike, Golf Digest *(1994)*

Do not be ashamed of choking. Any golfer who has never choked on a golf course should be in an asylum.

Jack Nicklaus

The greatest of champions have all been ex-chokers.

Peter Dobereiner

The ball sits there and says, "Now, idiot, don't hit me in the hazard. Don't hit me over there...hit me on the green. You think you can, idiot? I doubt if you can. Especially when you are choking your guts out."

Davis Love III

During the 1970 Masters—Even the CBS announcers are choking.

Tony Jacklin

CONFIDENCE

**Confidence has to be the golfer's
greatest single weapon on the green.**
Jack Nicklaus

Your confidence is the fifteenth club in your bag. You'd like it to be a thick-headed driver...but it sometimes seems like a pretty weak stick.

Peter Jacobsen (1995)

You cannot play scratch golf, or better, till you are as full of confidence as an egg full of meat.
Andra Kirkaldy

DISHONESTY

Golf is like solitaire.
When you cheat, you cheat only yourself.
Tony Lema (1966)

The rules invite cheating.... It's like trying to keep up with the tax code.
Peter Andrews

It's all over but the lying.
Anonymous

The latest statistical survey of golfers' height, conducted on behalf of a major sportswear company, reveals that the average player is seldom as tall as his stories.
Anonymous

When ground rules permit a golfer to improve his lie, he can either move his ball or change the story about his score.
Anonymous

Golf: A game where the ball lies poorly and the players well.
Art Rosenblum

Isn't it fun to go out on the golf course, and lie in the sun?
Bob Hope

The life of the golfer is not all gloom;
There's always the lies in the locker room.
> *Sammy Cahn and Jimmy van Heusen,*
> "Straight Down the Middle"

Golf is based on honesty. Where else would you admit to a 7 on a par 3?
> *Jimmy Demaret*

Bond frowned. The only remedy against a cheat at golf is not to play with him again.
> *Ian Fleming,* Goldfinger *(1959)*

Income tax has made more liars out of the American people than golf.
> *Will Rogers*

Golf liars have one advantage over fishing liars...they don't have to show anything to prove it.
> *Anonymous*

I never exaggerate. I just remember big.
> *Chi Chi Rodriguez*

Golf taught me perseverance; it taught me not to cheat—no easy thing for a boy when he's two down and his ball is deep in the woods.
> *James Reston*

One reward golf has given me, and I shall always be thankful for it, is introducing me to some of the world's most picturesque, tireless, and bald-faced liars.
> *Rex Lardner*

Some lies are believable and some are not. The technique of lying and the timing of lies are at least as important as mastering the drive.

Rex Lardner

At first a golfer excuses a dismal performance by claiming bad lies. With experience, he covers up with better ones.

P. Brown

You don't necessarily have to bring your clubs to play golf: just lie about your score.

Lon Simmons

Golf is the hardest game in the world to play...and the easiest to cheat at.

Dave Hill

DREAM ON

Every kid learning how to play golf dreams about winning the Masters, about winning the Open, not about being the leading money-winner. I've never shortchanged myself on dreams.

Tom Kite

All night I dreamed of millions of mean, sliced-up old balls all resembling my mother-in-law. The next day, I broke 90 for the first time in my life.

Dick Brooks

Don Quixote would understand golf. It is the impossible dream.

   Jim Murray (1988)

The game can be played in company or alone. Robinson Crusoe, on his island with his Man Friday as a caddie, could have realized the golfer's dream of perfect happiness—a fine day, a good course, and a clear green.

   Henry E. Howland, Scribner's *magazine (1895)*

Dream golf is simply golf played on another course. We chip from glass tables onto moving stairways; we swing in a strait-jacket, through masses of cobweb, and awake not with any sense of unjust hazard but only with a regret that the round can never be completed, and that one of our phantasmal companions has kept the scorecard in his pocket.

   John Updike, "Golf Dreams," in The New Yorker *(1979)*

Some golfers lie awake at night
And brood on what went wrong;
I'd rather think of what went right.
It doesn't take as long.

   Dick Emmons

The wretched golfer, divot-bound,
Persists in dreams of the perfect round.
And that is why I wander alone,
From tee to green to tee.
For every golfer I've ever known
Is too good or too bad for me.

   Ogden Nash

I visualize hitting the ball as far as JoAnne Carner, putting like Amy Alcott, looking like Jan Stephenson, and having Carol Mann's husband.

> *Dinah Shore (1982)*

ETIQUETTE

I'd like to be known as a gentleman first, and then as a golfer. That's all.
Ben Hogan

Gentlemen play golf. And if you aren't a gentleman when you start, after the crushing events of the game, you surely become one.

> *Bing Crosby*

Sometimes you'd like to just stand there in the middle of the green and scream as loud as you can. But we're the perfect gentlemen.

> *Ray Floyd (1984)*

Golf etiquette is kind of like the second verse of the national anthem...good stuff but read by practically nobody.

> *Herb Graffis*

Just as your opponent sometimes gives you unsolicited—and unwanted—assistance in finding your ball, you may get a chance to return the favor by helping him lose his.

> *Leslie Nielsen,* Bad Golf: My Way *(1996)*

Golf is a game of blows and weapons. In order that the game continue, we must make amends for every single act of destruction. In a golf club everyone knows the player who does not replace his divot. One can guess how he leads the rest of his life.

Michael Murphy, Golf in the Kingdom *(1976)*

Even in foursomes where fifty yards is reckoned a good shot, somebody must be away.

P. G. Wodehouse, Chester Forgets Himself *(1923)*

Honor: The privilege of being laughed at first on the tee.

Henry Beard, A Duffer's Dictionary *(1987)*

Gimme: An agreement between two losers who can't putt.

Jim Bishop

His version of golf's three worst words—Still your shot.

Dave Marr

There's an old saying: If a man comes home with sand in his cuffs and cockleburs in his pants, don't ask him what he shot.

Sam Snead

FUN

Keep your sense of humor. There's enough stress in the rest of your life to let bad shots ruin a game you're supposed to enjoy.

Amy Alcott

Golf is the worst damn fun anybody ever had.

Cy Manier

The fun you get from golf is in direct ratio to the effort you
don't put into it.
  Bob Allen (1950)

Golf is played by twenty million mature American men
whose wives think they were out having fun.
  Jim Bishop (1970)

Half of golf is fun. The other half is putting.
  Peter Dobereiner

Golf should not be a battle in the lifemanship war, or a vir-
ility test, or a social asset or an excuse for gambling, or a
character-building hobby, or a reason for not taking the family out on Sundays, although it may contain elements of all of
them.
  Peter Dobereiner

People who say golf is fun are probably the same people who
rationalize the game by saying they play it for their health.
What could be fun about a game in the entire history of
which nobody has ever shot the score he thought he should
have?
  Charles Price

Golf is a way of testing ourselves while enjoying ourselves.
  Arnold Palmer

Be funny on a golf course? Do I kid my best friend's mother
about her heart condition?
  Phil Silvers

It's no fun to watch me play. In fact, it's painful.
  Herman Keiser (1946)

Only the other day I actually saw someone *laugh* on a posh golf course in Surrey.

> *Michael Green,* Even Coarser Sport *(1978)*

LOVE

**Golf is a fickle game
and must be wooed to be won.**
Willie Park, Jr.

Golf is like a love affair. If you don't take it seriously, it's not fun; if you do take it seriously, it breaks your heart.

> *Arnold Daly*

Golf is like love. One day you think you're too old, and the next you can't wait to do it again.

> *Roberto de Vicenzo*

When you fall in love with golf, you seldom fall easily: it's obsession at first sight.

> *Thomas Boswell*

Love has had a lot of press-agenting from the oldest times, but there are higher, nobler things than love. A woman is only a woman, but a hefty drive is still a slosh.

> *P. G. Wodehouse,* A Woman Is Only a Woman

What is Love compared with holing out before your opponent?

> *P. G. Wodehouse,* Archibald's Benefit

I'm in love with golf, and I want everybody else to share my
love affair.
   Arnold Palmer

MENTAL EDGE

**Golf is played as much with
the head as with the hand.**
   Andra Kirkaldy

Golf has drawbacks. It is possible, by too much of it, to
destroy the mind.
   Sir Walter Simpson, The Art of Golf *(1887)*

The brain controls the mind. The mind controls the body.
The body controls the club.
   Mike Hebron

Let's face it, 95 percent of this game is mental. A guy plays
lousy golf, he doesn't need a pro; he needs a shrink.
   Tom Murphy

The game requires a certain cold toughness of mind, and
absorption of will. There was not an athlete I talked to from
other sports who did not hold the professional golfer in complete awe, with thanksgiving that golf was not their pro-
fession.
   George Plimpton, The Bogey Man *(1968)*

Once you step onto the course, you may be playing against par, your opponent, the elements, and the topography of the land, but your chief opponent is yourself. This is the game's enduring appeal and why it reveals far more of a person's character than any psychiatrist could worm out in umpteen sessions on an expensive Manhattan couch.

Chris Plumridge, The Lure of Golf

Golf is the only game that pits the player against an opponent, the weather, the minutest detail of a large chunk of local topography, and his own nervous system, all at the same time.

Mike Seabrook, A Good Walk Spoiled?

The human mind is the most powerful thing in this world, and scientists say we only use 10 percent of it. Well, I'm sure that's certain in golf. You've got more electrical connections in your head than a whole city. You'll do anything to keep 'em from going blooey on you in the crunch.

Joe Inman

The worst club in my bag is my brain.

Chris Perry

I didn't know you needed a mind to play golf. I thought all you did was kill the ball.

John Daly (1997)

Yes, it is a cruel game, one in which the primitive instincts of man are given full play, and the difference between golf and fisticuffs is that in one the pain is of the mind and in the other it is of the body.

Henry Leach

Don't worry about par. The practice of printing par figures is literally a mental hazard.
Bobby Jones

Competitive golf is played mainly on a five-and-a-half-inch course, the space between your ears.
Bobby Jones

I'm about five inches from being an outstanding golfer. That's the distance my left ear is from my right ear.
Ben Crenshaw (1976)

[Ben Crenshaw obviously had a smaller head than Bobby Jones.]

In playing a golf shot it always helps if the player can shut out from his mind all worry over the result of the effort, at least while he is in the act of playing the shot. After taking stance, it is too late to worry. The only thing to do then is to hit the ball.
Bobby Jones, "The Mental Hazards of Golf,"
from Vanity Fair *(1929)*

At golf you've got to be mentally alert. You can't lean against a tree that isn't there.
Doug Sanders

Every day, I try to tell myself this is going to be fun today. I try to put myself in a great frame of mind before I go out. Then, I screw it up with the first shot.
Johnny Miller (1984)

The golfer has more enemies than any other athlete. He has fourteen clubs in his bag, all of them different; eighteen holes to play, all of them different every week; and all around him are sand, trees, grass, water, wind, and 143 other players. In addition, the game is 50 percent mental, so his biggest enemy is himself.
Dan Jenkins

MULLIGANS

The First Shot, Part II: The Mulligan.
Leslie Nielsen, Bad Golf: My Way *(1996)*

Mulligan: Invented by an Irishman who wanted to hit one more twenty-yard grounder.
Jim Bishop (1970)

There were two things that made golf appealing to the average man: Arnold Palmer and the invention of mulligans.
Bob Hope, Confessions of a Hooker *(1985)*

Call me old-fashioned or starchy or whatever you will, but two things in this world I just can't grow accustomed to are: a man and a woman living together without being married...and taking a mulligan at golf.
Harvey Penick, And If You Play Golf, You're My Friend *(1993)*

Always keep in mind that if God didn't want a man to have mulligans, golf balls wouldn't come three to a sleeve.
Dan Jenkins

NERVES

Nerves are like some diseases:
some people are prone to them, others are not.
Gary Player

Tournament golf is a compromise of what your ego wants you to do, what experience tells you to do, and what your nerves let you do.
Bruce Crampton (1976)

If you could bottle nervous energy and use it at the right time, you could hit shots you didn't think you were capable of hitting.

Nick Price

After finishing second in the 1994 British Open—At Turnberry, I was so nervous on the final day that all I was concerned about was breaking 90.

Jesper Parnevik (1998)

Some guys get so nervous playing for their own money, the greens don't need fertilizing for a year.

Dave Hill, Teed Off *(1977)*

It's that you lose nerves, not nerve. You can shoot lions in the dark, and yet you can quiver like a leaf and fall flat over on a four-foot putt.

Johnny Farrell

PRESSURE

How would you like to meet the top 143 people at what you do each week in order to survive?

Bruce Crampton

Pressure is something every golfer feels at one time or another. Sometimes when I putted, I looked like a monkey trying to wrestle a football.

Sam Snead (1970)

The pressure gets worse the older you get. The hole starts to look the size of a Bayer aspirin.

Gary Player

The PGA Tour isn't pressure. Pressure is when you're playing
for $10 when you don't have a dime in your pocket.
    Lee Trevino

Anytime you play golf for whatever you've got, that's pressure. I'd like to see H. L. Hunt go out there and play for $3
billion.
    Lee Trevino

I walk too quickly, swing too quickly, and breathe too
quickly under pressure.
    Tom Watson

When I go out in the first round and my heart beats, I
chuckle and say, "Hey, Muffin, it's only Thursday. Your
heart's not supposed to beat until Sunday."
    Muffin Spencer-Devlin

On curtailing his drinking habits—I've been really stressed.
Pressure never bothered me until I was sober.
    John Daly (1993)

I have found, in my own matches, that if you keep throwing
consistent, unvarying bogeys and double bogeys at your opponents, they will crack up sooner or later from the pressure.
    Rex Lardner, Out of the Bunker and into the Trees *(1960)*

Winners know from experience how they will react to the
excitement and pressure of a final-round shoot-out. They
find a way to perform when their legs and arms go rubbery
and their heartbeats make the logos on their shirt jump up
and down.
    Peter Jacobsen

Mediocrity knows no pressure.
    Gary McCord

A good teaching professional can teach a young man to hit a golf ball with a stick pretty near perfectly every time. But how do you teach that man to hit that tiny ball with a long, whippy stick, when 15,000 people are jammed around him like a crowd at a six-alarm fire, and a quarter of a million dollars is riding on the next shot that he hits?

Tony Lema

QUITTERS NEVER WIN

My golf is woeful, but I will never surrender.
Bing Crosby

Golf is a game everybody quits, but nobody stops playing.
Bill Davis

He enjoys that perfect peace, that peace beyond all understanding, which comes at its maximum only to the man who has given up golf.
P. G. Wodehouse

Advice to a slow-learning pupil—Lay off for three weeks and then quit for good.
Sam Snead

No matter what happens—never give up a hole....In tossing in your cards after a bad beginning, you also undermine your whole game, because to quit between tee and green is more habit-forming than drinking a highball before breakfast.
Sam Snead

My ultimate desire is to retire from the game...because it drives me berserk.

David Feherty

[Also quoted as: "I play this game because my sole ambition is to do well enough to give it up."]

Orders to his caddie, after badly topping three shots in a row—
Pick up the ball...have the clubs destroyed...and leave the course.

Viscount Castlerosse

I forget when it happened, but in the middle of a round, which I was regarding with the usual distaste, a small voice within me said, "You don't have to do this." And I thought, "No, by God, I don't!" A great wave of relief came over me, and on D-Day, 1968, I put the clubs up in the loft with the water tanks, closed the hatch, removed the steps, and walked away. Nor have I for one second regretted it. It was rather like having sucked a very good orange dry and realizing you were eating the peel. Why not chuck it away and try an apple instead? Which is what I did.

Henry Longhurst, My Life and Soft Times

*On speculation of his retirement before he reaches forty—*I'll still play golf...it'll just be every Tuesday at 8 o'clock at the club.

Fred Couples (1998)

I retired from competition at twenty-eight, the same age as Bobby Jones. The difference was that Jones retired because he beat everybody. I retired because I couldn't beat anybody.

Charles Price

In some ways it takes more guts to quit than it does to carry on. Some people carry on playing tournaments because they have nothing else to do.

Tony Jacklin (1985)

When a player retires, his wife gets twice the husband but
only half the income.

    Chi Chi Rodriguez

"Mortimer, you must choose between golf and me."
"But darling, I went round in a hundred and one yesterday.
You can't expect a fellow to give up golf when he is at the top
of his form."

    P. G. Wodehouse, The Clicking of Cuthbert *(1922)*

I can tell you now. I'll know exactly when I want to retire,
but when I reach that time I may not know.

    Jack Nicklaus (1977)

After his 1980 U.S. Open victory, aged forty—It would be a
perfect way to go, except I don't really plan to go just yet.

    Jack Nicklaus

After his sixth Masters win in 1986, aged forty-six—It would be
the smartest thing to quit now. But I'm not that smart.

    Jack Nicklaus

I adore the game of golf. I won't ever retire. I'll play until I die.
Then I want them to roll me into a bunker, cover me with
sand, and make sure nobody's ball lands in there for a while.

    Lee Trevino (1985)

If I do retire, I'm going to get a pair of gray slacks, a white
shirt, a striped tie, a blue blazer, a case of dandruff and go
stand on the first tee so I can be a USGA official.

    Lee Trevino

If you don't succeed at first, don't despair. Remember, it takes
a lifetime to learn to play golf; most players spend their entire
lifetime finding out about the game before they give it up.

    Stephen Baker, How to Play Golf in the Low 120s *(1962)*

On his only attempt to take up the game—I tried...I
swung...I never tried again.
    Alexsandr Solzhenitsyn

After a bad round—Oh well, no matter what happens, I can
always dig ditches for a living.
    Arnold Palmer

Competitors take bad breaks and use them to drive themselves just that much harder. Quitters take bad breaks and use
them as reasons to give up. It's all a matter of pride.
    Nancy Lopez

After an abominable round of golf a man is known to have
slit his wrists with a razor blade and, having bandaged them,
to have stumbled into the locker room and inquired of his
partners, "What time tomorrow?"
    Alistair Cooke

RELAXING

Real golfers go to work to relax.
    George Dillon

The most advanced medical brains in the universe have yet to
discover a way for a man to relax himself, and looking at a
golf ball is not the cure.
    Milton Gross

On his habit of arriving late for his matches—When I have a match to play, I begin to relax as soon as I wake up. Everything I do, I do slow and easy. That goes for stroking the razor, getting dressed, and eating my breakfast. I'm practically in slow motion. By the time I'm ready to tee off, I'm so used to taking my time that it's impossible to hurry my swing.

Walter Hagen

SLOW PLAY

Oh, hang it! With so many things to be thought of all at once, steady play is impossible.
Sir Walter Simpson, The Art of Golf *(1887)*

If golfers keep on playing so slowly, on the green particularly, one way to correct the situation is to knock the ball into the S.O.B.s. There will be a slight delay while you have a hell of a fight, but from that point on you will move faster.

Horace G. Hutchinson, Hints on the Game of Golf *(1886)*

If the average American player would only realize how much easier it is to play well when he is swinging along at a good rate, he would surely gird up his loins and walk a little faster.

H. J. Whigham, The Common Sense of Golf *(1910)*

By the time you get to your ball, if you don't know what to do with it, try another sport.

Julius Boros

Play is conducted at a snail's pace. Some golfers today remind
me of kids walking to school and praying to be
late. . . . Golfers used to check the grass on the greens; today
they study the roots under each blade.

   Jimmy Demaret, My Partner, Ben Hogan *(1954)*

Don't you just hate it when a television announcer describes
a player as being "deliberate," when, in fact, he really means
that he's *slow*!

   Mike Purkey, Golf *magazine (1995)*

The slow-play habit is like the cigarette habit. It is so hard to
break that a man is wisest not to begin it.

   Jack Nicklaus (1969)

Your professional golfer . . . does not even think of hitting a
ball until he has conducted a geological and meteorological
survey of the situation . . . circling the ball warily, as though it
were a terrorist device, checking it out from every possible
angle; squatting and squinting; checking the wind; taking soil
samples; analyzing satellite photographs; testing the area for
traces of O. J. Simpson's DNA, etc. Your professional golfer
takes longer to line up a six-foot putt than the Toyota
Corporation takes to turn iron ore into a Corolla.

   Dave Barry, Washington Post *(1995)*

On Nick Faldo's slow progress during the 1995 Ryder Cup—They
ought to invoke the same-day rule.

   Paul Azinger

*After slow play in the 1997 Ryder Cup resulted in incomplete match-
es by nightfall*—Yet again the pace of some of the play was positively funereal, encouraging the thought that perhaps the Ryder
Cup should not have come to Spain but gone instead to Arku-
reyri in the north of Iceland in June, when the sun never sets.

   Alister Nicol

I have often been accused of being a slow player. I prefer to think that I am meticulous, that I think carefully before each shot and give myself the best possible chance of striking the ball well. This way I end up playing fewer shots per round, and that, in turn, makes me quicker rather than slower.

Bernhard Langer

His excuse for arriving late for a New York Giants' football practice—Don't blame me. Blame the foursome ahead of me.

Lawrence Taylor

SPORTSMANSHIP

**It's good sportsmanship to not pick up
lost golf balls ... while they are still rolling.**
Mark Twain

Is my friend in the bunker or is the bastard on the green?

Anonymous

Men trifle with their business and their politics, but never trifle with their games. They cannot pretend that they have won when they have lost; nor made a magnificent drive when they foozled it.

George Bernard Shaw

To brag a little; to show well,
To improve gently given luck.
To pay up, to own up
And to shut up if beaten.
These are the virtues of the sporting man.

Walter Travis

If your adversary is a hole or two down, there is no serious
cause for alarm in his complaining of a severely sprained
wrist. Should he happen to win the next hole, these symp-
toms will in all probability become less troublesome.
    Horace G. Hutchinson, Hints on the Game of Golf *(1886)*

If the following foursome is pressing you, wave them
through...and then speed up.
    Deane Beman

When five up express, as is polite, regret at laying a stymie,
but rejoice in your heart.
    Sir Walter Simpson, The Art of Golf *(1887)*

I have often been gratefully aware of the heroic efforts of my
opponent not to laugh at me.
    Bernard Darwin (1934)

If you think it's hard meeting new people, try picking up the
wrong golf ball.
    Jack Lemmon (1986)

On searching for a lost ball—It's a small thing, but you should
never have your hands in your pockets at the moment of discovery.
    Leslie Nielsen, Bad Golf: My Way *(1996)*

The loudest noise you hear on the golf course is the guy jan-
gling coins to distract the player he bet against.
    Jim Murray

When you are putting well, you can't hear anything off the
green, but when you're putting badly, you can hear a man
jingle two coins in his pocket one hundred yards away.
    Nick Faldo

On Auric Goldfinger's rattling coins in his pocket—Bond smiled grimly. He said, "Could you stop shifting bullion till after my shot?"

    Ian Fleming, Goldfinger *(1959)*

Few pleasures on earth match the feeling that comes from making a loud bodily-function noise just as a guy is about to putt.

    Dave Barry

Golf, in fact, is the only game in the world in which a precise knowledge of the rules can earn one a reputation for bad sportsmanship.

    Patrick Campbell

Another thing to remember is that while the ethics of golf forbid coughing, talking, sneezing, snoring, or making any other sort of noise while the opponent addresses the ball, it is not illegal to use mustard gas or throw flares or tickle his ears with a wisp of straw.

    Ring Lardner

I never kick my ball in the rough or improve my lie in a sand trap. For that I have a caddie.

    Bob Hope

Golf is the infallible test.... The man who can go into a patch of rough alone, with the knowledge that only God is watching him, and play his ball where it lies is the man who will serve you faithfully and well.

    P. G. Wodehouse, The Clicking of Cuthbert *(1922)*

In my day, we didn't tell anyone anything. If the green was fast, we hoped they wouldn't find out until it had cost them some strokes. And the only thing we hoped about the other fellow was that he'd break both legs. That sort of spirit made golf.

    Gene Sarazen

On being paired with Mark Brooks in the President's Cup—If we can't beat them playing, we can always irritate them to death.
   Scott Hoch

TEMPERAMENT

What golf writers call "temperament," I call common sense.
   Andra Kirkaldy

Good golfing temperament falls between taking it with a grin or shrug and throwing a fit.
   Sam Snead

The poetic temperament is the worst for golf. It dreams of brilliant drives, iron shots laid dead, and long putts holed, while in real golf success waits for him who takes care of the foozles and leaves the fine shots to take care of themselves.
   Sir Walter Simpson, The Art of Golf *(1887)*

THINKING

The pro—watch him next time— is always thinking.
   Arnold Palmer, My Game and Yours *(1963)*

Thinking instead of acting is the number one disease in golf.
   Sam Snead

Experts who have studied the matter assure us that the mind can only think of one thing at a time. Obviously, they have never made a study of golfers, or they would lower their estimate.

Robinson Murray

If you thought about merely walking down the street the way you think about golf, you'd wind up falling off the curb.

John Updike

Thinking must be the hardest thing we do in golf, because we do so little of it.

Harvey Penick

The more time I have to think about a shot, the worse I'm going to hit it.

Larry Laoretti

I do much of my creative thinking while golfing. If people know you are working at home, they think nothing of walking in for a cup of coffee. But they wouldn't dream of interrupting you on the golf course.

Harper Lee

Nothing will be left to chance. You want to know the course so well that you know it by heart. In the end you want to go to sleep at night thinking about it.

Nick Faldo (1981)

I look into their eyes, shake their hand, pat their back, and wish them luck, but I am thinking, "I am going to bury you."

Seve Ballesteros (1989)

THROWING

**I don't play well enough to be
allowed to throw a club.**
Lou Holtz

Why, during those early days Arnold Palmer was on tour, he
threw them. I have to say that he was the very worst golf-
club thrower I have ever seen. He had to learn to play well;
he'd have never made it as a thrower....I had to take the boy
aside and teach him how to throw a club. He was so innocent, he'd toss them backwards. I had to explain that you'd
get worn out walking back to pick them up. You have to
throw in front of you if you're going to be a professional.
> *Tommy Bolt,* The Hole Truth *(1971)*

I've thrown or broken a few clubs in my day. In fact, I guess
at one time or another I probably held the distance records
for every club in my bag.
> *Tommy Bolt,* How to Keep
> Your Temper on the Golf Course *(1969)*

I never threw a lot of clubs. I just got credit for throwing a
lot...I only threw about six in my career.
> *Tommy Bolt*

*On why he handed Tommy Bolt a two- instead of the requested
seven-iron*—It's the only iron we have left.
> *Anonymous caddie*

I know you can get fined for throwing a club. What I want
to know is if you can get fined for throwing a caddie.
> *Tommy Bolt*

After Tommy Bolt had thrown a club into a nearby water hazard—You'd better throw a provisional—that one's likely to be lost.

    Anonymous playing partner

I've got this new driver—persimmon head, graphite shaft, twelve-degree loft. It goes ten yards farther than any other club I have thrown.

    Alan Egford

The most exquisitely satisfying act in the world of golf is that of throwing a club. The full backswing, the delayed wrist action, the flowing follow-through, followed by that unique whirring sound, reminiscent only of a passing flock of starlings, are without parallel in sport.

    Henry Longhurst, *********! *(1965)*

Keep your eye on the club. Nothing is more embarrassing than to throw a club and then have to ask a playing partner where it went.

    Glen Waggoner

I don't enjoy playing video golf because there's nothing to throw.

    Paul Azinger

Why am I using a new putter? Because the old one didn't float too well.

    Craig Stadler (1983)

[Also reported to have been said during the 1992 U.S. Open.]

After he threw his putter into a lake—It was time for the club to die.

    Ken Green

*Why he threw his driver into a lake during the 1996
Scandinavian Open*—I wasn't mad. I just didn't ever want to
see it again.
  John Daly

Few golfers are born with a natural talent for hitting the ball,
but every player is blessed with the God-given ability to
throw a club.
  Henry Beard, Mulligan's Laws *(1993)*

GOLFING
PEOPLE

PLActually PLAYERS

Many play golf, and one odd effect of that
pursuit is that they return to work manifestly
stupider than they were. It is, I think, the
company of other golfers.

G. W. Lyttleton

Golfer: A guy who can walk eight miles with a heavy bag of
clubs, but when he gets home he expects his dog to fetch his
slippers.

Anonymous

The ideal build for a golfer would be strong hands, big fore-
arms, thin neck, big thighs, and a flat chest. He'd look like
Popeye.

Gary Player

The Southwestern United States is a dry and arid place,
unsuited for habitation except by reptiles who come to
breathe the clean, pure air or perhaps simply to warm themselves in the sun, and golfers, an unsettled lot driven by perverse nature to periodic fits of distemper.

> *Bob Sommers,* USGA Journal

Some players would complain if they had to play on Dolly
Parton's bedspread.

> *Jimmy Demaret*

Real golfers never question their client's score.

> *Anonymous*

The truly great things happen when a genius is alone. This is
true especially among golfers.

> *J. R. Coulson*

The glorious thing is that thousands of golfers, in park land,
on windy downs, in gorse, in heather, by the many-sounding
sea, enjoy their imbecilities, revel in their infirmities, and
from failure itself draw that final victory—the triumph of
hope.

> *R. C. Robertson-Glasgow*

It is a wonderful tribute to the game or to the dottiness of
the people who play it that for some people somewhere there
is no such thing as an insurmountable obstacle, an
unplayable course, the wrong time of the day or year.

> *Alistair Cooke*

Every golfer has a little monster in him. It's just that type of
sport.

> *Fuzzy Zoeller*

The bravest, stupidest race in the world, the unconvincible, inextinguishable race of golfers.

Bernard Darwin

PROFESSIONALS

**Golf pro: An optimistic doctor
who has a cure for dying.**
Jim Bishop (1970)

Pro golfers are a bunch of vagabonds who wear polyester pants for a living.

Peter Jacobsen

Golf professional: A fellow who never knows what town he's in till he calls downstairs to the desk clerk in the morning...but can read you the left-to-right break on every green in the town from memory.

Jim Murray (1968)

If I had my way, the social status of professional golfers would be one notch below that of Nazi war criminals.

Andy Lyons, Melody Maker *(1988)*

The players themselves can be classified roughly into two groups: the attractions and the entry fees.

Jimmy Demaret (1954)

Seventy-five percent of players on the European Tour are clones who do not know on which side their bread is buttered.

Brian Barnes

In competition, I have not regarded seriously the tendency of some people to endow golfers with superhuman powers.

> *Bobby Jones*

Bet you have never heard of a tour player striking because they wouldn't give him the weekends off, have you?

> *Tommy Bolt,* The Hole Truth *(1971)*

On 1970s professionals—They look like they're wearing barbed-wire jockstraps.

> *Herb Graffis,* Esquire *magazine*

If any perfection
Exists on this earth
Immune from correction
Unmeet for our mirth—
The despair of the scoffer,
The doom of the wit,
A professional golfer,
I fancy is it.

> *E. V. Knox, "A Round with the Pro," in* Punch *magazine (1929)*

The gallery sways like a primitive throng at a ceremony
  pagan,
And murmurs the names of its ancient gods,
Ouimet and Jones and Hagen.
There swirls around the gods of today an argumentative
  chorus;
Can Player give muscle to Nicklaus?
Can Palmer give weight to Boros?

> *Ogden Nash*

They keep talking about the Big Four: Palmer, Nicklaus, Player, and Trevino. I just want to be the fifth wheel in case somebody gets a flat.

> *Chi Chi Rodriguez*

INDIVIDUALS

(U.S. unless otherwise stated)

Helen Alfredsson—Sweden (b 1965)

Personally, I'd rather play golf with Helen Alfredsson than with any man alive.

> *Tom Doak*

She's a lunatic.

> *Laura Davies*

Isao Aoki—Japan (b 1942)

The PGA Tour has a simple test to see if a player is on drugs—if Isao Aoki speaks and the player understands him, the player is on something.

> *Bob Hope*

George Archer (b 1939)

His personal life will never hurt his nerves. George's idea of a big night out is a hamburger at McDonald's and a science fiction movie.

> *Dave Hill,* Teed Off *(1977)*

Tommy Armour (1895–1968)

Tommy has a mouth like a steel trap, a nose like a ski jump, hands like the fins of a shark, and eyes which indicate he would enjoy seeing you get a compound fracture of the leg.... He is as temperamental as a soprano with a frog in her throat.

> *Clarence B. Kelland,* The American Golfer *(1935)*

Paul Azinger (b 1960)

When he turned pro back in 1981, it was as though the village idiot had announced his intention of investigating the possibility of a career in astrophysics.

> *Bill Elliot*

Paul Azinger is a true inspiration to all golfers. He plays with his heart as well as his mind. If Norman Rockwell had painted a family man/golfer, he would have done a portrait of Paul.

    Dave Stockton

The human stick insect.

    Peter Dobereiner

The PGA's Tom Sawyer.

    Glen Waggoner, Divots, Shanks, Gimmes, Mulligans... *(1993)*

Ian Baker-Finch—Australia (b 1960)

On carding an opening 92 in the 1997 British Open—He went out in 44 and came back in 48, which sounded like a man's service history in World War II.

    Dan Jenkins, Golf Digest *(1997)*

Severiano Ballesteros—Spain (b 1957)

Unless his putting stroke deserts him, Seve Ballesteros should become the richest Spaniard since Queen Isabella.

    Jim Murray, Los Angeles Times *(1976)*

Seve Ballesteros goes after a golf course the way a lion goes after a zebra.

    Jim Murray, Los Angeles Times

In Spain, when little, the other caddies sat playing boy's games and laughed when my brother Seve came in—how you say?—like a drowning rat, maybe five hours afterwards. They no laugh today. They still carry bags.

    Manuel Ballesteros (1979)

*After Ballesteros hit several wayward shots during the 1979
British Open*—The winner, Severiano Ballesteros, chose not
to use the course but preferred his own, which mainly consisted of hay fields, car parks, grandstands, dropping zones,
and even ladies' clothing.
>   *Colin MacLaine (1979)*

When Ballesteros triumphed at the British Open in 1979, for
his first major win, he hit so few fairways off the tee that he
was often mistaken for a gallery marshal.
>   *Dan Jenkins,* Sports Illustrated *(1983)*

Nickname given to him after winning the 1979 British Open—
The Car Park Champion.

He was one of the best-looking young men in sport. He
didn't fall into the blond-and-boring category of young
Americans all trying to look like Johnny Miller.
>   *Ed Barner*

After his 1980 Masters win—He was like a Ferrari and made
us all look like Chevrolets.
>   *Tom Kite*

Seve doesn't hit the ball; he strokes it.
>   *Paul Way (1984)*

The only place Seve Ballesteros turns up for nothing is at his
mum's for breakfast.
>   *Howard Clark (1987)*

On his 65 during the 1988 British Open at Lytham St. Annes—
It would not be possible to commemorate Seve's 65 with
plaques, for it would render the course unplayable....Lots of
golfers can shoot a 63 in the first round of the Mundane
Open. But who shoots the joint-lowest final round in Open
history, the lowest round of the week by no less than two
shots, to walk off with the glittering prize?

> *Derek Lawrenson,* Golf Monthly

*[Hale Irwin could not believe anyone had bettered his 68 in the
treacherous conditions—"He did what? Come on! He must have
missed out some holes."]*

Seve Ballesteros's way is to hit a bank shot against a brick
wall, blade a putt with a sand wedge, and make a pitch stop
in midair and sing a chorus of "Malagueña" before dropping
next to the flagstick for a tap-in birdie.

> *Glen Waggoner,* Divots, Shanks, Gimmes, Mulligans... *(1993)*

Seve can get up and down to the flag from places a pot-holer
considers unsafe, but he could also—speaking in a strictly
golf sense, of course—start a fight in an empty house if he
felt like it.

> Total Sport *magazine (1996)*

Seve—the greatest thing to come out of Spain since a painting by Picasso that made sense.

> *Dan Jenkins*

Seve is a genius, one of the few geniuses in the game. The
thing is, Seve is never in trouble. He's in the trees quite a lot,
but that's not trouble for him. That's normal.

> *Ben Crenshaw*

During the 1993 German Open—I was in the hotel lobby talking to Seve Ballesteros, and the receptionist came over and asked me, "Are you Mr. Ballesteros?"
I said, "No, he is," of course.
The next day, I go out and shoot 67 because someone thinks *I* am Seve Ballesteros.
    David Feherty

Seve Ballesteros drives into territory Daniel Boone couldn't find.
    Fuzzy Zoeller

He hits the ball into the trees on three consecutive holes and keeps on scoring, but that's the way he is. He has this happy-go-lucky reputation. But I'll tell you what, he doesn't look that happy coming down the eighteenth when he's scored 74.
    Nick Faldo (1993)

On his diminishing success—He's nearer forty than thirty, and everyone, no matter who, only has so many bullets in his gun.
    Peter Alliss (1994)

On his antics as 1997 Ryder Cup captain—Ballesteros was so conspicuous, he was almost beside himself. When he gave Ian Woosnam a lift in the captain's golf cart, the Welshman complained about the speed of the Spaniard's driving. . . .
Considering he's hardly hit a fairway all year, driving has not been one of Seve's strong points.
    Tim Glover, London Independent

A hero who is no longer just a dewy-eyed Lancelot greeting the dawn, but a doleful Don Quixote facing the dusk.
    Ed Weathers, Golf Digest *(1997)*

How to spot him: He'll be under a tree, in the car park, on the members' practice ground, behind a fish-and-chip stall, arguing with a referee, bending his shots around grandstands on his knees. Just don't bother looking for him in the middle of the fairway.

> Fore! *magazine (1998)*

Miller Barber (b 1931)

His swing reminds me a lot of a machine I once saw at a county fair making saltwater taffy. It goes in four directions, and none of them seem right.

> *Buck Adams (1984)*

When Barber swings, it looks as if his golf club gets caught in a clothesline.

> *Ben Crenshaw (1984)*

Miller Barber's swing looked like a guy in a dark room flailing at a Mexican piñata with a short stick.

> *Gary McCord,* Golf Digest *(1996)*

Andy Bean (b 1953)

He's a superstar from the neck down.

> *David Ogrin (1984)*

Andy Bean, looking too big to be out there, and with his perennially puzzled expression seeming to be searching for a game more his size.

> *John Updike,* Thirteen Ways of Looking at the Masters *(1980)*

Frank Beard (b 1939)

He looks like a bad doctor from Elko, Nevada, whose chemistry set blew up and he's golfing for penance.

> *Don Rickles*

Chip Beck (b 1956)

He is such a positive, upbeat person, if a car ran over and killed his dog, he'd marvel at how peaceful the poor beast looked.

Gary McCord

Deane Beman (b 1938)

On his return to the Senior Tour—Did you ever think you'd see Deane Beman busting his hump to become the next Jim Colbert?

George Peper, speech at the 1996 GWAA Awards dinner

Thomas Bjorn—Denmark (b 1971)

On the Dane's surprise impact at the 1997 Ryder Cup—Tiger wasn't alone in his frustration. Other...stars, like Tom Lehman, Fred Couples, and Phil Mickelson, also took lumps from guys with v's and z's in their names, guys whose names end in vowels, guys who sound like waiters. A Dane, for God's sake! Bjorn. Guy with a j wandering around in his name.

Dan Jenkins, Golf Digest

Jane Blalock (b 1945)

Tell her to get off the tour. Nobody who swings like Shirley Temple can make a living out of this game.

Richie Ferraris (1969)

Tommy Bolt (b 1918)

What Gerald Ford was to the shanked drive, Tommy Bolt was to the Flying Persimmon. Terrible Tommy. Thunder Bolt. The Man Who Threw Clubs.

Glen Waggoner, Divots, Shanks, Gimmes, Mulligans... (1993)

Tommy threw clubs with class.

Don January

His clubs spend more time in the air than Lindbergh.

Jimmy Demaret

If Tommy Bolt had not become a touring pro, he would in all probability have been married to Bonnie Parker.

Dan Jenkins

If we could have screwed another head on his shoulders, he would have been the greatest golfer that ever lived.

Ben Hogan

Julius Boros (b 1920)

Julius is all hands and wrists, like a man dusting the furniture.

Tony Lema

He's Perry Como's kid by another marriage.

Don Rickles

James Braid—U.K. (1870–1950)

There are hitters who are reminiscent of howitzers in action, beneath whose feet the earth trembles; Braid seemed to impart the velocity of a bullet. It must have been a strain on the solid ball to have to pull itself together and refrain from bursting into pieces.

H. N. Wethered

Gay Brewer (b 1932)

Gay Brewer swings the club in a figure of eight. If you didn't know better, you'd swear he was trying to kill snakes.

Dave Hill

Gay Brewer sounds like a fag wine-maker from Modesto.

Jimmy Demaret

Ken Brown—U.K. (b 1957)

A walking one-iron.

> *Lee Trevino*

JoAnne Carner (b 1939)

The ground shakes when she hits it.

> *Sandra Palmer (1982)*

Her weight is a state secret.

> *John P. May (1982)*

Billy Casper (b 1931)

Billy could putt in a plowed field.

> *John Schlee (1968)*

After his 1959 U.S. Open win in which he one-putted thirty-one greens—If you couldn't putt, you'd be selling hot dogs out there.

> *Ben Hogan*

Billy Casper, currently one of the best putters from 400 yards in to the hole that the tour has ever seen.

> *Tony Lema (1964)*

On his impressive putting record—I feel sorry for Casper. He can't putt a lick. He missed three thirty-footers out there today.

> *Gary Player*

It takes a lot of guts to play this game, and by looking at Billy Casper, you can tell he certainly has a lot of guts.

> *Gary Player*

On the victorious 1979 Ryder Cup captain—He fouled up once. He never got the bar set up in the players' lounge.
  Lee Trevino

Bobby Clampett (b 1960)
His swing had more moves than an erector set.
  Jimmy Ballard (1984)

He is a tall, slender young man who, from a distance, looks a bit like Harpo Marx in double knits.
  Jim Moriarty, Sport *(1982)*

Bobby Cole—South Africa (b 1948)
The second shortest South African on the pro tour—He is one inch taller than Gary Player and a million dollars poorer.
  Dick Schaap, Massacre at Winged Foot *(1974)*

Henry Cotton—U.K. (1907–1987)
You couldn't tell whether Cotton was in the right or left side of the fairway, because his ball was so close to the middle.
  Bob Toski, Golf Digest *(1983)*

Henry Cotton wore Savile Row clothes and silk mono-grammed shirts. He drove a large motorcar, which he had a tendency to park opposite a sign saying "No Parking."
  Henry Longhurst

Fred Couples (b 1959)
Even his bad shots are good. That's the secret of golf.
  Johnny Miller

He just steps up to the golf ball, takes a deep breath to relax, takes it back, and whomps it. Then he goes and finds it and whomps it again. And when you add up the whomps, the total is usually lower than that of the other 143 whompers.
  Peter Jacobsen

Since his divorce, Fred Couples is now known as Fred Singles.
> *Bernard Guirk (1993)*

I'd like to have Fred Couples's face, Fred Couples's body, Fred Couples's swing...and Fred Couples's ex-wife's bank account.
> *Rocky Thompson*

Nearly thirty-eight...Couples is an appealing Peter Pan whose singular charm has always been that he would rather be thought of as just another one of the Lost Boys.
> *Tom Callahan,* Golf Digest *(1997)*

On his prospects for the 1998 British Open—He is, frankly, the hardest American to come over here since Hard Harry Hardman from Hardsville, Tennessee.
> Fore! *magazine*

Ben Crenshaw (b 1952)
He hits in the woods so often, he should get an orange hunting jacket.
> *Tom Weiskopf*

I've told him he might have a tan like mine, if he didn't spend so much time in the trees.
> *Lee Trevino*

Ben Crenshaw has the best grip, the best stance, and the best swing I've ever seen. Besides that, he's nice.
> *Lee Trevino (1979)*

Ben Crenshaw invented the fifteen-foot gimme.
> *Dan Jenkins,* Fairways and Greens *(1994)*

Ben is the best damn second- and third-place finisher in the majors the world will ever know.

Kevin Cook, Playboy *(1982)*

Comparing two playing partners in the opening rounds of the 1998 British Open—Both in power and range, Crenshaw may be an alto to Colin Montgomerie's grand tenor, but the Texan has three things Montgomerie would die for: the deadliest putter in the world and two major titles—the 1984 and 1995 Masters.

Simon Hughes, London Telegraph *(1998)*

John Daly (b 1966)
John Daly's driving is unbelievable. I don't go that far on my holidays.

Ian Baker-Finch (1992)

On his distance off the tee—Man! I can't even point that far!

Gay Brewer

I couldn't hit it where he hits it on a runway.

Fred Funk

He's longer than Fred Couples. He's longer than Greg Norman. He's even longer than *War and Peace.*

Bob Verdi, Chicago Tribune

On his awesome power during the 1993 British Open at Sandwich—When John Daly hits an iron, he takes a cubic yard of Kent as well. His divots go farther than my drives.

David Feherty

By the time we walk up to his drive, my clothes have gone out of fashion.

Fuzzy Zoeller

On his full swing—If you want to try this shot, you'd better have a backbone of steel, the strength of an ox, and be younger than thirty years old.

> *Peter Alliss*

On the difference in caddying for Daly after carrying Curtis Strange's bag—Let's just say that I walk to a different set of sprinkler heads.

> *Greg Ritz*

Like a hurricane, his arrival came without warning, and his game spells danger wherever he plays.

> *David Leadbetter*

John Daly's way is to grip it and rip it to set up an eagle or a triple bogey, depending on the phase of the moon.

> *Glen Waggoner,* Divots, Shanks, Gimmes, Mulligans... *(1993)*

Americans took one look at Daly's victory in the 1991 PGA Championship and spent a month's rent on a driver with a head the size of a cantaloupe. When Daly cracked his drives, he practically invited you next to the ropes to bellow, "You da man!"

> *Michael Farber,* Sports Illustrated *(1997)*

The best seat in all golf is to be right behind Daly on the practice tee. His drives seem to suck all the air off the range and send the ball spiraling over the horizon.

> *Chris Hodenfield,* Golf Digest *(1997)*

Beth Daniel (b 1956)
Chasing Beth Daniel is like swimming upstream against the current.

> *Bonnie Lauer (1982)*

Eamonn Darcy—Ireland (b 1952)

No one has had a swing like Eamonn since Quasimodo gave up golf to concentrate on bell ringing.

Bill Elliot

He swings like an octopus falling from a tree.

TV commentator

Laura Davies—U.K. (b 1963)

She is five foot ten inches tall, broad-shouldered, with big feet. I don't know how much she weighs, but, as my dear departed grandfather would say, she'd crush some grass.

Michael Parkinson, London Telegraph *(1994)*

Jimmy Demaret (1910–1983)

If Jimmy had concentrated on golf as much as laughing, he might have won more, but I wouldn't have liked him as much.

Ben Hogan

Not only did Jimmy never practice, I don't think he ever slept.

Sam Snead

If Jimmy Demaret had won the money, he would have been eight to five to leave it in a bar or blow it on a handmade pair of orange and purple saddle oxfords.

Dan Jenkins

Best Wind Player: This one easily goes to Jimmy Demaret. He could come in first place in this category just using his mouth.

Charles Price, Golf *magazine (1975)*

Jim Dent (b 1939)

Jim Dent is the longest hitter around today. He not only has a graphite shaft, he has graphite arms as well.

> *George Bayer,* Golf *magazine (1974)*

This big guy just knocks the dog water out of the ball.

> *Dave Hill,* Teed Off *(1977)*

Nick Faldo—U.K. (b 1957)

Of course, Nick Faldo is as neurotic as a long-tailed cat in a room full of rocking chairs, and pretty much No Fun.... You wouldn't want him for a brother-in-law...but he won the Ryder Cup.

> Total Sport *magazine (1995)*

On being the "am" in a pro-am—Some players are famous for not talking to you. I can't mention names, but his initials are Nick Faldo.

> *Kevin Whately*

The only time Nick Faldo opens his mouth is to change feet.

> *David Feherty (1992)*

Faldo is as much fun as Saddam Hussein.

> *Scott Hoch*

Yes, Nick Faldo's boring. He's never in the trees or in the water.

> *Fred Couples (1993)*

He'd probably be like that if he was writing a poem. He'd spend two days at that and want to make it perfect. I'm not like that. I'd be happy with, "Roses are red, Violets are blue, I'm at Augusta, And so are you!"

> *Fred Couples*

He has two moods:

1. Annoyed
2. About to be annoyed.

    Rick Reilly, Sports Illustrated

Faldo gets involved in controversies as often as a child walks through puddles.

    John Hopkins, Times *(London)*

On his reputation for slow play—You start your soft-boiled eggs by the time he's ready.

    Johnny Miller

On playing with Faldo in the 1992 U.S. Open—It was like playing by yourself, except it took an hour longer.

    Steve Pate

Raymond Floyd (b 1942)

He's the most intimidating player I've ever played against. He plays every shot like it's the last shot of his life. He's like a black leopard, stalking the jungle.

    Mark O'Meara

After being beaten in the 1986 U.S. Open—Raymond Floyd has not seen the Taj Mahal, the Great Wall of China...or the last of me.

    Payne Stewart

Lots of hair, Banlon shirt, and the half-glazed stare of a demonic accountant. His eyes were everything. Raymond's swing took on the curvilinear arc of an abandoned amusement park ride. There were dips and sways in all sorts of places.

    Gary McCord, Golf Digest *(1996)*

On the forty-nine-year-old playing in the 1991 Ryder Cup—Less than a year before joining the Senior Tour, Ray Floyd was bouncing around the sand dunes like a kid on a trampoline.

    Philadelphia Enquirer

Jim Furyk (b 1970)

Instead of taking the club away like a normal human being, Furyk throws it out away from him, like a cowboy initiating a rope trick....If the ball were a small animal trying to escape slaughter, it wouldn't have a chance. First, because the club seems to come from every which direction at once; and second, because the critter would be standing slack-jawed in amazement that anyone would swing a club like that in public.

    John Paul Newport, Golf Digest *(1996)*

The dipsy-doodle, Gumbyesque antics of Jim Furyk...look like a tilt-a-whirl amusement ride gone haywire. You're supposed to keep the shaft on a constant plane, but Jim changes planes more than most flight attendants.

    Gary McCord, Golf Digest *(1996)*

Al Geiberger (b 1937)

On his PGA tour record 59 in the 1977 Memphis Classic—There are certain things you don't believe in. The Easter Bunny. Campaign promises. The Abominable Snowman. A husband with lipstick on his collar. And a guy who tells you he shot a 59 on his own ball—out of town, of course.

    Jim Murray

David Graham—Australia (b 1946)

His walk is a little stiff, and his setup to the ball reminds me of someone adjusting a machine.

    Peter Alliss, 100 Greatest Golfers *(1989)*

Hubert Green (b 1946)

Hubert Green swings like a drunk trying to find a keyhole in the dark.

> *Jim Murray,* Los Angeles Times

On hearing a distant chain saw—Ah, that's just Hubert over there fixing his swing.

> *Fuzzy Zoeller (1983)*

Putting, he splits his hands on the shaft, spreads his legs, and hunkers over the ball like a chicken laying an egg.

> *Dave Hill,* Teed Off *(1977)*

Hubert Green just fidgeted thirty-six times, sneaking a peek at the flag, as he addressed his shot. Hubie's the king of peekers. Someday he's going to be wiggling and waggling, turning his head fifty times as he gets ready to pull the trigger, and he's not going to be able to hit it. He's just going to keep turning that head until it falls off, or until they send somebody out to bring him in.

> *Dave Stockton*

He was so ugly when he was a baby that his mother tied a pork chop around his neck to get the dog to play with him.

> *Larry Ziegler*

[Lee Trevino said a similar thing about J. C. Snead.]

He'll talk to a tree. . . . He'd be happy in a closet with a six-pack of beer.

> *Lee Trevino,* They Call Me Super Mex *(1982)*

Walter Hagen (1892–1969)

Walter is not a religious man. I know he believes in God, but if I ever wanted to go looking for him, I wouldn't start with a church. I have an idea he's broken eleven of the Ten Commandments.

    Fred Corcoran (1940)

Hagen was the first professional I knew that earned a million dollars at the game—and the first to spend it. Snead earned one million, too—but he saved two million.

    Fred Corcoran

Hagen spent money like a King Louis with a bottomless treasury. In the credit card age, he might have broken American Express. As it was, he got by.

    Al Barkow (1974)

Making a million or having the return of his laundry delayed by fiscal factors, nothing bothers Hagen. He could relax sitting on a hot stove. His touch was sensitive as a jeweler's scale.

    Tommy Armour (1935)

He carried it off big. He was gorgeous. One got the impression that he had invented the game.

    Charles Price, The World of Golf *(1962)*

Typically, for a man who might spend three-quarters of an hour shaving, the Haig spent more than six years of his retirement writing his autobiography, five of which were devoted to searching for just the right title.

    Charles Price, The World of Golf *(1962)*

Hagen played in tournaments as though they were cocktail parties.

> *Charles Price (1979)*

Sir Walter Hagen was the greatest golfer that ever lived. I truly believe this, greater than even Vardon, and Vardon went three and one-half years without hitting a sand trap.

> *Wilfrid Reid (1953)*

I think he was, without question, the greatest putter of all time. He could putt any kind of green under any conditions.

> *Gene Sarazen (1975)*

Walter Hagen goes down in history as the greatest exponent of the dramatic art of turning three shots into two.

> *Henry Longhurst*

His golf was fallible and impertinent, which endeared him to the common man.

> *Henry Longhurst*

Walter Hagen never knew where his ball was going. He had to invent six or seven new shots every time he played just to get his ball back into play.

> *Peter Dobereiner (1990)*

Clayton Heafner (1914–1960)

Clayton was the most even-tempered golfer I ever saw. He was mad all the time.

> *Sam Snead*

Dave Hill (b 1937)

In my time in the States, I found a lot of small-minded guys—and I'm afraid Dave Hill was one of them—who didn't like foreigners on their tour.

> *Tony Jacklin*

Scott Hoch (b 1955)
A poor man's Ted Turner.
> *John Hawkins,* Golf Digest *(1998)*

Ben Hogan (b 1912)
People are always wondering who's better, Hogan or
Nicklaus. All I know is that Nicklaus watches Hogan prac-
tice, and I never heard of Hogan watching Nicklaus practice.
What's that tell you?
> *Tommy Bolt (1978)*

Ben has probably hit more good shots and fewer bad shots
than any man in history.
> *Jack Nicklaus*

*On finding Ben Hogan on the practice tees after shooting a 64 in
the 1941 Rochester Open*—What are you trying to do, man?
You had ten birdies today. Why, the officials are still inside
talking about it. They're thinking of putting a limit on you.
> *Jimmy Demaret*

After his road accident—Ben, you sonofabitch! Just because I
beat you in a play-off, you didn't have to get so mad that you
tried to run a bus off the road.
> *Jimmy Demaret (1949)*

On Hogan's postaccident comeback at the 1950 L.A. Open—His
legs weren't strong enough to carry his heart around.
> *Grantland Rice*

*After Hogan won the 1951 U.S. Open following the auto acci-
dent*—Well, Ben, you've started a new trend. We're all going
out tonight and try to get hit by a bus.
> *Tommy Bolt*

Nobody ever covered the flag like Ben.
> *Gene Sarazen*

Ben Hogan would rather have a coral snake rolling inside his shirt than hit a hook.
> *Claude Harmon*

When you played Ben, he never walked for the left or right of the fairway; he walked down the center of the fairway. He never missed a shot.
> *Roberto de Vicenzo*

Ben Hogan just knows something about hitting the golf ball the rest of us don't know.
> *Mike Souchak*

I thought I was a hard fighter. I thought Hagen and Sarazen were. We're not in a class with this fellow, Hogan. When he has a ninety-yard shot to play, he expects to hole it.
> *Bobby Jones*

The answer to Hogan is, I fancy, that if Hogan means to win, you lose.
> *Henry Longhurst*

Watching Hogan ... we were almost convinced that, if he hit a shot into a bunker, well, that's the way the hole should be played.
> *Robert Sommers*

Ben Hogan ... came the closest of any human being on this planet to making the golf ball respond the way he wanted when he hit it. He dedicated his whole life to making the golf ball behave to his will.
> *Ben Crenshaw*

We can never establish who was the greatest player ever, but I don't know how you'd prove that anyone was a better golfer than Ben Hogan.

> *Peter Alliss,* 100 Greatest Golfers *(1989)*

Ben Hogan was the greatest striker of the ball that ever existed, and although he was never a great putter, he still won tournaments by the length of a street.

> *Chris Plumridge*

Ben Hogan played a golf course the way a locomotive runs down a railroad track, making only scheduled stops.

> *Bernard Darwin*

It is possible to play golf, and in fact win, by hitting an awful lot of bad shots if somehow you make up for them with spectacular recoveries or fantastic putting. But Hogan would play a whole tournament, sometimes for four days, without a single bad shot.

> *Peter Thomson*

When I want to hit a nice, boring trajectory on a long iron, I'll try to think of Hogan.

> *Phil Mickelson (1997)*

Hale Irwin (b 1945)
Hale Irwin, the picture-book golfer with the face of a Ph.D. candidate.

> *John Updike,* Thirteen Ways of Looking at the Masters *(1980)*

Hale Irwin isn't the sort of golfer who celebrates victories by buying champagne for the house. His idea of a party is drinking a sugar-free cola and contemplating prudent ways of investing his latest paycheck.

> *Fred Corcoran (1984)*

Don January (b 1929)

Don January's playing with all the passion and verve of a meter reader.

Vin Scully

Robert Tyre "Bobby" Jones Jr. (1902–1971)

What we talk about here is not the hero as golfer, but that something Americans hungered for: the best performer in the world who was also the hero as human being, the gentle, wholly self-sufficient male.

Alistair Cooke

On meeting him for the first time—I met Bobby Jones and started to talk but couldn't. I was in a daze. I never thought I'd ever shake hands with Bobby Jones. I just stood there like a dope.

Sam Snead

Bobby Jones stands to the ball as if engaged in conversation.

Anonymous

An uncomplicated man, who simply stands up and gives it one.

Henry Longhurst

One might as well attempt to describe the smoothness of the wind as to paint a clear picture of his complete swing.

Grantland Rice

Bobby Jones was the most genuinely modest person I have ever met. When one had talked with him a short time, he gave you the feeling that the only difference between your game and his was that he had been much more lucky.

Raymond Oppenheimer

A match against Bobby Jones is just as though you got your hand caught in a buzz saw. He coasts along serenely, waiting for you to miss a shot, and the moment you do, he has you on the hook and you never get off. He can drive straighter than any man living. He is perfectly machinelike in his iron play, and on the greens he is a demon.

Francis Ouimet

To deprecate Jones's record would be a little like saying the Civil War wasn't on the level.

Charles Price, The World of Golf *(1962)*

It is nonsense to talk about who was the greatest golfer in the world. All you can say is that there have been none greater than Bobby Jones.

Tommy Armour

The flavor of the Masters reflects the personality of Robert T. Jones Jr., and Bob has always epitomized the best in golf.

Gene Sarazen

At a New York civic reception in his honor—Here you are, the greatest golfer in the world, being introduced by the worst one.

Mayor James J. Walker (1930)

Betsy King (b 1955)
Before her victory in the 1991 LPGA Championship—The way Betsy is playing, Rin Tin Tin could carry her clubs and it wouldn't make any difference.

Gary Harrison

Tom Kite (b 1949)
On his repeated (early) failure to win a major—If Tom had a fifty-gallon drum of potential, he's using forty-eight gallons of it.

Peter Jacobsen

Matt Kuchar (b 1978)

On his even-par score in the 1998 Masters—He was a refreshing reminder that the PGA Tour used to seem like enjoyment for most of the guys on it. Before the law firm of Greedy and Grim took over, of course.

Dan Jenkins, Golf Digest *(1998)*

Bernhard Langer—Germany (b 1957)

The chess world must hope that Langer never takes up chess. His games might take years to finish.

Charleston News *(1991)*

Commenting on the German's chin stubble after a slowly played round—He was clean-shaven—when we teed off.

Lee Trevino (1992)

David Leadbetter—U.K. (b 1958)

His promotional material refers to him as "The King of Swing," which is a bit of a cheek if you happen to be a fan of Benny Goodman.

Michael Parkinson, London Telegraph *(1994)*

Tom Lehman (b 1959)

Are you going to yell "You da man!" at Tom Lehman? He wears Dockers! People who wear Dockers can be lots of things—except, by definition, *da man.*

Michael Farber, Sports Illustrated *(1997)*

Tom Lehman has been in more spots than Bob Hope.

Gary McCord

During the 1997 Ryder Cup—Yesterday Lehman holed putts the length of Route 66.

Alister Nicol

Wayne Levi (b 1953)

On his singles loss in the 1991 Ryder Cup—Wayne Levi—losing to Seve Ballesteros—looked like a Sunday hacker.

    Washington Post

Gene Littler (b 1930)

On watching him practice—Doesn't take long for a Rolls Royce to warm up, does it?

    Tommy Aaron (1970)

On his apparent anonymity—There's no such guy as Littler. He mails in his scores.

    Bob Drum (1975)

Bobby Locke—South Africa (b 1917)

Bobby was the prime example of someone who could not hit the ball but really could play golf.

    Henry Cotton

He was not like Jack Nicklaus, who careens along the fairway, then takes eons over the shot. Locke has just two speeds for everything—leisurely and slow.

    Ken Bowden (1972)

This guy from the bush duck-hooks every shot...including his putts.

    Anonymous

The son-of-a-bitch Locke was able to hole a putt over sixty feet of peanut brittle.

    Lloyd Mangrum (1982)

Nancy Lopez (b 1957)

Her looks are perfect for the part. Arnold Palmer was attractive and virile. Nancy Lopez is attractive and vibrant.
> *Frank Deford*

It's not just that Nancy Lopez is pretty; it's that she is pretty in everything she does.
> *Betsy Rawls*

They've got the wrong person playing Wonder Woman on television.
> *Judy Rankin (1978)*

Nancy Lopez is planning to marry a sportscaster. I thought she had more taste than that.
> *Dick Schaap,* Sport *magazine (1979)*

On "attempts" to beat her—We've all been trying to steal Nancy's birth-control pills, but so far we've been unsuccessful.
> *JoAnne Carner (1980)*

Her backswing reminded me of someone trying to push open a garage door.
> *Gary McCord,* Golf Digest *(1996)*

Davis Love III (b 1964)

He belongs at Wimbledon, in whites, booming first serves as swift as his tee shots are long. He even has a patrician tennis name right out of a British drawing-room mystery.
> *Thomas Boswell,* Golf *magazine (1996)*

Graham Marsh—Australia (b 1944)

As befits a former teacher of mathematics, he seems to go round golf courses with a pair of compasses, a protractor, dividers, and a slide rule.

> *"Laddie" Lucas*

Casey Martin (b 1972)

On the PGA Tour's original refusal to allow him to ride in a cart—Of course, Martin should get a cart. Anybody with a bus token for a heart knows that. Golf fans want to see golfers play golf. I've never heard anybody yet say, "Hey, let's get over to nine and watch Seve walk!"

> *Rick Reilly,* Sports Illustrated *(1998)*

Billy Maxwell (b 1929)

Billy leaps at the ball like a panhandler diving for a ten-spot.

> *Tony Lema (1964)*

Cary Middlecoff (b 1921)

Middlecoff the dentist doesn't hit irons; he drills them. Every time he wins another tournament, he raises his dental rates. We only hope he fills cavities faster than he plays golf.

> *Mark Mulvoy and Art Spander,*
> The Passion and the Challenge *(1977)*

Cary, a splendid champion, was forever a slow player. A joke on the tour used to be that Cary gave up dentistry because no patient could hold his mouth open that long.

> *Dan Jenkins*

Johnny Miller (b 1947)

When I play a round with Mormon Miller, I must always remind myself never to talk about birds or booze.

> *Jack Newton (1976)*

He doesn't smoke, drink, cuss, or wink at strange girls. He plays pool—but only in Billy Casper's recreation room.

Dave Hill, Teed Off *(1977)*

On his fluid swing—As smooth as a man lifting a breast out of an evening gown.

Phil Harris (1974)

I was going to buy me one of them Johnny Miller leisure suits, but the dude said the fire marshal took 'em off the racks.

Lee Trevino (1978)

As comfortable in the desert as a cactus.

Nick Seitz (1978)

Larry Mize (b 1958)

His cap seems a couple of sizes too big. It makes him look as though his clothes were laid out by his mother.

David Owen, Golf Digest *(1996)*

Colin Montgomerie—U.K. (b 1963)

Mrs. Doubtfire.

U.S. PGA Tour nickname (1997)

The goon from Troon.

Sports Illustrated *(1997)*

The Scot in the Harpo wig.

Tom Callahan, Golf Digest *(1997)*

On being asked to wear shorts during the 1993 World Championships (in Jamaica)—I would be too sexy to wear shorts. There would be trouble from the gallery. And anyway, Monty in shorts...no thanks!

Nick Faldo

Colin Montgomerie smiles with his entire body. He beams. Of course, he frowns the same way.

> *Tom Callahan,* Golf Digest *(1998)*

I get along with him and have no problems, but it seems he is only at his happiest when he is complaining.

> *Brad Faxon (1996)*

Colin has the temper of a warthog that has been stung by a wasp...and a face like a bulldog licking piss off a nettle.

> *David Feherty (1992)*

Best Attribute: No filter from brain to mouth.

> Golf Digest *(1998)*

Poor Monty. He has tried everything to break his Major duck. New coach, no coach, lots of practice, hardly any practice, go on a calorie-controlled diet, take Prozac...OK, I lied about the Prozac.

> *Simon Hughes,* London Telegraph *(1998)*

Orville Moody (b 1933)
On his surprise 1969 U.S. Open success—It was like unhitching a horse from a plow and winning the Kentucky Derby, or a guy stepping out of the audience, removing his coat, and knocking out the heavyweight champion of the world.

> *Jim Murray,* Los Angeles Times

If you had to pick one man you would not want putting for your life, he would be it.

> *Bruce Devlin (1984)*

Nor did his cross-handed putting method particularly recommend him, since no man had ever putted cross-handed and won more than a kick in the ass with a cold boot.

> *Dan Jenkins*

Walter Morgan (b 1941)

He plays golf like a man with nothing to do but smell roses all day.

Lee Pace, Golf Magazine *(1996)*

Old Tom Morris—U.K. (1821–1908)

Old Tom is the most remote point to which we can carry back our genealogical inquiries into golfing style, so that we may virtually accept him as the common golfing ancestor who has stamped the features of his style most distinctly on his descendants.

Horace G. Hutchinson (1900)

Young Tom Morris—U.K. (1851–1875)

Tommy Morris eclipsed his contemporaries and totally changed their conception of how well the game could be played—like Vardon, Jones, and Hogan in later generations.

Michael Hobbs

Byron Nelson (b 1912)

I wouldn't bet anyone against Byron Nelson. The only time he left the fairway was to pee in the bushes.

Jackie Burke

At my best, I never came close to the golf Byron Nelson plays.

Bobby Jones

Larry Nelson (b 1947)

Most weeks he couldn't putt the ball into a two-car garage.

Dan Lauck (1984)

Jack Nicklaus (b 1940)

Nicklaus exudes the killer instinct peculiar to sports immortals. The breakfast of champions is not cereal; it's your opponent.

Nick Seitz, PGA Tour Annual *(1977)*

Palmer and Player played superbly, but Nicklaus plays a kind of golf with which I am not familiar.

Bobby Jones

The first time I saw Jack Nicklaus in person, he reminded me of the Alamo...neither is anywhere as big as I had expected.

Glen Waggoner

Nothing breaks his concentration. He can almost will the ball into the hole.

Ben Crenshaw

There's Nicklaus...only five strokes back. I wouldn't feel safe unless Nicklaus was in a wheelchair.

Dan Jenkins, Dead Solid Perfect *(1974)*

The greatest player who ever wore a slipover shirt.

Dan Jenkins

I would rate Adlai Stevenson and Jack Nicklaus as the two most decorous losers to play on the world stage.

"Laddie" Lucas

To win the things he's won, build golf courses around the world, be a dad to all those kids, and be a hell of an investor, too, it's phenomenal. Hey, stick a broom in his rear end, and he could probably sweep the U.S.A.

Jackie Burke (1981)

Jack Nicklaus is like a young Toots Shor—a victim of circumference.

Jimmy Demaret

Nicklaus may be the only pro in the world who can frighten other pros with his practice shots.

Dick Schaap, Massacre at Winged Foot *(1974)*

On caddying for his father—Do I ever disagree with him on course strategy? Never...unless he's wrong.
  Gary Nicklaus

Chasing Nicklaus is like chasing a walking record book.
  Tom Weiskopf (1975)

The only way we're going to beat this guy is if he signs the wrong card.
  Lee Trevino

If Jack Nicklaus had to play my tee shots, he couldn't break 80. He'd be a pharmacist with a string of drugstores in Ohio.
  Lee Trevino

So, how did Nicklaus win so much? Because he could finish a hole better than anyone else. As a player he's the greatest of all time, but as a golfer I can't even put him in the first fifty.
  Wild Bill Mehlhorn

In Ohio, Nicklaus would win a popularity contest over a parlay card of Mother Teresa, Johnny Carson, and Elvis back from the dead.
  Peter Jacobsen

If I had to have someone putt a twenty-footer for everything I own—my house, my cars, my family—I'd want Nicklaus to putt for me.
  Dave Hill

He wouldn't three-putt a supermarket parking lot.
  Dave Hill, Teed Off *(1977)*

I'm not fit to lace Jack Nicklaus's shoes.
  Hubert Green

You know he's gonna beat you, he knows he's gonna beat
you, and he knows you know he's gonna beat you.
Leonard Thompson

When Jack plays well, he wins; when he plays badly, he
comes second; when he's playing terrible, he's third.
Johnny Miller

It's one thing to beat the young guys, but when you beat Jack
Nicklaus on national television, it is real sweet.
Johnny Miller (1983)

There have been better golfers than Jack Nicklaus, but there
has never been a better winner.
Tom Weiskopf

Most of the time, he plays with the timidity of a middle-
aged spinster walking home through a town full of drunken
sailors, always choosing the safe side of the street.
Peter Dobereiner, London Observer *(1975)*

Jack has become a legend in his own spare time.
Chi Chi Rodriguez

On being asked how the food was in a restaurant—Like Jack
Nicklaus. Very good...and very slow.
Roberto de Vicenzo

Greg Norman—Australia (b 1955)
If I get to be Greg Norman, somebody please stop me.
Davis Love III

He looks like one of the guys they used to send after James
Bond.
Dan Jenkins

Golf kicks Norman from pillar to post. In other sports, good fortune is denied a place in the history books. The Royal and Ancient game offers three categories: lucky golfers, unlucky golfers, and a stratum below that belonging solely to Norman.

Derek Lawrenson, Golf Monthly

Norman is an Aussie's ideal of an ideal Aussie: 6'1", hair the color of whipped cream, and shoulders so wide that he has to edge sideways through the average doorway. He is deeply "religious," which in Australian terms means he is a sports freak.

Peter Dobereiner, Golf Digest *(1984)*

On a barren run of form—The American players have a new name for the "Great White Shark." Greg Norman is referred to as the "Carp."

Guy Hodgson, Independent on Sunday *(1990)*

[Fellow Australian golfer Jack Newton called Norman "The Great White Fish Finger."]

If Greg Norman's the Great White Shark...I'm the Loan Shark.

Chi Chi Rodriguez

On the news that Norman went shark shooting—I don't mind playing golf with Greg Norman, but I'll be damned if I'll go swimming with him.

Lee Trevino

He is thirty-nine years old and on top of the world, yet...he is still pursued by demons. In the past two years he has changed his swing, his coach, his caddie, and his management team. Everything except his wife.

Michael Parkinson, London Telegraph *(1994)*

After losing to Norman, on the second extra hole, in the 1990 World Matchplay—I played crap, he played crap. He just out-crapped me.
> *Wayne Grady*

After his 1993 British Open win—Greg Norman will be the toast of Sandwich tonight.
> BBC *Radio Five commentator*

Moe Norman—Canada (b 1930)
He can not only get the ball up and down from the ball washer, he could, if motivated, play it out of the cup and back into the ball washer.
> *Peter Dobereiner,* Golf Digest *(1983)*

Andy North (b 1950)
Andy North has indeed won the U.S. Open twice. Apart from those triumphs he has achieved little except managing to consistently tie his shoelaces and hoist his pants on the right way round.
> *Bill Elliot*

Golfer Andy North's sister, Pamela, yesterday married Mr. Dick South.
> UPI *Press Report (1977)*

Christy O'Connor Sr.—Ireland (b 1924)
Christy has as much rhythm as an old blues singer.
> *Paddy Skerrit*

Mac O'Grady (b 1951)
Anytime you talk to him, you'll hear three words you never heard before.
> *Mike Nicolette,* Sports Illustrated *(1984)*

Jose Maria Olazabal—Spain (b 1966)

After hitting a variety of shots on the eighteenth at Valderrama
during the 1997 Ryder Cup, while under the overwatchful eye of
his team captain—Ollie not only made a barkie, a chippie, a
droppie, and a sandie, but he also survived a Seve, which
ought to be worth an Emmy.

    Rick Reilly, Sports Illustrated *(1997)*

Arnold Palmer (b 1929)

Arnold Palmer is the biggest crowd-pleaser since the invention of the portable sanitary facility.

    Bob Hope

He first came to golf as a muscular young man who could
not keep his shirttail in, who smoked a lot, perspired a lot,
and who hit the ball with all the finesse of a dockworker lifting a crate of auto parts. Arnold Palmer did not play golf, we
thought. He nailed up beams, reupholstered sofas, repaired
air-conditioning units.... We were as wrong about him as
the break on a downhill six-footer, as wrong as his method
seemed to us to be wrong: hit it hard, go find it, hit it hard
again.

    Dan Jenkins, The Dogged Victims of Inexorable Fate *(1970)*

On playing against him—It's like riding a lion down the road,
whipping him with a rattlesnake, while trying to get away
from a mean guy behind you.

    Doug Sanders (1961)

Palmer lashes into the ball with such explosive force that he
almost falls off the tee after his follow-through. The word
caution is not in his vocabulary.

    Billy Casper (1967)

Arnold Palmer had everything except a brake pedal.
   Peter Dobereiner, Golf Digest *(1982)*

Arnold Palmer, whose blitzkrieg attitude to an immobile golf
ball in the rough is to take about half a ton of flora and
fauna with it in restoring it to where it should be.
   Ian Wooldridge, Golf Illustrated

Arnold Palmer has a swing once impolitely described as looking like someone wrestling with a snake.
   Brian Viner, London Mail on Sunday *(1998)*

Palmer, he of the unsound swing, a hurried slash that ends as
though he is snatching something hot from the fire.
   John Updike, Thirteen Ways of Looking at the Masters *(1980)*

Arnold swung the club as though he were playing tug-of-war
with Zeus.
   Gary McCord, Golf Digest *(1996)*

Palmer not only makes a golf tournament seem as dangerous
as an Indianapolis 500, but he crashes as often as he finishes
first.
   Mark McCormack (1967)

You have to be aggressive, and that's the way I've been play-
ing recently. I've been reading some articles about Arnold
Palmer, and how he became so great. If they put a flag on the
Titanic, Arnie would buy a scuba-diving outfit and go for it.
   Chi Chi Rodriguez (1987)

Like us golfing commoners, he risks looking bad for the sake
of some fun.
   John Updike, Golf *magazine (1980)*

Under a new USGA rule, anyone using the word *charisma* in writing about Palmer is henceforth subject to a two-stroke penalty and loss of down.

> *Herbert Warren Wind,* Golf Digest *(1975)*

The most charismatic figure I have ever seen ... swinging, punching, slashing his way round the golf courses of the world.

> *Peter Alliss,* Golf World *(1997)*

Being paired with Arnold Palmer is like a two-shot penalty.

> *John Schlee (1973)*

On the *rivalry*—It's as if God said to Jack Nicklaus, "You will be the greatest player who ever lived," and then whispered to Arnold Palmer, "but they'll love you more."

> *Tom Callaghan*

I remember one night we got to kicking each other's shins under the table. I kicked him. He kicked me. Neither would give. We ended up with the biggest damned bruises. We used to do the stupidest stuff.

> *Jack Nicklaus*

I don't think I can ever be another Arnold Palmer. No one could. He can hitch up his pants or yank on a glove, and people will start oohing and aahing. When I hitch up mine, nobody watches.

> *Jack Nicklaus*

Golf was a comparatively sexless enterprise before Palmer came a-wooing. His caveman approach took the audience by storm. He was Cagney pushing a grapefruit in Mae Clarke's face, Gable kicking down the door to Scarlett O'Hara's bedroom.

> *Jim Murray,* Los Angeles Times *(1974)*

In the 1961 U.S. Open, at Rancho Park, Arnold hit four of the longest drives of his life. Unfortunately, they were all on the ninth hole...out-of-bounds. Arnold wasn't partial. He hit two to the left and two to the right. Seven fans in his "Army" were so dismayed, they threw themselves off George Archer.

Bob Hope, Confessions of a Hooker *(1985)*

He has won almost as much money playing golf as I have spent on lessons.

Bob Hope

I can still see him marching up the hill toward us, shoulders slightly hunched, head thrust forward, shirttail hanging out. That walk, that look, have been so much a part of golf for so long, it's easy to forget that they were once new. Back then, pro golfers looked like our fathers. Not Palmer. Palmer looked like your best friend's older brother, the one who had the '55 stick-shift Olds and who would sometimes let you hang out with him on Friday night.

Glen Waggoner

Palmer usually walks to the first tee quite unlike any other pro on the circuit. He doesn't walk onto it so much as climb into it, almost as though it were a prize ring; and then he looks around at the gallery as though he is trying to count the house.

Charles Price, The World of Golf *(1962)*

Arnold Palmer is a bit of a mystery because he won a few championships and his trousers were in constant danger of falling down. He was forever hitching them up, and the only explanation I can offer for his success is that he must have worn very tight underpants. I must ask him that someday.

Peter Dobereiner, Golf World *(1984)*

I would rather watch Arnie shoot 80 than Tiger Woods shoot 60, and I don't know anyone who doesn't feel the same.

> *Peter Kessler (1998)*

The Palmer Salad (iceberg lettuce, Roquefort dressing, and blue cheese crumbles) at the Bay Hill Club in Orlando, Florida, costs $3.95, which is 45 cents more than the Caesar Salad. It figures, Caesar might have looked good on a chariot, but he never mounted a charge like Arnie.

> *Brian Viner,* London Mail on Sunday *(1998)*

Jesper Parnevik—Sweden (b 1965)

The whacko Swede in his silly cap and skinny tap dancer's pants always looks like the last guy to climb out of the clown car at the circus.

> *Dan Jenkins,* Golf Digest *(1997)*

Out of Stockholm and the '60s has come a retro Roy Orbison wearing pegged pants and what appear to be old Munsingwear golf shirts, reprising the spirit of white plastic pocket-penholders and eyeglasses held together with adhesive tape, rendering his trademark pop-top cap comparatively unremarkable.

> *Tom Callahan,* Golf Digest *(1997)*

Jerry Pate (b 1953)

On being paired with him in the 1982 Ryder Cup—Jerry had everything...from the neck down. With my brains and his swing, we were unbeatable.

> *Lee Trevino*

After he jumped into the lake upon winning the Memphis Open—I'm surprised he didn't drown, because he can't keep his mouth shut.

> *Jack Nicklaus*

Billy Joe Patton (b 1922)

Bareheaded, bespectacled, grinning...with a faster swing
than a kitchen blender.

> *Dan Jenkins,* The Dogged Victims of Inexorable Fate *(1970)*

Corey Pavin (b 1959)

Corey Pavin is a little on the slight side. When he goes
through a turnstile, nothing happens.

> *Jim Moriarty (1984)*

If swinging the club really was as simple and natural as, say,
swinging a hammer, Corey Pavin would be making $8.47 an
hour.

> *Henry Beard,* Mulligan's Laws *(1993)*

Corey Pavin is the only golfer whose practice swing is worse
than his actual swing.

> *Johnny Miller (1995)*

This must be the swing of the future, for sure as hell, I
haven't seen anything like it in the past.

> *Charles Price*

He manufactured shots, he showed great skill and nerve, and
when asked to speak, he strung words together as if he'd
actually been to school.

> *Peter Alliss*

He plays the game as if he has a plane to catch. As if he were
double-parked and left the meter running. Guys move slower
leaving hotel fires.

> *Jim Murray*

He has the perfect temperament to play guard in the NBA. Maybe Pavin is too much of a gentleman to head-butt anybody, like Knicks guard John Starks. But just imagine how much you'd hate to learn Pavin was going to cover you man-to-man.

Thomas Boswell, Golf *magazine (1996)*

He's like a little dog that gets hold of your pants leg and won't let go.

Mark O'Meara

If my son wants to learn golf, I'll send him to Corey.

Nick Price

Calvin Peete (b 1943)
He has a crooked left arm...until he reaches out for the paycheck.

Lee Trevino

Alf Perry—U.K. (1904–1974)
He dresses like a gardener and usually plays like one.

Henry Cotton

After his 1935 British Open victory—He came from nowhere and went back there.

Anonymous

Gary Player—South Africa (b 1935)
Gary Player is all right if you like to see a grown man dressed up as Black Bart all the time.

Don Rickles

[But as Player himself says: "I wear black because I loved Westerns, and the cowboys always looked good in black."]

Player, varying his normal black outfit with white slacks, his bearing so full of fight and muscle, he seems to be restraining himself from breaking into a run.

> *John Updike,* Thirteen Ways of Looking at the Masters *(1980)*

He runs and lifts weight and eats health foods. That's all well and good, but I get tired of hearing him brag about it. So what if he has the most perfect bowel movements on the tour?

> *Dave Hill,* Teed Off *(1977)*

Gary solicits far too much advice on the practice tee....I've seen him taking a lesson at the U.S. Open from a hot dog vendor.

> *Dave Hill,* Teed Off *(1977)*

The best sand player I have ever seen is, without doubt, Gary Player. Playing against him, you begin hoping he'll be on grass rather than in sand anytime he misses the green.

> *Jack Nicklaus*

As much as I want to win as many tournaments as I can, I am not prepared to play, week in, week out, year after year, as Gary Player does.

> *Tony Jacklin (1971)*

If he doesn't have an obstacle to clear, he will erect one to keep up his interest, and at positive thinking he could give Norman Vincent Peale two a side.

> *Nick Seitz*

Renee Powell (b 1946)

When Renee Powell is playing in a northerly direction, and I am observing from the south, if any member of the constabulary in the vicinity happens to be a mind reader, I could go to jail for my thoughts.

> *Peter Dobereiner,* For the Love of Golf

Nick Price—Zimbabwe (b 1957)

A player who competes with Ben Crenshaw for the title of Nicest Guy in Golf.

> *Dan Jenkins,* Golf Digest *(1997)*

Ted Ray—U.K. (1877–1943)

He was usually as dour as an elephant with a sore foot.

> *Grantland Rice*

Costantino Rocca—Italy (b 1956)

After Rocca beat Tiger Woods in the 1997 Ryder Cup singles—
Come on, Europe, get real with the bragging. You really want to let Costantino Rocca, an old guy from an Italian box factory, play Tiger Woods for a living? Sure, Rocca beat him, 4&2, in a crucial singles match at Valderrama, but so did everybody else.

> *Dan Jenkins,* Golf Digest *(1997)*

Juan "Chi Chi" Rodriguez—Puerto Rico (b 1935)

He hits the ball so straight. It's from hitting it in those Puerto Rican alleys.

> *Dave Stockton (1984)*

Chi Chi's swing always looked like he was in a room filled with flies and his flyswatter wasn't big enough.

> *Gary McCord,* Golf Digest *(1996)*

*On his postputt swaying motion—*That's called "Body Spanish."

> *Bob Murphy*

Paul Runyan (b 1908)

Watch Paul's unhurried swing. It's as lazy as a Spanish siesta, as delicately fashioned as a flower petal.

> *Horton Smith*

Doug Sanders (b 1933)

Look at John Daly's swing. It's not possible. He's made of
rubber. Look at Jack's swing—flying right elbow. Arnie's flat.
Doug Sanders—he could swing inside a telephone booth and
not break a window. In the end, it's all in the head.

> *Gary Player (1995)*

Doug Sanders braces himself with a wide stance that looks
like a sailor leaning into a northeast gale and takes the club
back barely far enough to get it off the ground.

> *Tony Lema (1964)*

He is a dashing Southerner with a fetching smile and a ready
eye for the ladies. Put him on the North Pole, and he'll have
every Eskimo around at a party within twenty-four hours.

> *Dan Hruby (1984)*

On his flamboyant dress sense—The man looks like a jukebox
with feet. In fact, even his feet look like jukeboxes.

> *Tommy Bolt*

The only guy on tour who could have more fun than the leg-
endary Jimmy Demaret.

> *Melanie Hauser,* Golf *magazine (1996)*

Gene Sarazen (b 1902)

The name speaks for itself. He stands for all the good there is
in golf.

> *Jimmy Demaret*

If it wasn't for golf, Sarazen would be back on a banana boat
between Naples and Sicily.

> *Jimmy Demaret*

Gene Sarazen tears the ball through the wind as if it did not exist.

Bernard Darwin

The boldness of Gene Sarazen's play leaves him no middle ground. He has to go for the flag.

Bobby Jones

Tom Sieckmann (b 1955)

In 1981, Tom Sieckmann won the Philippine Open, the Thailand Open, and the Singapore Open, leaving him second only to the U.S. Marines for victories in the Pacific.

Gary Nuhn, Dayton Daily News

Charlie Sifford (b 1923)

There are days when he could putt better with a rake.

Jim Murray (1968)

Jeff Sluman (b 1957)

Jeff Sluman, 5'7" of nonexplosive dynamite, lists his special interests as: the Stock Market and the Tour Policy Board. He probably hasn't discovered crochet, yet.

Bill Elliot

Macdonald Smith (1890–1949)

If we all played golf like Mac Smith, the National Open Championship could be played on one course every day in the year and never a divot mark would scar the beautiful fairway. He has the cleanest twenty-one-jewel stroke in golf. He treats the grass of a golf course as though it were an altar cloth.

Tommy Armour, The American Golfer *(1935)*

J. C. Snead (b 1941)

Seldom confused with his uncle Sam.

Dave Hill, Teed Off *(1977)*

On his second-place finish in the 1978 U.S. Open—He played almost the entire final round without putting his spikes on the fairway. He spent so much time in the sand that if you held his wedge to your ear, you could hear the ocean.

  Joe Gergen

Sam Snead (b 1912)

I've just watched a kid who doesn't know anything about playing golf, and I don't want to be around when he learns how.

  Gene Sarazen

Sam Snead did to the tee shot what Roger Bannister did to the four-minute mile.

  Byron Nelson

It's called color. Some people have it and some don't. As for Slammin' Sam Snead, he has enough color to outfit a couple of rainbow factories.

  Rex Lardner, The Great Golfers *(1970)*

On learning that Snead received only $500 for his 1946 British Open victory—Of course, he's still got it.

  Dave Marr

Sam Snead's got more money buried underground than I ever made on top. He's got gophers in his backyard that subscribe to *Fortune.* He's packed more coffee cans than Brazil.

  Arnold Palmer

If the legend is true that Sam keeps all his wealth buried in tomato cans, the designated site must be an area as big as Fort Knox.

  Robert Trent Jones

If you could get the digging rights to Sam's backyard, you'd never have to work again in your life.

> *Doug Sanders*

Sam was born with a natural ability to keep his bar bills as low as his golf score.

> *Jimmy Demaret (1954)*

When I dine with Mr. Snead, he always suggests that I order as if I was expecting to pay for it myself. I have known many great destroyers of money, but Mr. Snead is not among them.

> *George Low*

Sam was born warmed up. If you cut him, 3-in-1 oil would come out, not blood.

> *Gardner Dickinson*

Watching Sam Snead practice hitting golf balls is like watching a fish practice swimming.

> *John Schlee,* Golf Digest *(1977)*

Anyone who would pass up an opportunity to see Sam Snead swing a golf club at a golf ball would pull down the shades when driving past the Taj Mahal.

> *Jim Murray,* Los Angeles Times

Snead, with his rakishly tilted panama and slightly pushed-in face—a face that has known both battle and merriment—swaggers around the practice tee like the Sheriff of Golf Country.

> *John Updike,* Thirteen Ways of Looking at the Masters *(1980)*

While he has yet to read *War and Peace,* Snead wasn't any more a hillbilly than Shirley Temple was a midget.

> *Charles Price (1983)*

I never saw Byron Nelson play, and I've only seen Ben Hogan hit balls, but I've played a lot with Sam, and he plays the game the way it's supposed to be played—the way you dreamed about playing just once in your life.

Ben Crenshaw

Like classic plays and symphonies, Sam Snead doesn't just belong to a generation. His mark will be left on golf for an eternity.

Peter Thomson

Hollis Stacy (b 1954)
Shirttail hanging out, hair blowing in the wind, dragging on a cigarette. That's sex appeal.

Arnold Palmer (1981)

Craig Stadler (b 1953)
Some guys hope to shoot their age. Craig Stadler hopes to shoot his waist.

Jim Murray, Los Angeles Times (1980)

How can I not like Craig? He's the best thing that ever happened to me. He makes me look good.

Tom Weiskopf (1982)

On a heavily perspiring "Walrus"—It certainly is warm, and from the looks of that shirt, he's been dressed by the dreaded sisters—Polly and Esther.

Dave Marr, ABC TV

Jan Stephenson—Australia (b 1951)
Hell, if I were built like Jan, I'd show it off too.

JoAnne Carner (1982)

Payne Stewart (b 1957)

Payne Stewart has developed an infinite capacity for self-destruction.

Ben Wright

Dumbest-Dressed Player on Tour: Payne Stewart and his NFL-logo knickers. Can't really blame him, though. For $350,000 a year, I'd wear my underpants outside my clothes.

Glen Waggoner, Divots, Shanks, Gimmes, Mulligans... *(1993)*

He's tremendously confident right now. He'd need to be to dress the way he does.

Colin Montgomerie

He's the only pro never to be asked: "How much would you have to be paid to dress like Payne Stewart?"

Fore! *magazine (1998)*

Dave Stockton (b 1941)

Everyone complains about his putting, but Dave Stockton doesn't know how dangerously he's living when he moans. He's such a great putter, someday someone's gonna hit him in the head with a club.

Dan Sikes

Dave Stockton has as much confidence as John Elway, Deane Beman, and Hillary Clinton combined.

Rocky Thompson

Hal Sutton (b 1958)

After he had complained about local British crowds at the 1985 Ryder Cup—I bet Sutton can't wait to get back to America and head straight for McDonald's.

Tony Jacklin

If God were a teenager and descended to give us the word,
He'd probably look like Hal Sutton.

    Nathaniel Crosby (1983)

Cyril Tolley—U.K. (b 1895)

One has the impression of wide and irresistible shoulders acting like a great flywheel, revolving with such titanic force that
if a golf ball had any volition of its own, it would disappear
into space without wanting to be crushed into submission.

    H. N. Wethered

Katsuyoshi Tomori—Japan

During the 1995 British Open—He plays golf like Willie
Nelson sings. You don't think he can do it, but he goes and
does it quite well.

    Peter Alliss, BBC TV

Walter Travis—Australia (1862–1927)

*After he became the first Australian to win the British Open in
1904*—Never since the days of Caesar has the British nation
been subjected to such humiliation.

    Lord Northbourne

Travis holed out from such immeasurable distances that his
opponents claimed he could putt the eyes out of a chipmunk.

    Charles Price, Golfer-at-Large *(1982)*

Travis could go weeks without missing a fairway and play
through a hurricane wearing a ten-gallon hat.

    Charles Price, Golfer-at-Large *(1982)*

Lee Trevino (b 1939)

Lee's swing always looked like he was pulling a heavy load
with a skinny horse.

    Gary McCord, Golf Digest *(1996)*

He's done it all with a swing that suggests a lumberjack going after the nearest redwood.

> *Curry Kirkpatrick*

[Sentiments with which Trevino agrees: "No one who ever had lessons would have a swing like mine."]

More people turn up to watch Lee Trevino change shoes than to watch me tee off.

> *Orville Moody*

During the Masters—If you don't shut up, Lee, I'm going to tell where you swam across the border.

> *Doug Sanders*

Lee Trevino is the only man I know who talks on his backswing.

> *Charley McClendon,* Sports Illustrated *(1972)*

He makes Joan Rivers sound like Calvin Coolidge.

> *Bob Hope*

Lee Trevino relieves his tension by talking all the time—to other people, to himself, even sometimes in midswing. Man, how he talks!

> *Jack Nicklaus*

Lee's got more lines than the Illinois Railroad.

> *Fuzzy Zoeller (1979)*

He has the gift, unusual among top sportsmen, for the *bon mot*, and his delivery is that of an ace comedian.

> *John Ballantine (1970)*

If he didn't have an Adam's apple, he'd have no shape at all.

> *Gary Player (1972)*

Trevino, so broad across, he looks like a reflection in a fun-
house mirror, a model of delicacy around the greens and a
model of affable temperament everywhere.

    John Updike, Thirteen Ways of Looking at the Masters *(1980)*

On his 1971 Canadian Open play-off win over Art Wall—
Trevino and Wall...not until Julia Roberts married Lyle
Lovett has there been such an unlikely pairing.

    Jerry Tarde, Golf Digest *(1996)*

Harry Vardon—U.K. (1870–1937)
He was the epitome of confidence. Often, he would play a
shot and then replace his divot before bothering to see where
the ball had gone. He didn't have to see. He knew.

    Gene Sarazen

After the 1931 U.S. Open—The groove in his swing was so
obvious, you could almost see it. I was so impressed that during the last round, when my swing started to leave me, I
started imitating his. And it worked, too. Fact is...I almost
caught him with his own swing.

    Walter Hagen

A grand player up to the green, and a very bad player when
he got there. But then, Vardon gave himself less putting to
do than any other men.

    Bernard Darwin

He held on to the club as though it were a garden rake, addressed
it as though he were about to pick up a piano, and swung it as
though he were trying to get out of the way of something.

    Charles Price, Golfer-at-Large *(1982)*

He never threw a tantrum, never gave an alibi—he just came
to play.

    Charles Price

Glenna Collett Vare (b 1903)

No one else quite so adequately expressed how far women's golf had come since those far-off days when women swung at the ball as though they were beating off purse-snatchers with an umbrella.

> *Charles Price,* The World of Golf *(1962)*

Lanny Wadkins (b 1949)

Lanny is a self-confessed optimist, the kind who, if he falls in a sewer, checks his pockets for fish.

> *Mickey Herskowitz (1983)*

Lanny is back home in Maine painting his house. As fast as he does everything, what's he going to do on the second day?

> *Dan Jenkins (1985)*

On being paired with Lanny Wadkins—Cripes! They're going to have to hire a third person just to smile for us.

> *Curtis Strange*

Playing against Lanny is like having a bulldog tied to your ankles.

> *Dave Stockton (1991)*

He's the most tenacious player I've ever seen. You put a pin in the middle of a lake, and Lanny will attack it.

> *John Mahaffey (1983)*

The Speedy Gonzalez Fastest Player on Tour Award: Lanny Wadkins. Nobody else is even close. Lanny is halfway down the fairway before his tee hits the ground after his drive.... You like to watch a man being tortured? Watch Lanny Wadkins waiting to hit.

> *Glen Waggoner,* Divots, Shanks, Gimmes, Mulligans... *(1993)*

Duffy Waldorf (b 1962)

On his swing—He looks like someone delivering a pizza.

> Ben Wright

Tom Watson (b 1949)

Any self-respecting golf tournament wants to be won by Tom Watson.

> *Jim Murray,* Golf *magazine (1983)*

Watson scares me. If he's lying six in the middle of the fairway, there's some kind of way he might make five.

> *Lee Trevino (1979)*

Watson's close friends enjoy describing him as the worst walker and worst dresser in golf.

> *Herbert Warren Wind,* The New Yorker *(1981)*

Watson walks about his golf course business like a young trial lawyer going from one courtroom to the next.

> *Al Barkow,* Golf's Golden Grind *(1974)*

To call him complex would be to call the Rubik's cube slightly taxing.

> *Larry Dorman*

There's no right speed for everyone...if I tried to play at Tom Watson's breakneck speed, I'd self-destruct before I finished playing the front nine.

> *Nancy Lopez*

Tom Watson...pensive Tom Sawyer, who, while the other boys were whitewashing fences, has become, politely, but firmly, the best golfer in the world.

> *John Updike (1980)*

Tom Watson is a hell of a golfer, but he sure could use a choreographer. Watching him shoot a 66 is like watching the president sign a bill.

> *Jay Cronley,* Playboy *(1981)*

When you drive into the left rough, hack your second out into a greenside bunker, come out to within six feet of the hole, and sink the slippery putt...when you do that, you've made a Watson par.

> *Andy Bean (1984)*

Tom Weiskopf (b 1942)

On the golf course at the peak of his game, Tom Weiskopf was one part Jack Nicklaus, one part Tommy Bolt, and, for better or worse, one part Tom Weiskopf, which was always something of a problem.

> *Dan Jenkins,* Fairways and Greens *(1994)*

Tom Weiskopf is getting ready to issue his first quote of the year, and I don't want to miss it.

> *Dan Jenkins,* Sports Illustrated *(1971)*

He knows more ways of choking than Dracula.

> *Colman McCarthy (1977)*

His swing was made in heaven, part velvet, part silk, like a royal robe, so sweet you could pour it over ice cream.

> *Jim Murray,* Los Angeles Times

Lee Westwood—U.K. (b 1973)

Lee Westwood has the smile of the moment...his teeth appear to have been hammered into his head by a drunken cobbler.

> *Tom Callahan,* Golf Digest *(1998)*

Before he won the 1998 Loch Lomond Invitational—He's a big boy...six feet tall and not anorexic....If he'd been in the circus, he'd be the strongman.

> *Peter Alliss,* BBC TV

Joyce Wethered—U.K. (b 1901)

She could hit a ball 240 yards on the fly while standing barefoot on a cake of ice.

> *Willie Wilson*

Tiger Woods (b 1975)

I saw talent in Tiger when he was three days old. When he got out of the high chair, he had a golf swing.

> *Earl Woods*

On being asked his opinion of fifteen-year-old Tiger Woods—I don't know. I never played the course.

> *Sandy Lyle*

Both Arnold and I agree that you could take my [six] Masters and his [four] and add them together, and this kid should win more than that.

> *Jack Nicklaus (1996)*

After his record win in the 1997 Masters—Ten Steps to Stop or
Slow Down Tiger Woods:
1. Make him wear Harry Vardon's tweed suit.
2. Make him wear Greg Norman's planter's hat.
3. Make him read a David Leadbetter instruction article.
4. Make him use Phil Mickelson's clubs.
5. Make him play the gutty.
6. Make him wear Tom Kite's glasses.
7. Make him read every word of the new Jack Nicklaus
   autobiography.
8. Make him go to dinner with Mark Rolfing.
9. Make him attend the annual golf writers' dinner.
10. Make him get married and have to go to Ace Hardware
    a lot.

    Dan Jenkins, Golf Digest *(1997)*

If Tiger Woods didn't exist, Nike would have invented
him.... He's got a name that sounds like it's straight from the
credits of *Tin Cup.* Tiger Woods? Are you kidding me? That's
like having a baseball star named "Slugger Bats."

    Richard Roeper, Chicago Sun-Times *(1997)*

After his 1–3–1 record in the 1997 Ryder Cup—It was Tiger
Woods becoming the first cat to lay an egg.

    Rick Reilly, Sports Illustrated *(1997)*

Tiger: Not The Full Monty.

    European fans' T-shirt at the 1997 Ryder Cup

Tiger could probably be world champion in the 400 m, kicking Michael Johnson's ass. If you think his swing is pretty,
you should see him run.

    Earl Woods

Ian Woosnam—U.K. (b 1958)

Woosnam is a product of the oriental art of miniaturizing professional golfers, but there is nothing bonsai about the scale of Woosnam's golf.

> *Peter Dobereiner*

If he ever grows up, he'll be one hell of a player.

> *Seve Ballesteros (1987)*

The typical golfer on the tour is thirty-five years old, stands $5'11''$...all of them tower over Ian Woosnam, who, at, $5'4^1/_2''$, is only slightly taller than Bruce Lietzke's putter.

> *Glen Waggoner,* Divots, Shanks, Gimmes, Mulligans... *(1993)*

On partnering Ian Woosnam for all four rounds of the 1994 Masters—It's the longest relationship I've ever had.

> *John Daly*

On his 1997 Ryder Cup singles match—The tone for the match was set off the first tee, from which Fred Couples hit a corker and Woosnam hit a cork tree. His recovery shot hit another one so violently that the two people perched in it did well not to fall out. One down, and very nearly two spectators down.

> *Martin Johnson,* London Telegraph

Mildred "Babe" Zaharias (1914–1956)

There's only one thing wrong about Babe and me. I hit the ball like a girl, and she hits like a man.

> *Bob Hope*

She made women's golf. She put the hit in the swing.

> *Patty Berg*

On her leaving athletics for a golfing career—
The Texas Babe now shifts her scene,
Where slashing drives are far,
Where spoon shots find the distant green
To break the back of par.
> *Grantland Rice*

Larry Ziegler (b 1939)

If Larry ever dreamed that he beat me, he'd apologize when he woke up.
> *Lee Trevino*

Francis Urban "Fuzzy" Zoeller (b 1951)

When I catch my driver and Fuzzy catches his one-iron, I can get within thirty yards of him.
> *Hale Irwin (1981)*

Maybe Fuzzy Zoeller plays golf the way everybody should. Hit it, go find it, hit it again. Grin, have a smoke, take a sip, make a joke, and every so often win a major championship.
> *Dan Jenkins,* Sports Illustrated *(1984)*

AMATEURS

Amateurs are always short.
Walter Hagen

Amateur golfer: One who moves heaven and earth whilst playing golf.
> *Anonymous*

An amateur golfer is one who plays for honor—in my mind, that's tougher than playing for money.

Willie Turnesa

INDIVIDUALS

[U.S. unless otherwise stated]

Spiro Agnew—Vice president

The last time I played with Vice President Spiro Agnew, he hit a birdie...an eagle, a moose, an Elk, and a Mason.

Bob Hope (1970)

At least he can't cheat on his score...because all you have to do is look back down the fairway and count the wounded.

Bob Hope (1971)

Prince Andrew—British Royal

Fergie apparently expected her husband to be a fun-loving companion: by all accounts, he has become an indifferent couch potato and, worse, yet, a golfer!

Newsweek

Request aimed at Prince Andrew, obstructing the gallery's view of the seventeenth at Valderrama, during the 1997 Ryder Cup—
By order of the Queen, will Your Royal Highness kindly sit down!

Anonymous fan

Johnny Bench—Baseball player

The only soft spot in his game is that his putter has the "take" sign on all the time.

Gary McCord, Just a Range Ball in a Box of Titleists *(1997)*

Jack Benny—Comedian

Jack Benny had only one golf ball the whole of his golfing career. He finally lost it when the string came off.

Bob Hope

George Burns—Comedian

George, you look perfect...that beautiful knitted shirt, an alpaca sweater, those expensive slacks...you've got an alligator bag, the finest matched irons, and the best woods money can buy. It's a damned shame you have to spoil it all by playing golf.

Lloyd Mangrum

George Bush—President

After he played a round of golf prior to the Gulf War—It's nice to see a president improving his golf game with the nation on the brink of war. On the eve of Fort Sumter, they say Lincoln was so nervous, he was blowing routine six-foot putts.

Gerald Nachman

He'd rather face Congress than a three-foot putt.

Ken Raynor

After her husband had hit two spectators—As if we don't have enough violence on television.

Barbara Bush (1995)

Bill Clinton—President

Clinton plays golf...he wore jogging shoes, and his shirt was hanging out over painter's pants. Golf needs Clinton like it needs a case of ringworm.

Rick Reilly, Sports Illustrated *(1992)*

Clinton can't possibly practice enough to hit the ball straight unless he's out there with O. J. hitting sand shots in the middle of the night. Golf isn't politics, where Clinton can get to the center just by throwing Hillary over the side. Golf takes work.

Tony Kornheiser (1995)

The way he plays, acts, dresses is a snapshot of a new player being attracted to golf.

Golf Digest (1998)

Bing Crosby—Singer

He invented the pipe, the shirt worn outside the pants, the cocked hat. He is so rich, even his caddies subscribe to *Fortune.*

Bob Hope

Vic Damone—Singer

He would be a fine player, but he's too busy looking in the grass to see if he can find a mirror.

Don Rickles

Vic's golf swing has the same flow as one of his soft ballads but has the power of PeeWee Herman. Beautiful to watch, but the club doesn't make enough noise on the downswing.

Gary McCord, Just a Range Ball in a Box of Titleists *(1997)*

Sammy Davis Jr.—Singer

Sammy Davis Jr. hits the ball 130 yards and his jewelry goes 150.

Bob Hope

Prince Edward [VIII]—British Royal

While playing with Edward, the Prince of Wales—Here, Eddie, hold the flag while I putt out.

Walter Hagen (c. 1930s)

Dwight D. Eisenhower—President

As an intellectual, he bestowed upon the games of golf and
bridge all the enthusiasm and perseverance that he withheld
from his books and ideas.

> *Emmet John Hughes*

Augusta is the course Ike Eisenhower usually plays on. That's
proof enough for me that he is a man with good taste.

> *Jimmy Demaret,* My Partner, Ben Hogan *(1954)*

No administration ever had more suntanned Secret Service
men.... You could always find his farm at Gettysburg because
it was the one completely surrounded by divots.... During
his White House years there was a rumor going round that
the new dollar bill would have Ben Hogan's face on it.

> *Bob Hope*

He has given up golf for painting...it takes fewer strokes.

> *Bob Hope*

Golf has long symbolized the Eisenhower years—played by
soft, boring men with ample waistlines who went around rich
men's country club courses in the company of wealthy busi-
nessmen and were tended by white-haired dutiful Negroes.

> *David Halberstam*

Gerald Ford—President

In the Bob Hope Golf Classic the participation of President
Gerald Ford was more than enough to remind you that the
nuclear button was at one stage at the disposal of a man who
might have either pressed it by mistake or else pressed it
deliberately in order to obtain room service.

> *Clive James,* London Observer *(1981)*

A droll TV commentator remarked that the president had turned golf into a "combat sport" and that the security men were coming in handy to keep track of the ball.

Clive James, London Observer *(1981)*

Gerald Ford doesn't realize he can't hit a ball through a tree trunk.

Jack Nicklaus

And the name that is synonymous with Ford . . . "Fore!"

Vin Scully (1984)

He has assaulted more people with a golf club than Jack Nicholson. Who can remember those days at the Bob Hope Golf Classic when President Ford would tee off of the first hole and send a Scud into the gallery, and some lucky senior citizen would be marked ceremonially by the imprint of his golf ball?

Gary McCord, Just a Range Ball in a Box of Titleists *(1997)*

Gerald Ford—the most dangerous driver since Ben Hur—has made golf a contact sport. There are forty-two golf courses in the Palm Springs area, and nobody knows which one Gerald Ford is playing until after he has teed off. It's not hard to find Gerald Ford on a golf course—just follow the wounded.

Bob Hope

Bob Hope says I have made golf a combat and contact sport. But I know I'm getting better at golf because I'm hitting fewer spectators.

Gerald Ford, People *(1983)*

I call him the "PGA Hit Man." But it's wonderful being able to get back some of the money I gave to the government.

Bob Hope

When I play with Gerald Ford, I usually try to make it a foursome...the president, myself, a paramedic, and a faith healer.

Bob Hope

Whitey Ford—Baseball player

He golfs like he pitches. He puts the ball where he wants it...low and away.

Jim Murray

Joe Garagiola—Baseball announcer

On the inaugural Joe Garagiola Tucson Open—It's the first time a .200 hitter ever had anything named after him.

Bob Hope

Frank Gifford—Sportscaster

Frank, either you have to get better soon or quit telling people I'm your teacher.

Dave Marr

Jackie Gleason—Actor

Jackie's such a generous guy that he donated a sweater to charity as a pro-am prize, and now there's a family of refugees living in it.

Bob Hope

[Confirming what Gleason had already said about his own expansive waistline: "When I tee the ball where I can see it, I can't hit it. And when I put it where I can hit it, I can't see it."]

Billy Graham—Evangelist

Pretty hard to beat a guy who gets a ball out of a sand trap just by looking up and muttering a few words.

Bob Hope

Michael Jackson—Singer

I have this notion that if Michael Jackson had ever taken up golf, he would never have felt the need to have lunch with orangutans—or even with Elizabeth Taylor.

Dan Jenkins, Fairways and Greens *(1994)*

Lyndon B. Johnson—President

You'd better be careful anytime you play golf with President Johnson...he always brings his own Birdies.

Hubert H. Humphrey (1968)

Michael Jordan—Basketball player

As good as Jordan is at golf—and he's not that bad—there are dozens of guys with comb-overs and 35 percent body fat whose games would make His Airness look like Mugsy Bogues on the golf course.

Ed Sherman, Chicago Tribune *(1998)*

Sandy Koufax—Baseball player

He could hit a ball farther off line than any man I ever knew. When Sandy practiced, he would blanket three fairways, three hundred yards out and three hundred yards wide. He was like a one-man hailstorm.

Mac Hunter (1982)

Christopher Lee—British actor

For an old geezer you don't half give it a f***ing whack.

Wayne Riley

Jack Lemmon—Actor

*On watching him swing a club—*My God, he looks like he's beating a chicken.

Byron Nelson

During the 1959 Crosby Pro-Am at Pebble Beach—Now here's Jack Lemmon, about to play an all-important eighth shot.
    Jim McKay

My lasting memory of Jack Lemmon will be in that crouched putting stance, eyes narrowly focused, poised over a six-foot putt on the seventeenth hole at Pebble Beach, shaking like a Mexican space shuttle, for an 8.
    Gary McCord, Just a Range Ball in a Box of Titleists *(1997)*

Jack Lemmon has been in more bunkers than Eva Braun.
    Phil Harris

After caddying for him—When he gets the ball into a tough place, that's when he's most relaxed. I think it's because he has so much experience at it.
    Don Christopher

Ivan Lendl—Czech tennis player
After the clay-court specialist hit five golf balls into the water—Remember, grass isn't his best surface.
    Roger Maltbie (1996)

Dean Martin—Actor
On his decision to quit Bel-Air G.C.—The departure of a Dean Martin from a golf course is comparable to a near-sighted millionaire leaving a crap game in a smoky room.
    Jim Murray

George Meany—Union leader
He plays like a union man. He negotiates the final score.
    Bob Hope

Joe Montana—Football player

Suggesting how her husband could improve his accuracy off the tee—What we have to do is get Dwight Clark to stand in the middle of the fairway about two hundred yards away. Joe would hit him out of habit.

    Cass Montana (1983)

Bill Murray—Comic actor

On the clown Prince of the PGA Tour—One Bill Murray is good for the tour; two would be a disaster.

    Johnny Miller

Richard M. Nixon—President

Nixon could relate to the ordinary guy who plays. Hell, I even once caught him cheating a little bit...moving the ball when he didn't think nobody could see him. All hackers do that.

    Sam Snead

Tom O'Connor—British comedian

To his pro-am partner—Try to slow your swing down to a blur.

    Sandy Lyle

Shaquille O'Neal—Basketball player

On his receiving some extra-long Taylor Made clubs from his Florida neighbor Mark O'Meara—His Shaqness doesn't play the long game. He's never done well outside fifteen feet.

    Mike Purkey, Golf *magazine (1996)*

Joe Pesci—Actor

His swing has more positions than a Craftmatic adjustable bed.

    Gary McCord, Just a Range Ball in a Box of Titleists *(1997)*

O. A. "Bum" Phillips—Football coach
On his ultra-crew-cut hairstyle—It reminds me of a good three-wood lie.
> *Carol Mann*

George Plimpton—Writer
During the Bing Crosby Pro-Am—You were hitting some shots out there that weren't making any noise.
> *Dave Marr*

Charley Pride—Singer
I only see Charley Pride when we get to the greens. Charley hits some good woods...most of them trees.
> *Glen Campbell*

J. Danforth Quayle—Vice-president
Scorecard.
> *Quayle's Secret Service code name*

An empty suit that goes to funerals and plays golf.
> *H. Ross Perot*

Anyone who knows Dan Quayle knows he would rather play golf than have sex any day.
> *Marilyn Quayle (1992)*

After partnering with the former VP in a losing-money foursome match—Let me get this, Dan; you're unemployed now.
> *Mark O'Meara*

I wonder if golfer Dan Quayle would be happy to learn that ten pros list "family" as their number one special interest? (I wonder if anyone still cares what Dan Quayle thinks? I wonder if anyone still remembers who he is?)
> *Glen Waggoner,* Divots, Shanks, Gimmes, Mulligans... *(1993)*

Mickey Rooney—Actor

Shorter guys have lower centers of gravity, which Isaac
Newton or somebody figured out is better for swinging a
club. This principle of swing dynamics has its limits, as anyone who has ever watched Mickey Rooney play in the Bob
Hope Classic will readily attest.

> *Glen Waggoner,* Divots, Shanks, Gimmes, Mulligans... *(1993)*

Telly Savalas—Actor

During the 1984 Bob Hope Classic—Telly Savalas, struggling under
an 18 handicap, now needs a three-ax to get out of this trouble.

> *Vin Scully,* NBC TV

O. J. Simpson—Football player and actor

On April 14, 1865, President Abraham Lincoln was assass-
inated at Ford's Theater by a deranged actor. O. J. Simpson
was playing golf at the time.

> *David Letterman*

Emmitt Smith—Football player

*After the Dallas Cowboy's perfect first drive during a pro-am
tournament*—Don't pick up your tee so fast. You ought to
stand there and admire it.

> *Lee Trevino*

Harry S. Truman—President

He never backed off from anything, and I like that. No way
would he ever have been penalized for slow play. He'd just
step up and knock the hell out of the ball.

> *Lee Trevino,* They Call Me Super Mex *(1982)*

John Wayne—Actor

After he suddenly quit golf—How could a guy who won the
West, recaptured Bataan, and won the Battle of Iwo Jima let
himself be defeated by a little hole in the ground?

> *James E. Grant*

Andy Williams—Singer
I love to play with Andy, but he can be very distracting. Have you ever tried to pitch over a water hazard while your partner is humming "Moon River"?
Bob Hope

THE AVERAGE GOLFER

The average weekend golfer is far too greedy.
Gary Player

The average golfer doesn't play golf. He attacks it.
Jack Burke

This made him two up and three to play. What an average golfer would consider a commanding lead. But Archibald was no average golfer. A commanding lead for him would have been two up with one to play.
P. G. Wodehouse, Archibald's Benefit *(1919)*

The average golfer, if I am a fair specimen, is hooked when he hits his first good shot; the ball climbs into the air all of its own, it seems—a soaring speck conjured from the effortless airiness of an accidentally correct swing. And then, he or she, that average golfer, spends endless frustrating afternoons, whole decades of them, trying to recover and tame the delicate wildness of the first sweet swing. Was ever any sporting motion so fraught with difficulty and mystery?
John Updike

A leading difficulty with the average player is that he totally misunderstands what is meant by concentration. He may think he is concentrating when he is merely worrying.

Bobby Jones

The average golfer would rather play than watch. Those who don't play can't possibly appreciate the subtleties of the game. Trying to get their attention with golf is like selling Shakespeare in the neighborhood saloon.

Bob Toski, The Sporting News *(1983)*

DUFFERS

Golf is so popular simply because it is the best game in the world at which to be bad. At golf it is the bad player who gets the most strokes.

A. A. Milne, Not That It Matters *(1919)*

In playing a pitch, chip, or shot from a bunker near the green, there is one significant difference to be noted between the method of the expert player and that of the duffer; in one case, the swing is amply long, smooth, and unhurried; in the other, it is short and jerky, because the club has not been swung back far enough.

Bobby Jones

Golf is the only game where the worst player gets the best of it. He obtains more out of it as regards exercise and enjoyment, for the good player gets worried over the slightest mistake, whereas the poor player makes too many mistakes to worry over them.

David Lloyd George

My tournament lineup would include anyone who never finished a par 5 with the same ball as he started...any guy who has just bought a new club called a Birdie-Seeker or FlagJammer or a putter that looks like something you'd fix the plumbing with...any guy who never got out of a sand trap in fewer than six strokes.

Jim Murray, Los Angeles Times *(1983)*

A golfer might as well turn in his clubs if he can't find some excuse for his own duffery.

Milton Gross

OFFICIALS

There are seemingly only three professions where you do not lose your job for consistent poor performance: TV weathermen in the U.K., tournament professional golfers, and the PGA officials who set flag positions.

Tony Johnstone

Tom Finchem—PGA commissioner

Tom Finchem, the commissioner, has a smile as hard as a pawnbroker's.

Tom Callahan, Golf Digest *(1998)*

If Ben Hogan was the homicide inspector viewing the body, Finchem is the body.

Tom Callahan, Golf Digest *(1998)*

ARCHITECTS

They don't build courses for people.
They build monuments to themselves.
George Archer

The first golf course architect was a 15-handicapper with a whippy swing from Scotland named Father Nature.
Art Spander (1977)

Golf architects make me sick. They can't play golf, so they try and rig the courses so that nobody else can play either.
Sam Snead

There are as many course architects as there are golfers. Everyone is an architect in his Walter Mitty dreams.
Robert Trent Jones Jr.

When someone tells me his new course measures more than 7,000 yards, it is usually said with the pride of a new father, as if distance, or wasting of land, is something to boast about.
Gene Sarazen

The real trick of golf course architecture is to lure the golfer into a false sense of security.
Pete Dye, Golf Digest *(1979)*

Answering critics of his complex course designs—Golf is not a fair game, so why build a fair golf course?
Pete Dye

I think I'll go cold turkey in the end and build golf courses.
I'll torture other people.
David Feherty

That's how golf architects make their money, always going
back to fix what they don't do right in the first place.
Lee Trevino (1981)

If I were designing a golf course for myself, there'd be a dog-
leg right on every hole, and the first hole wouldn't count;
that would be a warm-up hole.
Lee Trevino (1983)

By all means screw their women and drink all their booze,
but never write one word about their bloody awful golf
courses.
Henry Longhurst

It is easier to tell a man that there's something wrong with his
wife and child than with his golf course.
Frank Hannigan, Chicago Tribune *(1984)*

Next time you run into Pete Dye or Tom Fazio or Rees Jones,
if you can't say something nice, shut up. A golf architect
would rather you criticize his kids than criticize his courses.
George Peper, Golf *magazine (1995)*

The trick for the developer, as devised through his architect,
is to build something that is photogenically stunning, however impractical, extravagant, or absurd. Never mind the
golfer, that most gullible of citizens.
Peter Thomson

Individuals

Pete Dye

Pete Dye's true hallmark is the use of railroad ties, telephone poles, or planking to shore up his greens, sand traps, and his banks of water hazards. He uses so much wood that one of his courses may be the first to ever burn down.

> *Barry McDermott (1982)*

On his island hole at TPC Sawgrass—Those who think Arnold Palmer invented golf back in the 1950s probably think Pete Dye invented golf-without-a-safety-net in the 1980s.

> *Ron Whitten,* Golf Digest *(1996)*

Robert Trent Jones

Early golf courses had no bunkers. They are strictly a man-made invention, and the larger ones, such as those that stretch across an entire dairy farm, were the invention of a demented man named Robert Trent Jones.

> *Dan Jenkins*

He must have a permanent crick in his neck. Every time he walks down a fairway, he's looking behind him to see how he can make the hole longer.

> *Gene Sarazen*

He was the first architect to make a million dollars designing courses and two million redesigning them.

> *Nick Seitz*

Speaking to Ione Jones, after winning the 1951 U.S. Open— Mrs. Jones, if your husband had to play golf on the courses he designs, your family would be on the breadline.

> *Ben Hogan*

Charles Blair Macdonald

He was so rugged in his thinking that he probably wore his tweed knickerbockers without any underwear.

Charles Price

Jack Nicklaus

On his trademark golf course design—His courses are like Jack himself, grim and humorless, with sharp edges.

Peter Thomson

Asking Nicklaus to redesign Augusta was like asking Andy Warhol to repaint the Sistine Chapel.

David Feherty

Arnold Palmer

Before the Bob Hope Classic—Have you ever noticed that when Arnold plays a course he designed, Ed Seay has to show him where the first tee is?

Lanny Wadkins

[Seay is Palmer's design partner.]

A. W. Tillinghast

Maybe if A. W. Tillinghast had designed the Alamo, and the USGA had toughened it up, the Mexican siege would have failed.

Dick Schaap, Massacre at Winged Foot *(1974)*

CADDIES

No man is a hero to his caddie.
Dudley Doust

A caddie is someone who accompanies a golfer and didn't see the ball either.

Anonymous

Caddie: Individual who carries bags for golfers and assists them
in the playing of the course. Ideally, a caddie should possess the
eyes of a big-game hunter, the strength of a linebacker, the
patience of a diplomat, and the memory of a Mafia witness.

Henry Beard, A Duffer's Dictionary *(1987)*

The Royal Hong Kong Club caddies hit the nail on the head;
their term for golf: Hittee ball, say damn.

Dick Anderson

On the local caddies—In Scotland, he is as much of an insti-
tution as the player himself. He has grown up on the links,
and is guide, counselor, and friend of the player whose clubs
he carries. One of his principal qualifications there is that he
should be able to conceal his contempt for your game.

Henry E. Howland, Scribner's *magazine (1895)*

I have never had a caddie over fourteen years of age who did
not look disgruntled when he was paid. Under fourteen, they
are still financially innocent, and grateful for anything green.

John Updike, Golf Digest *(1993)*

There are three rules for a caddie to live by: show up, keep
up, shut up.

Paul Jungman

Few people carry a heavier burden farther than a golf caddie.

Stephen Nolan

If I needed advice from my caddie, he'd be hitting the shots
and I'd be carrying the bag.

Bobby Jones

It was a great honor to be inducted into the Golf Hall of
Fame. I didn't know they had a caddie division.

Bob Hope

Caddies are part valet, part coach, part psychiatrist, and mostly invisible. From behind the gallery ropes, spectators seldom notice them. Shouldering golf bags big enough to hold supplies for an Arctic expedition, they trudge in the shadows of their golfers.

Dave Anderson

If a permanent caddie is heroin, if you're going to break out in a cold sweat because you don't have him, then you'd better get one.

Frank Beard

There were three things in the world that he held in the smallest esteem: slugs, poets, and caddies with hiccups.

P. G. Wodehouse, Rodney Fails to Qualify *(1924)*

Real golfers, no matter what the provocation, never strike a caddie with the driver. The sand wedge is far more effective.

Huxtable Pippey

My game is so bad, I gotta hire three caddies—one to walk the left rough, one for the right rough, and one down the middle. And the one in the middle doesn't have to do much.

Dave Hill

The average caddie can find five balls while looking for yours—which he can't find.

Robinson Murray

*On seeing Amy Alcott kissing her caddie after winning the U.S. Women's Open—*So, that's the secret of winning an Open. First thing Monday, I'm gonna fire old Larry and get me a caddie I can smooch.

Lou Graham

If each time a player and caddie split up was actually a divorce, most tour players would have been "married" more times than Zsa Zsa and Liz combined.

Peter Jacobsen

If your caddie coaches you on the tee, "Hit it down the left side with a little draw," ignore him. All you do on the tee is try not to hit the caddie.

Jim Murray

While tearing off
A game of golf
I may make a play for the caddie.
But when I do
I don't follow through
'Cause my heart belongs to daddy.

Cole Porter, "My Heart Belongs to Daddy" (1938)

The Ball no question makes of Ayes or Noes,
But right or wrong, as strikes the Player, goes;
The supercilious Kadi with your clubs
Could tell exactly Why—He knows, He knows!

*Thomas Risk, "The Golfaiyat of Dufar Hy-Yam,"
from* The Lyric of the Links

From men who have adopted carrying as a trade, the golfer is entitled to expect the highest standard of efficiency. If he carries for you regularly, he ought to know what club you intend to take, and to give it without being asked. When you are in doubt about how to play your shot, he ought to confirm you in the opinion you have formed regarding it. He must never show the just contempt he has for your game.

Sir Walter Simpson, The Art of Golf *(1887)*

The player may experiment about his swing, his grip, his stance. It is only when he begins asking his caddie's advice that he is getting on dangerous ground.

    Sir Walter Simpson, The Art of Golf *(1887)*

My own experience as a caddie imparted lasting knowledge to me in only two areas: sex and poker.

    Larry Sheehan

The driving range is the sadistic relief center for golf. Here is where golfers line up to try and hit some poor unfortunate, locked in a steel cage built around an old jeep. The guy who picks up balls in this contraption is usually a former caddie who talked too much about his client's indiscretions of scoring. Most golfers feel this punishment is too light.

    Herbert I. Kavet

During a Bing Crosby Pro-Am—I was lying ten and had a thirty-five-foot putt. I whispered over my shoulder, "How does this one break?" And my caddie said, "Who cares?"

    Jack Lemmon

Nobody but you and your caddie care what you do out there, and if your caddie is betting against you, he doesn't care either.

    Lee Trevino

Caddies are a breed of their own. If you shoot a 66, they say, "Man, we shot a 66!" But go out and shoot 77 and they say, "Hell, he shot a 77!"

    Lee Trevino

On his heavyweight caddie—I always know which side a putt will break. It always slopes toward the side of the green where Herman [Mitchell] is standing.

    Lee Trevino

On carding a double bogey during the 1924 U.S. Open—I have been playing golf three hundred and seventy five **** years, and after all that time I reach the day where I ask a twenty-five-year-old caddie what club to use.

    Bobby Cruikshank (1924)

Never let your caddie tell you anything more than how deep the hole is and what time it is.

    Jim Murray (1968)

FANS

I wish they'd make the gallery ropes out-of-bounds. We're the only sport that plays in the audience.
Lee Trevino

Even if you are seven feet tall, have the vision of an eagle, can run like a cheetah, and are able to abide legions of unidentified Republicans telling you to "SShhhhh!!" all the time, watching a golf tournament in person just may be the single most frustrating spectator experience in the whole wide world of sports...and that includes luge and curling.

    Glen Waggoner, Divots, Shanks, Gimmes, Mulligans... *(1993)*

Without the people, I'd be playing in front of trees for a couple of hundred dollars.

    Fuzzy Zoeller, Sports Illustrated *(1984)*

After carding a woeful 78—My gallery at the end consisted of my two opponents, three caddies, and some guy who was in the Army with me and wanted to borrow ten bucks.

    Cary Middlecoff (1949)

In a stroke play tournament, with so much going on all over the course simultaneously, more often than not an observer finds himself stationed intently just where nothing is happening.

Herbert Warren Wind, Nine Strokes in 27 Holes *(1961)*

Golf fans have a remarkable sixth sense that tells them what is happening elsewhere on the course, often a mile away. Some sort of telepathic wizardry takes place that not even the Soviet Union's KGB could figure out.

Dan Hruby, San Jose News *(1983)*

One of life's great mysteries is just what do golfers think they are playing at. But even more mysterious is what those spectators, who traipse around golf courses, are looking for.

Michael Parkinson

Rule One: Whenever a spectator seeks out a really good vantage point and settles down on a shooting stick or canvas chair, the tallest, fattest golf watcher on the course will take up station directly in front.

Peter Dobereiner, Golf World *(1975)*

On his traveling fan base—You have heard of Arnie's Army. Well, these are Dean's Drunks.

Dean Martin

On the partisan galleries at the 1981 British Open—I told them, if you want to laugh, you have two choices: either go to a circus or I'll bury this eight-iron in your head.

David Graham

On partisan British crowds—Individually, they are pretty nice folks. But get them together and they are about as miserable a bunch of people as you could ever have the misfortune to run into in a supposedly civilized world.

Tommy Bolt

British galleries understand the game and are very respectful. In my opinion, it's the last civilized country left in the world.
Tom Watson (1983)

With the huge excited crowd surging all around him, it is only natural that the player should come in for a good deal of buffeting about. It may come as a surprise to many people to know after a big tournament my ankles and shins are black and blue.
Harry Vardon

On Arnold Palmer's band of followers, "Arnie's Army"—If Arnold asked all of those people to go jump into the river for him, they would march straight to the river and jump.
Gary Player

On Arnie's Army—The hero-worshipers in his gallery ought to appreciate that somebody has to play along with Arnold to keep his score, if nothing else.
Dave Hill, Teed Off *(1977)*

I drew a big gallery today. I was paired with Arnold Palmer.
Gene Littler

MEDIA

Dan Jenkins—Writer
Not to have read Dan Jenkins on golf is like playing golf in Scotland and missing out Carnoustie.
John Hopkins

Henry Longhurst – British commentator (1909–1978)
His voice practically wore plus fours. It was a fruity, affably
charming, old bufferish voice. It drew upon reminiscence
fathoms deep; it spoke of golf in the days of gutta-percha
when men were men and sand wedges were niblicks. It was
like hearing about music from someone who had known
Brahms.

Edward Pearce, Love-Hate

I just don't know about the guy. He looks like W. C. Fields in
drag. But he happens to be the best in the business.

Frank Chirkinian

He was fond of a regular sip. The Americans dubbed him
Henry "Don't mind if I do" Longhurst or "Henry
Longthirst."

Peter Alliss

TOURNAMENTS, TOURS & RULES

TOURNAMENT GOLF

**There are two kinds of golf:
golf and tournament golf . . .
and they are not at all the same.**
Bobby Jones

Golf—the plain variety—is the most delightful of games, an
enjoyable, companionable pastime; tournament golf is
thrilling, heartbreaking, terribly hard work—a lot of fun
when you are young with nothing much on your mind, but
fiercely punishing in the end.
   Bobby Jones

Casual golf and tournament golf are as different as ice
hockey and tennis.
   Ben Hogan

THE MAJORS

When you lose a major,
it's like a death in the family.
Ken Venturi

Golf championships are a good deal like omelettes. You cannot have an omelette without breaking eggs, and you cannot have a golf championship without wrecking hopes.

O. B. Keeler

Even though you are playing in a tournament and you try to block out the major championship that's a week or two away, and you say you'll concentrate on this tournament and worry about the majors when you get there, that's a lot of baloney. Believe me, your mind is on the major.

Lee Trevino

Most of us would give up our wives, our firstborn, and our favorite putters just to finish in the top ten of a major.

Lee Trevino (1981)

I was interested in one thing—majors—because I know they live long. You could win a million dollars, and that will go. But when you win the U.S. Open or the British Open or the Masters or the PGA, that title goes to your grave.

Gene Sarazen

Prior to winning his first major—Unfortunately, when you are assessed at the end of your career, it's majors that count, not money in the bank.

Tom Kite

THE MASTERS

On naming it the "Masters"—I must admit the
name was born out of a touch of immodesty.
Bobby Jones

If you didn't know better, six hours of the Masters on CBS could
leave you with the feeling that Augusta National Golf Club is a
holy land and the winner of the tournament will be passing
through a corridor where no mere mortal will ever tread.
Tom Gilmore (1984)

At my first Masters, I got the feeling that if I didn't play well,
I wouldn't go to heaven.
Dave Marr

If they renamed it the Hartford Open, everyone would shoot
265 [over 72 holes]. Take away the pressure, and all those
young bucks would shoot the lights out.
Lee Trevino

On blowing a lead in the 1954 Masters—Hell, it ain't like
losing a leg!
Billy Joe Patton

After finishing second—On the fifteenth hole I started thinking about the green jacket. They gave it to Charles Coody.
Johnny Miller (1971)

Finishing second in the Masters was like getting kicked in the
head.
David Duval (1998)

I've never been to heaven, and thinking back on my life, I probably won't get a chance to go. I guess winning the Masters is as close as I'm going to get.

Fuzzy Zoeller

Green grass, green grandstands, green concession stalls, green paper cups, green folding chairs and visors for sale, green and white ropes, green-topped Georgia pines. If justice were poetic, Hubert Green would win it every year.

John Updike, Thirteen Ways of Looking at the Masters *(1980)*

[. . . and wear the Green jacket?]

I told Hord Hardin I was getting too old to play in the Masters, but he kept saying, "Gene, they don't want to see you play; they just want to see if you're still alive."

Gene Sarazen [aged 90]

The Masters is more like a vast Edwardian garden party than a golf tournament.

Alistair Cooke, TV Guide *(1983)*

The reason I always watch the Masters is to see if it's really true that a bird has never crapped on the golf course.

Jay Cronley, Playboy *(1981)*

I don't mind being the ex-Masters champion. It feels a lot better than not being an ex-Masters champion.

Sandy Lyle (1989)

You start to choke when you drive through the front gate. On the first tee you just want to make contact with the ball.

Hale Irwin

The crowds are so large, especially around the name players, that one can travel eighteen holes and never see a shot. But it's the finest tournament you'll ever hear.

Art Spander and Mark Mulvoy (1977)

I've won ten tournaments, and I'd gladly give up any five of those titles to win the Masters. If pressed, I'd probably be willing to give up all ten. That's how much the Masters means.

Frank Beard

U.S. OPEN

**Nobody ever wins the National Open.
Somebody loses it.**
Bobby Jones

After his 1956 win—Nobody wins the Open. It wins you.
Cary Middlecoff

After his second U.S. Open victory—Any player can win the U.S. Open once, but it takes a helluva player to win two.
Walter Hagen (1919)

If you like driving in Memorial Day weekend traffic and going to movies like *Glory* where everybody gets killed at the end, you'll love the Open. It isn't a golf tournament; it's a survival test.

Nick Seitz

The U.S. Open is the greatest title there is. The course should be so hard, nobody can win it.

John Oswald (1951)

That's the way it is in the U.S. Open golf tournament. Whoever's in the lead feels like the first guy onto the beach at Normandy on D day.

> *Gary Nuhn,* Daytona Daily News *(1979)*

The U.S. Open gallery revels in disaster. "Palmer just took an 8!" will ring through it from time to time, and the town criers who hurry from fairway to fairway with the bad news are as happy as an old maid reporting a new divorce.

> *Jim Murray (1968)*

On the severity of the courses—The fringe around the greens isn't fringe at all, but long grass.... The scrambler is better off back home eating beer nuts and watching it on television.

> *Dan Gleason (1976)*

On the severity of the courses—We're not trying to humiliate the greatest players in the world. We're trying to identify them.

> *Frank "Sandy" Tatum (1984)*

On a typical U.S. Open course—Fairways trimmed closer than Michael Jordan's head, Formica-hard greens coated with Teflon, and rough up to Ian Woosnam's chin.

> *Glen Waggoner,* Divots, Shanks, Gimmes, Mulligans... *(1993)*

The NFL doesn't make the field 200 yards long just because it's a Super Bowl. The NBA doesn't raise the baskets eleven feet for the Championship series. But this week at the U.S. Open, the USGA will have the rough deeper than an elephant's eye, the greens slicker than Telly Savalas's head, and the fairways as narrow as a supermarket aisle.

> *Tim Rosaforte*

At the Augusta Masters, I just take three deep breaths and hit it as hard as I can. You don't have to worry about rough, because there isn't any. Do that [at the U.S. Open], and you might never be heard of again.

Lee Trevino

If the Masters is an offensive show, the U.S. Open is the greatest defensive test in golf.

Peter Jacobsen

*After Orville Moody's surprising win in 1969 following Lee Trevino's win the previous year—*What does it matter who Orville Moody is? At least he brought the title back to America.

Dave Marr

Playing in the U.S. Open is like tippy-toeing through hell.

Jerry McGee

BRITISH OPEN

If you don't win the British Open, there's a gap in your record.

Gene Sarazen

What do I want with prestige? The British Open paid the winner $600 in American money. A man would have to be two hundred years old at that rate to retire from golf.

Sam Snead, The Education of a Golfer *(1962)*

*On the poor attendance of U.S. golfers in the 1950s—*It's a rickety event in which Peter Thomson beat half a dozen guys from Stoke Poges.

Dan Jenkins

The British Open probably would have died if the American stars hadn't started going over to play in it more regularly the last fifteen years. Arnold Palmer saved it, but as far as I'm concerned, he didn't do us any favors.

Dave Hill

It's almost like the eighth wonder of the world playing that event.

Lee Trevino

What do you think on the last tee before winning an Open championship? Does your life flash through your mind? Do you think of your parents, your wife, your schoolteacher, your first job? No, you just think of hitting your last drive straight.

Tony Jacklin (1970)

On the one major he has not won—If I could make a pact with the devil, I'd take a British Open, then happily retire the next day.

Raymond Floyd

On his 1991 Open victory—Just to play in it is great. To do well is fantastic. To win it is a dream.

Ian Baker-Finch

Wind is part of the British Open. It is an examination, and it took me a long time to pass the examination. Eighty percent of the fellows out there have not passed the test.

Gary Player (1974)

PGA CHAMPIONSHIP

The PGA Championship is simply an American tour event with ideas above its station.

> *Peter Dobereiner,* London Guardian *(1983)*

I don't think a tournament with such a long history and tradition of its own wants to be thought of as "U.S. Open: The Sequel."...It's perceived as a U.S. Open wannabe. The PGA sets up golf courses just as the Open does, with baked-out greens and pet cemetery rough.

> *Peter Jacobsen*

On his play-off loss to Jerry Barber in 1961—I guess I was just plain scared to win that dude.

> *Don January (1961)*

On the 1987 PGA at Palm Beach—Call it the Perspiring Golfers of America Championship. It might be easier to complete a triathlon than seventy-two holes on this swamp monster. The Bermuda rough is said to be deadlier than the Bermuda Triangle.

> *Tim Rosaforte*

THE PLAYERS CHAMPIONSHIP

On being asked the difference between the Players Championship and the British Open—120 years!

> *Sandy Lyle*

No matter how much the Players Championship covets similar [major] status, tradition cannot be painted onto a championship as a coat of paint is added to a wall.

John Hopkins

RYDER CUP

Ryder Cup play is always tighter
than Jesper Parnevik's pants. . . . There is no
Poulan Weedeater Ryder Cup. No Budweiser
kickoffs. No tortuous halftimes during which
the California Raisin is constantly bumping
into Snow White. . . . Unlike soccer's World Cup,
the Ryder Cup doesn't take a month, thirty-two
countries, and three riots to play. . . . And, best
of all . . . No annoying mascot!

Rick Reilly, Sports Illustrated *(1997)*

Let's face it, if the Europeans didn't keep winning or retaining the Ryder Cup, it wouldn't be nearly so much fun for those of us who derive perverse pleasure out of seeing some of our spoiled, pampered American millionaires get dusted every two years by a bunch of guys whose names are hard to spell, harder to pronounce, and no doubt grew up learning the best use for something as curious as a golf club was to herd goats.

Dan Jenkins, Golf Digest *(1997)*

On the Ryder Cup selection procedure—The U.S. PGA is as archaic as the hickory-shafted baffy.

Gene Sarazen (1949)

In America the Ryder Cup rates somewhere between the Tennessee Frog Jumping Contest and the Alabama Melon-Pip Spitting Championship, although the players themselves have always taken it seriously until Tom Weiskopf declined to play in favor of a week's holiday shooting sheep.

   Peter Dobereiner (1978)

On learning that George Bush had hosted a presidential dinner for the U.S. Ryder Cup team—We have had no such threats of that kind from Mrs. Thatcher.

   Tony Jacklin (1989)

On the U.S. team spirit—We are even cheering for Ken Green.

   Curtis Strange (1989)

After a tie saw Europe retain the 1989 Ryder Cup—Big Mouth Yanks Get Their Own Butts Kicked.

   Headline in the London Daily Star

On caddying for Bernhard Langer, whose final missed putt gave victory to the U.S.A.—People ask me how Bernhard Langer stood up to all that pressure over the last three holes of the Ryder Cup. How about me? I not only had to stand up, I had to carry the bag as well.

   Peter Coleman (1991)

The country's pride is back! We went over and thumped the Iraqis, and now we have won this.

   Paul Azinger (1991)

I only played three matches [at Oak Hill] and hit only three fairways. My biggest contribution was to get the team colors for Sunday changed from green to my lucky blue.

   Seve Ballesteros (1995)

On Seve Ballesteros's press conference announcement that Spain, not Ireland, would host the 1997 Ryder Cup—Seve poured so much oil on troubled waters yesterday that he was in danger of creating an environmental disaster to rival the *Exxon Valdez.*
> *Dermot Gilleece,* Irish Times

Mark O'Meara reckoned that players deserve to be paid for playing in the Ryder Cup, which to me sounds about as daft as saying sumo wrestlers deserve to be fed before the world's famine victims.
> *Jock Howard,* Golf World *(1997)*

The beginning of the end is here, for Europe is on its last ankles, creaking ones.
The Ryder Cup goes back to being a snore now, a given like sunrise, for Europe has too many old Faldos and Langers and no youthful duplicates. The replacement parts go by Bjorn, a tennis name, and Westwood, a wizard's address.
> *Jeff Rude,* Golf Week *(1997)*

Before the final-day singles in 1997—By nightfall, Europe led 9–4, which in a Ryder Cup is like saying Dallas 52, Buffalo 7 halfway through the third quarter. There were fifteen matches left, in which the Americans would need to score 10 $^1/_2$ points. In other words, they were slightly more dead than Franco.
> *Rick Reilly,* Sports Illustrated *(1997)*

On the American defeat in 1997—To us, golf is not a team game. You don't pass the ball around; you just pass the blame around.
> *Art Spander (1997)*

Most Americans don't think we lose the Ryder Cup even when Europe wins the Ryder Cup.
> *Dan Jenkins,* Golf Digest *(1997)*

"'Next time,' I advised Tom Kite, "start off against an easier land mass...like Saudi Arabia or Antarctica."
"The Good Doctor," Inside Sports *(1998)*

PGA TOUR

**Playing on the American PGA Tour
is like being in the Army.**
Seve Ballesteros

The PGA Tour always was, and still is, a total accident—like oysters, or two-putting from forty feet.
Dan Jenkins, Fairways and Greens *(1994)*

Professional golf has become a game with too much character and not enough characters.
Thomas Boswell, Washington Post *(1979)*

On the many changes to the tour—Next the Golf Journeyman's Union will put in belly dancers, the tattooed lady, and Jojo the dog-faced boy to make more money and degrade a sport that was once distinguished by class.
Herb Graffis, Golf Digest *(1983)*

There's an old saying on tour, "Set fire to the trees and cover the greens with broken glass, put the pros out there in gasoline-soaked pants and barefooted, and someone will break par."
Tommy Bolt, The Hole Truth *(1971)*

I wonder how I had the nerve to start out on the tour or stay with it as long as I did. Most of the players at least got in on the ground floor. I climbed in through a basement window.
Tony Lema

A bad week on the tour is when demons dance through your swing thoughts. In the real world, a bad week is when you wake up to find you're a steelworker in Youngstown.
Don Wade (1983)

Out here, you've got to realize that if you take an 8 on a hole, 90 percent of the other pros don't care, and the other 10 percent wish it had been a 9.
Mason Rudolph (1969)

SENIOR TOUR

The Senior Tour is a mulligan in life.
George Archer

No matter how old you get, you can probably still make money playing the Senile Old Golfers Pro Tour.
Dave Barry

On becoming eligible for the Senior Tour—Why would I want to be out there with all those young guns? No sense playing the flat bellies when you can play the round bellies.
Lee Trevino (1989)

The Senior Tour is the only place you can get a fresh start but know all the mistakes you made the first time.

Lee Trevino

On why, at seventy-seven, he gave up the Senior Tour—It's a grind trying to beat sixty-year-old kids out there.

Sam Snead (1989)

You know you're on the Senior Tour when your back goes out more than you do.

Bob Brue

On the introduction of the Senior Skins Game—I'm waiting for the Senile Skins Game.

Bob Hope

LPGA TOUR

The LPGA... has, in recent years, grown to where the women play for over a million dollars in... can we say purse money?
Al Barkow (1974)

The LPGA needs a player that looks like Farrah Fawcett and plays like Jack Nicklaus. Instead, they've got players who look like Jack Nicklaus and play like Farrah Fawcett.

Anonymous

They call women's pro golf the "Bitchy Bitch" circuit: it's more like the "Butchy Butch.'" They don't have separate dinner dates or anything. They all stick together in their groups, and if two of the girls who've paired off have a row, the atmosphere is terrible.

    Julie Welch (1977)

USGA

The United States Golf Association, which...stands in the same relation to golfers as the Securities and Exchange Commission does to inside traders.

    Henry Beard, A Duffer's Dictionary *(1987)*

On the usga toughening up U.S. Open Courses—If the USGA could put a lake in the middle of every green, they would.

    Dave Stockton

On attempts to change Pebble Beach for the 1992 U.S. Open—If the USGA people took over the Louvre, they'd paint a mustache on the Mona Lisa.

    Roger Maltbie

PRO-AMS

The safest place for spectators in celebrity tournaments is probably on the fairway.

    Joe Garagiola (1985)

When you're looking at the scores, start at the bottom.
Frank Dill (1983)

Thinking you can win the Bing Crosby Pro-Am with a high handicap makes as much sense as leaving the porch light on for Jimmy Hoffa.
Phil Harris

On the Bing Crosby Pro-Am—When they say they have a sudden death play-off, it's not just a figure of speech. You need penicillin in your bag more than a one-iron. It's known as the "Vapo-Rub Open."
Jim Murray (1968)

LOCAL RULES & SIGNS

Local rules: A set of regulations that are ignored only by players on one specific course rather than by golfers as a whole.
Henry Beard, A Duffer's Dictionary *(1987)*

If a ball comes to rest in dangerous proximity to a hippopotamus or crocodile, another ball may be dropped at a safe distance, no nearer the hole, without penalty.
Nyanza G.C. in British East Africa (1950)

A stroke may be played again if interrupted by gunfire or sudden explosion.
Anonymous course in Rhodesia (1972)

On the green, a ball lying in a hippo footmark may be lifted and placed not nearer the hole without penalty.
Jinga G.C. in Uganda

In competition, during gunfire or while bombs are
falling, players may take cover without penalty for ceasing
play.
The positions of known delayed-action bombs are marked by
red flags at a reasonably, but not guaranteed safe distance
therefrom.
A player whose stroke is affected by the simultaneous explosion of a bomb may play another ball from the same place.
Penalty: one stroke.

> *WWII temporary rules at Richmond G.C.*
> *in Surrey, England*

If a reindeer eats your ball, drop another where the incident
occurred.

> *Bjorkliden Arctic G.C. in Sweden*

Pitlochry (in Scotland) is the only course in Britain with a
sign saying "No skiing on the fairways."

> Fore! *magazine (1998)*

Remember the maxim for all you are worth,
"If you scuff with your iron, you put back the turf."

> *Sign at Royal Dornoch G.C. in Scotland*

It is easier to replace the turf than to returf the place.

> *Sign at anonymous English golf course*

Players on foot have no standing on the course.

> *Sign at Thunderbird G.C. in California*

RULES

**There is no surer nor more painful way to learn
a rule than to be penalized for breaking it.**
Tom Watson

Golf is a very serious game, but it has an amusing side to it.
We have things like snakes in some parts of the world, and
the word *snake* seems to conjure up things; we have a dead
snake as a loose impediment, and a live one as an outside
agency: one you can move, one you cannot. One incident
from the middle of Africa involved a golfer addressing the
ball when, unknown to him, a snake slid down a tree behind
him. As the player was starting his downswing, he spotted
the snake, and changing the path of his swing, he whacked
the snake's head off. His opponent said, of course, "Good
shot!," but the rules question was: was it a stroke or not? We
took the view that the intention of the player to strike the
ball had ceased on the way down, and that not only had he
not played a stroke, but that he had converted an outside
agency into a loose impediment!

John Glover (R&A rules executive)

The Rules of Golf are dumber than carrots.... A long time
ago a bunch of guys in coats and ties and funny accents
drank a vat of brandy and made up these *rules* that only Ben
Hogan could live by.

Dan Jenkins, Fairways and Greens *(1994)*

I think most of the Rules of Golf stink. They were written
by guys who couldn't break a hundred.

Chi Chi Rodriguez

The unfairest thing in golf is the two-stroke out-of-bounds penalty: if you shy away and play it safe, you can get by, but if you stand up and play it like a man, you can be in real trouble.

Tony Jacklin (1974)

Golf in Ireland is one of life's great pleasures, although given that it is overrun with Americans in the summer season, it is high time that the Irish Golf Association declared cigar butts to be a loose impediment rather than obstructions. The fairways in July and August are knee-deep in the things.

Martin Johnson, Obsession

You mustn't blow your nose when your partner is addressing the ball...otherwise the book of rules is mostly nonsense.

Henry Longhurst (1978)

GOLF COURSES

COURSE LANGUAGE

**An ideal or classical golf course
demands variety, personality, and above
all, the charm of romance.**
Charles B. Macdonald

What a beautiful place a golf course is. From the meanest
country pasture to the Pebble Beaches and St. Andrews of
the world, a golf course is to me a holy ground. I feel God in
the trees and grass and flowers, in the rabbits and the birds
and the squirrels, in the sky and the water. I feel I am at
home.

   Harvey Penick

I've been around golf courses all my life. They are the
Demaret answer to the world's problems. When I get out on
that green carpet called a fairway and manage to poke the
ball right down the middle, my surroundings look like a
touch of heaven on earth.

   Jimmy Demaret, My Partner, Ben Hogan *(1954)*

I tell you, turning your land into a golf course is the salvation of the farmer. The only thing to do with land now is just play golf on it. Sell your land and caddie.
Will Rogers (1928)

Approach the golf course as a friend, not an enemy.
Arnold Palmer

A good golf course is one that makes us pros look human. It's good to see the gallery think sometimes, "Hey, he's duffing it around just like I do." On the other hand, we don't want too much of it: we don't want every spectator saying, "Hell, I play as good as him: why should I waste time and money watching these jerks play?"
Arnold Palmer (1970)

A good golf course makes you want to play so badly that you hardly have time to change your shoes.
Ben Crenshaw

A great course should have the Atlantic Ocean on one side, the Pacific on the other, and Ben Hogan or Arnold Palmer winning a tournament on it.
Pete Dye

All truly great golf courses have an almost supernatural finishing hole, by way of separating the chokers from the strokers.
Charles Price, Golf *magazine (1981)*

The best way to build a golf course is to start two hundred years ago.
Peter Dobereiner

Golf courses are built by men, but God provides the venues.
Robert Trent Jones

A round of golf should inspire eighteen inspirations.
    A. W. Tillinghast

A decade from now, I think target golf will be looked back on as the disco music of golf course architecture. We'll simply laugh and wonder how we could ever have been so light-headed.
    Peter Jacobsen

Hell is standing on the most beautiful golf course that's ever been made and not having any golf clubs.
    Jim Meyers (1982)

After playing four rounds on different courses in the Bob Hope Classic—The only problem is that it's hell to find your way home every night.
    Lee Trevino

I've built golf courses and laid the irrigation system just by teeing off.
    Lee Trevino (1983)

On being asked to name the worst course he'd played on—I don't know what "worst" means. Every golf hole has got a cup and a flag…and you can get the ball in it eventually.
    Bobby Jones

A "classic" course is one that Bobby Jones may have played, and a "modern" course is one that was either designed by Jack Nicklaus or is located somewhere on the plains of Nebraska, but nowhere near a telephone.
    Dan Jenkins, Golf Digest *(1998)*

You don't go home and talk about the great tennis courts that you played, but you do talk about the golf courses you played.
    Hank Ketcham

A golf course is nothing but a poolroom moved outdoors.
  "Father Fitzgibbon" in Going My Way *(1944)*

A golf course outside a town serves an excellent purpose in
that it segregates, as though in a concentration camp, all the
idle and idiot well-to-do.
  Osbert Sitwell

What, after all, is a golf course, except a glorified lawn perfo-
rated by eighteen holes?
  Witold Rybzynski

Courses built for 300-yard-tee-shot artists are not great courses.
  Peter Thomson

LINKS

**It should be remembered that golf started by
the sea, it was played on a type of country
called "links," which is the link between the sea
and the land, and today most of our great golf
courses are links, but you cannot have links
anywhere else but by the sea.**
  Lord Brabazon

The grounds on which golf is played are called links, being
the barren sandy soil from which the sea has retired in recent
geological times. In their natural state links are covered with
long, rank bent grass and gorse. Links are too barren for cul-
tivation: but sheep, rabbits, geese, and professionals pick up a
precarious livelihood on them.
  Sir Walter Simpson, The Art of Golf *(1887)*

The Scots say that Nature itself dictated that golf be played
by the seashore. Rather, the Scots saw in the eroded seacoasts
a cheap battleground on which they could whip their fellow
man in a game based on the Calvinist doctrine that man is
meant to suffer here below and never more than when he
goes out to enjoy himself.
  Alistair Cooke

The key to British links golf is the word "frustration." You
can hit the perfect shot, and all of a sudden, it will bounce
straight right or, for no apparent reason, jump beyond the
hole. If I played over here for four straight weeks, I'd be a
raving lunatic.
  Tom Watson (1977)

Compared to American golf, whose courses are triumphs of
orthodonture, an English links is organic. The Americans
favor Target Golf, a series of tee, tree, bunkers, and hole,
composed as one might paint by numbers, the whole of it
given a final surface of laminate.
  Edward Pearce, Love-Hate

On a links course, you can have four seasons in four rounds.
  David Leadbetter

[On some British links courses, you can have four seasons in four holes!]

Americans are drawn to links courses like bears to honey. The
venture may sting a bit, but the sweet prize is ultimately
worth the pain.
  Jim Moriarty, Golf Digest *(1997)*

DIVOTS

When it comes to divot making, pros are to hackers what a brain surgeon is to a hog butcher. If both were dancers, pros would be Fred Astaire, hackers Chubby Checker.

Glen Waggoner, Divots, Shanks, Gimmes, Mulligans... *(1993)*

The only difference is at Augusta the divots tear loose on dotted lines.

John Updike, Thirteen Ways of Looking at the Masters *(1980)*

Sneaky little devil, Polts. Thought he was just a terrible player.... But he's laid a lawn front and back of his new bungalow, entirely out of divots.

J. R. Coulson

FAIRWAYS

Fairway: A narrow strip of mown grass that separates two groups of golfers looking for lost balls in the rough.

Henry Beard

Fairway: That which a player playing 6 on a long hole is heard to answer when asked how far it is to the flag.

Tim Brooke-Taylor, Golf Bag *(1988)*

Those fairways are so narrow, you have to walk down them single file.

Jimmy Demaret

They all lived in houses backing onto golf courses and all boasted, "There are Fairways at the bottom of the garden."

Frank Muir, Oh My Word

GREENS

**Putting greens are to golf courses
what faces are to portraits.**
Charles B. Macdonald

G is for *Green*, that's constructed to roll
In every direction away from the hole.
>*Richard Armour,* Golf Is a Four-Letter Word *(1962)*

Extremely large greens breed slovenly play.
>*A. W. Tillinghast*

Man, the greens were so fast, you had to hold the putter over
the ball and hit it with the shadow.
>*Attributed to a number of golfers*

Reading a green is like reading the small type in a contract. If
you don't read it with painstaking care, you are likely to be in
trouble.
>*Claude Harmon*

On reading greens—If I'm breathing heavy while walking on a
green, I'm going uphill. If I trip, I'm going downhill.
>*David Goldman (1979)*

Putting isn't golf. Greens should be treated almost the same
as water hazards. You land on them, then add two strokes to
your score.
>*Chi Chi Rodriguez (1983)*

*After diabolical weather at the 1992 U.S. Open at Pebble
Beach*—The greens were turning blue out there.
>*Tom Kite*

Greens near the ocean break imperceptibly toward the sea.
Ben Hogan

HOLES & PINS

**Really good golf holes are full of surprises,
each one a bit better than the last.**
Robert Hunter

There's just no way to make the hole look bigger.
Tommy Armour

The vital thing about a hole is that it should either be more difficult than it looks or look more difficult than it is. It must never be what it looks.
Sir Walter Simpson

There is absolutely no excuse for a featureless hole anywhere on any course. If it has not got anything about it that might make it respectable, it has got to have quality knocked into it until it can hold its head up in polite society.
A. W. Tillinghast

A great hole is one which puts a question mark into a player's mind when he arrives on the tee to play it.
Mackenzie Ross

Great golf courses should have at least one silly hole.
Frank Hannigan

Every hole should be a difficult par and a comfortable bogey.
Robert Trent Jones

The job of a finishing hole is as clearly defined as that of a dance hall bouncer. It has to maintain order, clear out the amateurs, and preserve the dignity of the game.

    Jim Murray, Golf *magazine (1983)*

Golf is a terrible, hopeless addiction, it seems: it makes its devotees willing to trudge miles in any manner of weather, lugging a huge, incommodious, and appallingly heavy bag with them, in pursuit of a tiny and fantastically expensive ball in a fanatical attempt to direct it into a hole the size of a beer glass half a mile away.

    Mike Seabrook, A Good Walk Spoiled?

On what changes he would make to the game—I would like to see the holes bigger.

    Fuzzy Zoeller

That sure is a small ball you're trying to swing at. And it sure is a long way to the green. And when you get there, that cup is not exactly as big as a corporation president's ego.

    Dan Jenkins, Dead Solid Perfect *(1974)*

On the 1975 Greater Greensboro Open—The pin placements weren't too tough, but whoever set them missed ten greens.

    Leonard Thompson

On the 1983 San Diego Open—If they used the same pin placements on a Saturday afternoon with municipal players, they'd be out here two weeks.

    Lee Trevino

What do I think of pin placements? I think every green should have a pin placement.

    Gary McCord (1985)

HAZARDS

> The strategy of the golf course is the soul of
> the game. The spirit of golf is to dare a hazard,
> and by negotiating it reap a reward.
> *George C. Thomas Jr.*

These are the hazards of golf: the unpredictability of your
own body chemistry, the rub of the green on the courses, the
wind and the weather, the bee that lands on your ball or on
the back of your neck while you are putting, the sudden
noise while you are swinging, the whole problem of playing
the game at high mental tension and low physical tension.

Arnold Palmer

Of all the hazards, fear is the worst.

Sam Snead

Hazards are like spices that a designer sprinkles on a course
to give it flavor.

Robert Trent Jones Jr.

The number one thing about trouble is...don't get into
more.

Dave Stockton

What goes up must come down...usually in a lake or a
bunker.

Anonymous

The difference between a sand trap and water is the
difference between a car crash and an airplane crash. You
have a chance of recovering from a car crash.

Bobby Jones

BUNKERS

There are no bunkers in the air.
Walter Hagen (1920)

On "friendlier" modern championship bunkers—The behavior
etiquette for a greenside bunker should go into reverse.
Players should be forbidden to smooth them in any way. The
bunker should be the fearful place it once was, not the perfect surface from which a pro expects to float his ball out
stone dead, something he doesn't expect when chipping.
Michael Hobbs

If I had my way, I'd never let the sand be raked. Instead, I'd
run a herd of elephants through them every morning.
Charles B. Macdonald

You have to be prepared to shoot your way out of the trouble
you shoot your way into.
Peter Thomson

There is no such thing as a misplaced bunker. Regardless of
where a bunker may be, it is the business of the player to
avoid it.
Donald Ross

Some (municipal) players think that the rake by the side of
the trap is a hazard itself and that it is a two-stroke penalty if
you touch it.
Jay Cronley

Why do people panic in bunkers? First of all, a bunker is
defined as a hazard by rules, and anything that's called a hazard must be hazardous, right?
Nancy Lopez

Bunkers serve two purposes. They are for framing a green—
to give it definition and to give the player an idea of the distance he is in hitting the green. And for beauty. They are *not*
for trapping *people*.

> Ben Hogan

Nobody practices bunker shots...don't fall into that trap.

> *Gary McCord,* Golf for Dummies *(1996)*

Jack Spratt could only drive; his wife could only putt.
So, between them both, you see, they had a lot of trouble in
bunkers.

> Anonymous

After winning the 1979 British Open—They say I get into too
many bunkers. But is no problem. I am the best bunker player.

> Seve Ballesteros

On encountering bunker trouble in the 1974 U.S. Open—The
sand was heavier than I thought, and it only took me four
swings to figure it out.

> Johnny Miller

We don't want quicksand, but it should still be a hazard.

> David B. Fay (1998)

Some golfers blast their ball from traps
With one adroit explosion,
But others, out in ten perhaps,
Depend upon erosion.

> *Richard Armour,* Golf Is a Four-Letter Word *(1962)*

The chip shot from a bunker is the lapidary's stroke of a diamond.

> Henry Cotton

Too much ambition is a bad thing to have in a bunker.
Bobby Jones

I use the word "bunker," meaning a pit in which the soil has been exposed and the area covered with sand. I regard the term "sand trap" as an unacceptable Americanization. Its use annoys me almost as hearing a golf club called a "stick." Earthworks, mounds and the like, without sand, are not "bunkers."
Bobby Jones

Sand trap: A deep depression filled with sand . . . filled with golfers in a deep depression.
Henry Beard, A Duffer's Dictionary *(1987)*

Mediocre players are just out there messing up the sand traps.
Lloyd Mangrum

Boy, if the phone should ring,
Or anyone come to call,
Whisper that this is spring,
To come again next fall.
Say I have a date on a certain tee
Where my friends the sand traps wait in glee.
Anonymous

WATER HAZARDS

Golf balls are attracted to water as unerringly as the eye of a middle-aged man to a female bosom.
Michael Green, The Art of Coarse Golf *(1967)*

Only bullfighting and the water hole are left as vestigial evidence of what bloody savages men used to be. Only in golf is this sort of contrived swindle allowed.

>   *Tommy Bolt,* Keep Your Temper on the Golf Course *(1969)*

Water creates a neurosis in golfers. The very thought of this harmless fluid robs them of their normal powers of rational thought, turns their legs to jelly, and produces a palsy of the upper limbs.

>   *Peter Dobereiner,* The Glorious World of Golf *(1973)*

When your shot has to carry over a water hazard, you can either hit one more club or two more balls.

>   *Henry Beard,* Mulligan's Law *(1994)*

After hitting two balls into the water—By God, I've got a good mind to jump in and make it four.

>   *Simon Hobday (1994)*

I've lost balls in every hazard and on every course I've tried. But when I lose a ball in the ball washer, it's time to take stock.

>   *Milton Gross,* Eighteen Holes in My Head *(1959)*

After Hale Irwin's tee shot ricocheted off the Pebble Beach rocks back onto the fairway—On the scenic and infamous par 5 eighteenth, he had one last chance, but from the way he struck his tee shot, it appeared as if he were trying to hit the ocean in regulation.

>   *Dan Jenkins (1984)*

Water holes are sacrificial waters where you make a steady gift of your pride and high-priced balls.

>   *Tommy Bolt*

If one of my patented cut-punch saw-bladed four-irons skips twice on the water, then sinks like a stone, I remark irritably, "Algae! It just takes the topspin off the ball."

Leslie Nielsen, Bad Golf: My Way *(1996)*

A wife always knows when her husband has had a bad round. He has pond weed in his socks.

P. Brown

ROUGH LUCK

The longer the grass, the shorter the temper.
Gerald Batchelor

Show me a hole that is dependent on rough for its defenses, and I will show you a bad hole.

Peter Dobereiner, London Observer *(1984)*

The real test of golf—and life—is not keeping out of the rough, but getting out after we are in.

Henry Lash

Rough should have high grass. When you go bowling, they don't give you anything for landing in the gutter, do they?

Lee Trevino (1979)

I'd like to see the fairways more narrow. Then everybody would have to play from the rough, not just me.

Seve Ballesteros (1979)

On his wayward form in the 1995 Ryder Cup at Oak Hill—I hit three fairways in three days, but cleared out a lot of rough for the members.

    Seve Ballesteros

On the rough at Winged Foot during the 1974 U.S. Open—I knew I was in trouble when I saw a bunch of USGA guys down on their hands and knees parting the rough trying to find my ball.

    Jim Colbert

On the rough at Bellerive during the 1992 PGA Championships —You're reduced to a hundred-yard swing, with your buttocks clamped at 2,500 psi, hoping that the recipient of the venomous swipe doesn't fly out like a wounded snipe across the green straight into the very same crap.

    David Feherty

Pebble Beach is one of the most beautiful places in the world to play golf, albeit attended by one of the world's worst golfing hazards, the *Mesembryanthemum nodiflorum*, otherwise known as ice plant. There are times when ice plant can look like a nice plant—it blooms prettily in purple and pink—but those times are not when one's ball is in it.

    David Davies, London Guardian *(1992)*

I may have been a bit greedy when I pegged the ball toward the flag instead of out into the fairway. It didn't even make the first cut, and now it's in super-heavy grass. Well, there's no need to waste time beating around the bush. Let's pop that thing out into the short grass.

    Leslie Nielsen, Bad Golf: My Way *(1996)*

TREES COMPANY

**He who insists on preserving a tree
where it spoils a shot should have nothing
to say about golf course construction.**
George C. Thomas Jr.

All trees are magnetic.
Beselink's Law

My turn-ons: big galleries, small scores, long drives, short
rough, fat pay checks, and skinny trees.
Peter Jacobsen, Golf *magazine (1983)*

If the tree is skinny, aim right at it. A peculiarity of golf is
that what you aim at you generally miss. The success of the
shot depending mainly, of course, on your definition of
"skinny."
Rex Lardner, Out of the Bunker and into the Trees *(1960)*

Before trying to play a shot out of a Pebble Beach tree—Where
the hell's Jane?
Nick Faldo (1992)

On being asked what club he used to play out of a tree—A tree
iron, of course.
Bernhard Langer (1993)

I never saw a good player from the trees.
Byron Nelson (1984)

*On a transplanted tree "appearing" on the course for the pga
Championship*—I thought only God could make a tree, but I
forgot about the PGA.
Chi Chi Rodriguez

I have discovered one important thing about the [Augusta National] course: those big pine trees don't move.

Fuzzy Zoeller (1979)

COURSES OF THE WORLD

**A golf course is something as mysterious
as St. Andrews, as majestic as Pine Valley, as
ferocious as Oakmont, as subtle as Hoylake,
as commonplace as Happy Knoll.**

Charles Price

Troon and Prestwick—Old and "classy"
Bogside, Dundonald, Gailes, Barassie.
Prestwick St. Nicholas, Western Gailes,
St. Cuthbert, Portland—memory fails—
Troon Municipal (three links there)
Prestwick Municipal, Irvine, Ayr.
They faced the list with delighted smiles—
Sixteen courses within ten miles.

Local Scottish rhyme

There are many potential black spots on the world's golf courses, and when the world's leading players set foot on such holes, the noise of the galleries can be likened to the squabbling of vultures awaiting their turn at the carcass. Among such holes could be listed the twelvth at Augusta with its swirling winds waiting to push the ball back into Rae's Creek; the seventeenth at Carnoustie with the insidious Barry Burn snaking across the fairway; the eighteenth at Pebble Beach where the Pacific Ocean washes away any stroke which has a hint of a hook.

Chris Plumridge

Alaska

Alaska would be an ideal place for a golf course—mighty few trees and damn few ladies' foursomes.

Rex Lardner, Out of the Bunker and into the Trees *(1960)*

Augusta National, Georgia

Augusta National is overexposed but not overrated. There are courses around the country as good, but they don't have the same exposure. That's because the Masters is Scarborough Fair, the gathering of eagles. Everyone wants to make the trip to mecca.

Bobby Jones

On how he designed the course—Two things were essential. First there must be a way around for those unwilling to attempt the carry; and second there must be a definite reward awaiting the man who makes it. Without the alternative route the situation is unfair. Without the reward it is meaningless.

Bobby Jones

There isn't a hole out there that can't be birdied if you just think. But there isn't one that can't be double-bogeyed if you stop thinking.

Bobby Jones

You can lick this course with your normal game—if you ever calm down enough to play your normal game.

Frank Beard (1970)

When you get on this Augusta course, it's a given fact that you're going to get nailed. The variable is how you accept it.

Joe Inman

Augusta National is like playing a Salvador Dalí landscape. I expected a clock to fall out of the trees and hit me in the face.

David Feherty

The Augusta National course reminds me of a mousetrap
with a piece of cheese in the middle. If you get too greedy,
the trap will crush you.

    Gary Player

If there's a golf course in heaven, I hope it's like Augusta
National. I just don't want an early tee time.

    Gary Player

Augusta is the closest thing to heaven for a golfer...and it's
just about as hard to get into.

    Joe Geshwiler, San Francisco Examiner *(1983)*

It's like a black widow spider. It seduces you, entices you,
romances you...and then it stings you, kills you emotionally.

    Mac O'Grady

Nothing funny ever happens at Augusta. Dogs don't bark and
babies don't cry. They wouldn't dare.

    Frank Chirkinian

The course is perfection, and it asks for perfection.

    Nick Faldo

If you don't have goose bumps when you walk into this
place, you don't have a pulse.

    Hal Sutton

Sam Snead won the Masters yesterday on greens that were
slicker than the top of his head.

    Dan Jenkins (1952)

The greens are the course! They are faster than a fart on a hot
skillet.

    Dave Hill, Teed Off *(1977)*

We could make the greens so slick, we'd have to furnish ice
skates on the first tee.

> *Hord Hardin (1981)*

During the 1994 Masters—They don't cut the greens here at
Augusta; they use bikini wax.

> *Gary McCord, CBS TV*

*[This quip led to McCord being "banned" from commentating on any
future Masters telecasts for CBS Sports.]*

Augusta is not my kind of course. With my game, I can't
play there. Every good course has a couple of holes where
everybody talks about the tough decisions to make in club
selection. But here, there are thirteen or fourteen holes like
that.

> *John Mahaffey*

Eleventh, Twelfth, & Thirteenth (Amen Corner)

Amen Corner looks like something that fell from heaven, but
it plays like something straight out of hell.

> *Gary van Sickle*

If you get around in par, you believe a little bit more in God.

> *Dave Marr*

Twelfth (155-yard par 3)

It is not necessarily impossible. It simply seems to require
more skill than I have at the moment.

> *Ben Hogan*

The meanest little hole in the world.

> *Lloyd Mangrum*

The twelfth has killed more guys than Audie Murphy.
    Don Wade, And Then Jack Said to Arnie *(1991)*

The most demanding tournament hole in golf.
    Jack Nicklaus

I kept telling Tom Kite, "Let's go ahead and hit before they
suspend play." That's one hole you don't want to wake up to.
    Mark Lye (1984)

On finding Rae's Creek, in front, during the 1993 Masters—I
hope I don't have to play that hole again. Next year I think
I'll lay up short.
    Dan Forsman

Ballybunion Old Course, Ireland
Golf architects should live and play here before they build
golf courses.
    Tom Watson

After playing Ballybunion for the first time, a man would
think that the game of golf originated here.
    Tom Watson

When a tourist drives through Switzerland, he is staggered by
its prodigal beauty; around the corner from the most wondrous view he has ever beheld, he comes upon a view that
surpasses it—and so on, endlessly. Ballybunion is something
like that. One stirring hole is followed by another and
another.
    Herbert Warren Wind, The New Yorker

Very simply, Ballybunion revealed itself to be nothing less
than the finest seaside course I have ever seen.
    Herbert Warren Wind

When the wind blows, anyone who breaks 70 here is playing better than he is able to play.

Christy O'Connor Sr.

At Ballybunion, in winter one of the wildest places in the British Isles, with the original Cruel Sea pounding away on the rocks, a high slice is swallowed by the Atlantic like a grain of sand. A big enough slice theoretically would see no land till it touched Long Island.

Henry Longhurst, Round in Sixty-Eight *(1953)*

FOURTEENTH (PAR 4)

The fourteenth, a par 4 that Tom Simpson enlivened by placing in the drive zone a mounded double bunker, which the members immediately dubbed "Mrs. Simpson."

Herbert Warren Wind, Following Through *(1985)*

Ballybunnion New Course, Ireland
Before building the New Course—This is the most natural golf terrain I have ever encountered...I will build you a great golf course, one of my best.

Robert Trent Jones

New Ballybunion is nothing less than the finest links course on earth.

Peter Dobereiner

Royal Birkdale, England
Lee Trevino, who won the Open at Birkdale, expressed the view that it was the most American of the British Open golf courses, an opinion presumably based on the fact that there is a McDonald's hamburger palace in [nearby] Southport.

Peter Dobereiner, London Guardian *(1983)*

*On his approach shots to the soft greens during the 1979 British
Open*—...like chipping into a basket of dirty clothing.
>   *Jack Nicklaus*

The clubhouse looks like the main terminal of Entebbe
Airport.
>   *Peter Ryde*

TWELFTH (183-YARD PAR 3)

Described by Tom Watson as "one of the great par 3s," this is
a lichen-clad moonscape with more humps and craters than a
Bosnian high street.
>   *Simon Hughes,* London Telegraph *(1998)*

FIFTEENTH (542-YARD PAR 5)

We put down my bag to hunt for the ball—found the ball,
lost the bag.
>   *Lee Trevino (1983)*

Broadmoor Resort, Colorado
Golf at the Broadmoor represents one of the most interesting
patch jobs since Baron Frankenstein started picking up free
samples at the local medical school.
>   *Peter Andrews*

The [Brookline] Country Club, Massachusetts
To me, the ground here is hallowed. The grass grows greener,
the trees bloom better, there is even warmth to the rocks.
Somehow or other the sun seems to shine brighter on The
Country Club than any other place I have known.
>   *Francis Ouimet (1932)*

Butler National G.C., Oak Brook, Illinois

If the USGA ever got its hands on this course, it would all be over.

Dave Stockton

I used to dream that I could be a waiter in a place like this.

Chi Chi Rodriguez

Cairo, Egypt

On the course he designed neighboring the pyramids—I call it the Sphinx Links.

Robert Trent Jones

Carnoustie, Scotland

Moody as Maria Callas, it rouses fury when the westerlies come roaring out of the Atlantic across the width of Scotland.

Fred Tupper

That brooding monster on Scotland's east coast.

Michael McDonnell, The Complete Book of Golf *(1985)*

Carnoustie is like an ugly, old hag who speaks the truth no matter how painful. But it's only when you add up your score, you hear exactly what she thinks of you.

Tom Watson

A good swamp spoiled.

Gary Player (1975)

On the undulating course—The elephants' burial ground.

Johnny Miller

During the 1953 British Open—I've got a lawn mower back home in Texas. I'll send it over.

Ben Hogan

There are several long ditches or trenches in the rough.
They're about three feet deep, and I'm surprised that there
aren't a lot more one-legged golfers because of those ditches.
    Ben Hogan

Their championship tees are called "Tiger" tees. I thought
this was because they were so far back in the heather and
gorse that only a tiger would be there.
    Ben Hogan

Carnoustie, which might be my favorite Scottish word. All at
the same time, it sounds like a castle you should see, something you might want to wear at a reunion of the old regiment, or something you might want to eat... "I'll just have
the carnoustie with a small green salad."
    Dan Jenkins (1970)

Every hole starts out like the one you've just played—
unreachable.
    Dan Jenkins (1970)

Chepstow St. Pierre, Wales
A perfectly pleasant little resort layout... but it's basically just
a deer park with a few fairways mown through.
    Golf Digest (1996)

Cherry Hills, Colorado
It had grass in it that looked like it was three feet deep. If
you got in there, you might never be found again. I mean it
was the kind of place where you hunted buffalo... not par.
    Arnold Palmer

Colonial Country Club, Fort Worth, Texas
Colonial is the halter-top capital of the world.
    Tom Brookshier (1977)

If you don't like what you see at Colonial, you're too old to be looking.

Norm Alden (1977)

FIFTH (459-YARD PAR 4)

The most notorious hole in Texas.

Dan Jenkins

Putting downhill on the heavily bunkered green ... is like trying to stop a ball in a bathtub before it hits the drain.

Alan Shipnuck, Sports Illustrated *(1998)*

Crooked Stick, Carmel, Indiana

I thought I had encountered every hazard, but on this course you have to take into account the curvature of the earth.

David Feherty (1991)

Cypress Point, Pebble Beach, California

The Sistine Chapel of golf.

Frank "Sandy" Tatum

The course is the most wonderful combination of beauty and beast.

Jack Lemmon

What a course. It has the looks of Christie Brinkley and the tenderness of Tokyo Rose.

Bob Hope (1983)

Frostily exclusive ... but staggeringly beautiful.

Cliff Michelmore

SIXTEENTH (233-YARD PAR 3)

Best long par 3. You can top your drive, but you can't top the
scenery.

Dan Jenkins, Fairways and Greens *(1994)*

The wind always howls, usually dead in your face, and rumor
has it the seals down on the rocks below raise one flipper to
call for a fair catch on all the balls dropping over the cliff.

Peter Jacobsen

EIGHTEENTH (342-YARD PAR 4)

On the "too easy" finishing hole—This is the best seventeen-
hole golf course in the world.

Jimmy Demaret

Sometimes a particular hole will cause you to choke—a
choke hole. Like the eighteenth at Cypress. It's like walking
into a certain room in a big dark house when you were a kid.
You get this fear that hits you.

Dave Marr

Delgany, Ireland
The nearest thing you can get to a perpendicular golf course.
You really need suckers rather than spikes on your shoes as
you struggle vertically upwards and then play the next hole
back down this precipitous gradient.

Peter Dobereiner

Royal Dornoch, Scotland

Forget Cypress Point and the others. This is easily the finest course in the world, the absolute number one. I am glad it is difficult to get here, and I am not going to tell anyone about Dornoch. I want to keep it to myself, the way it is, and come back every year until I die.

Anonymous U.S. course designer

Modesty forbids me saying more than it is the most beautifully situated links in the world, and that no American golfer should omit to go there, where he will find the best golf, a royal welcome, and no rabble.

Donald Ross, Golf Has Never Failed Me

When you play it, you get the feeling you could be living just as easily in the 1800s, or even the 1700s. If an old Scot in a red jacket had popped out from behind a sand dune, beating a feather ball, I wouldn't have blinked an eye.

Pete Dye, The New Yorker *(1964)*

El Fasher, Sudan, Africa

Of the four-hundred-odd courses on which I have played, including some on which no blade of grass had ever grown or ever will, El Fasher remains unique. There was no clubhouse, and no tees, but there were nine greens, each with a hole in, generally the metal rim sticking out of the sand, so that a local rule said: "On the rim counts in."

We teed off in the sand at the top of the bluff overlooking a magnificent view and played down to the first hole, marked by a small boy in a nightshirt holding what turned out to be the club's only flag. No use having permanent flags, they said. If you had wooden ones, the ants would eat them, and if you had metal, the locals would melt them instantly down for spears.

Henry Longhurst, My Life and Soft Times

Firestone Country Club, Akron

On the South Course—I just can't play this course. It eats my lunch. Firestone's a long iron course. I'd just as soon pull a rattlesnake out of my bag as a two-iron.

> *Lee Trevino (1979)*

The winner at Firestone? Par!

> *Headline in* Golf *magazine (1976)*

Formby Ladies, England

Don't ask for the gentleman's toilets in Formby Ladies' club-house. There aren't any.... For male visitors, Formby Ladies' clubhouse is a water hazard with a difference.

> *Michael McDonnell,* The World of Golf

Ganton, England

The 1949 Ryder Cup matches were played at Ganton, outside of London, and I can best describe the course as a sort of Pennsylvania Turnpike with tees.

> *Jimmy Demaret,* My Partner, Ben Hogan *(1954)*

[Ganton is actually just outside Scarborough in the north of England.]

Grand Cypress, Florida

It is like one of those hot-air hand dryers in toilets. It's a great idea, and everybody uses it once, but never again. It takes too long.

> *David Feherty*

Gullane, Scotland
Folks praise the links ayont the Forth—
St. Andrews, Elie, Leven:
About Carnoustie, Dornoch Firth,
Our ears they aft are deavin'.
But Gullane, oh, your wondrous charm
A' other links surpasses;
Inspired we climb your links as once
The ancients climbed Parnassus.

> *Scottish poem*

**Harbour Town Golf Links, Hilton Head Island,
South Carolina**
It's different, but then so was Garbo.

> *Pete Dye*

There is no denying that golf has put Hilton Head Island on the map. After all, how many homes can you build around a tennis court?

> *Charles Price*

It's pretty, but too golfy.

> *Hollis Stacy (1983)*

Harbour Town is so tough, even your clubs get tired.

> *Charles Price (1970)*

I like to putt the Harbour Town greens. They're so bumpy, the gallery can't tell when I have the yips.

> *Larry Ziegler (1978)*

Hazeltine National, Chaska, Minnesota

On the ten doglegs that litter the course—Robert Trent Jones must have laid out the course in a kennel.

    Bob Rosburg

After the 1970 U.S. Open—All you need is eighty acres of corn and some cows.

    Dave Hill

The greens resembled Indian burial mounds more than anything else. And their horses had been buried along with the Indians.

    Dave Hill, Teed Off *(1977)*

Houston Country Club, Texas

It has gold dust instead of sand in the traps, and the greens are irrigated with oil. It is home base for those hackneyed caricatures: the Texas zillionaire and his lady hung with ice cubes.

    Red Smith, A Hundred and Four Years Old *(1964)*

Hoylake, England

On the excellence of the greens—Their only fault is that they give no possible excuse for a missed putt.

    Bobby Jones (1930)

The opening tee shot at Hoylake is the most terrifying I've seen in my life.

    Peter Alliss (1998)

The K Club, Kildare, Ireland

On the newly opened, Arnold Palmer–designed course—Looks great. Has Arnold seen it yet?

    Jack Nicklaus

Instead of one signature hole, Palmer leaves his mark with a host of potential card wreckers which look as though they have been beamed straight from the U.S. majors.

Daniel Davies

The K Club leaves the visitor wanting nothing, except perhaps an extension to their overdraft facility.

Daniel Davies

Kiawah Island, Ocean Course, South Carolina

Probably the toughest course in America when the Atlantic exhales.

Brian McCallen, Golf *magazine (1996)*

This course is not like anything in Scotland or Ireland. It's like something in Mars.

David Feherty

During the 1991 Ryder Cup—The golf course is so hard, it's unbelievable. Nick Faldo and I have just said we don't know if we could have finished if we'd had a card in our hands.

Raymond Floyd

Lakeside County Club, Los Angeles

A requirement at Lakeside was that you be able to hold your booze. That was the club of the hard-drinking Irish, and the gag, standard for admission, was that you had to be able to kill a fifth in nine holes.

Jim Murray, Los Angeles Times

Los Angeles Area

Golf in and around Los Angeles tends to be—like the rest of the landscape—unreal. Part Royal and Ancient, part Disneyland. The Good Ship Lollypop with four-irons.

Jim Murray, Golf in Disneyland *(1973)*

Los Angeles Country Club

On being invited to play at this exclusive Club—Usually I play golf with the kind of people who rob banks, not own them.

    Jim Murray (1968)

It is said eligibility for membership is a Hoover button, a home in Pasadena, and proof-positive that you never had an actor in the family.

    Jim Murray

Royal Lytham and St. Anne's, England

To build an artificial sand hill is no light task, and it is characteristic of the wholehearted golfers of St. Anne's that they have raised several of these terrifying monuments to history.

    Bernard Darwin, The Golf Courses of the British Isles

Medinah Country Club, Illinois

After the 1991 U.S. Open—If we played a course like this every week, there wouldn't be anybody left at the end of the season. We'd all quit the game.

    Mark Calcavecchia

SEVENTEENTH (168-YARD PAR 3)

Golf architects dream about creating such a hole. Players dream of boiling such architects in oil.

    John Marshall

Royal Melbourne, Australia

The people of Royal Melbourne are proud of their greens. They can have them. The greens are the biggest joke since Watergate.

    Lee Trevino

Merion G.C., Ardmore, Pennsylvania

That course doesn't even belong in the Top 200! They have to grow rough up to your rear end to make it playable for the Open.

> Sam Snead

On why he didn't carry a seven-iron during the 1950 U.S. Open—There isn't a seven-iron shot at Merion.

> Ben Hogan

After winning the 1971 U.S. Open in a play-off with Jack Nicklaus—I didn't beat Merion. I just compromised with her, like a wife, trying not to let her have her own way too often.

> Lee Trevino

I love Merion, and I don't even know her last name.

> Lee Trevino (1971)

Merion wouldn't alter that course for the Second Coming, let alone another golf championship.

> Charles Price (1981)

ELEVENTH (369-YARD PAR 4)

If you hit this green with your second shot, you heave a sigh so deep that it is usually audible a mashie shot away.

> Bobby Jones

Muirfield, Scotland

You take a search warrant to get in, and a wedge and a prayer to get out.

> Harold Henning

On his 1980 British Open victory—You cannot love golf any more than you do when you come down the fairway of this golf course a champion.... There isn't one bad hole on this course.

　　Tom Watson

Muirfield without a wind is like a lady undressed. No challenge.

　　Tom Watson (1987)

Of Muirfield, a wise and able golfer once said that if he were at the peak of his form and had to play a match to save his life, he would choose Muirfield for the dueling ground.

　　Sam McKinlay, Golfer's Bedside Book

On the vast swathes of rough—I don't really want first prize...I just want the hay concession.

　　Doug Sanders

After trouble in a Muirfield bunker ended with a 10—I wouldn't say God couldn't have got out of it, but he'd have had to throw it.

　　Arnold Palmer (1987)

First (449-yard par 4)

One of the scariest opening holes in golf.

　　Tony Jacklin

Muirfield Village, Dublin, Ohio

They should have slippers at every hole and pass a rule that you have to take off your shoes before going on the green. They shouldn't be walked on with cleats.

　　Lee Trevino

The Muirfield Village Golf Course near Columbus, Ohio, site of last week's tournament, was in such immaculate condition that people would sooner have dropped cigarette butts on their babies' tummies.

Dan Jenkins, Sports Illustrated *(1977)*

There are eighteen bullies out there. You gotta beat them up one at a time. You beat up one, and here's another bully you got to beat up.

Jack Grout

It's a pretty jewel until it eats your lunch once or twice. Then, like a prom queen who loses her dentures when she bites into a cheeseburger, she never quite looks the same again.

Peter Jacobsen

Do you realize that water comes into play on eighteen shots?!

Tom Weiskopf

SIXTEENTH (204-YARD PAR 3)

On an approach shot during the Memorial—To illustrate how difficult this shot is, go out into your front yard and chip a ball from your lawn down onto the hood of your car and make it stop. Pretty hard to do, huh? Well, this is tougher.

Gary McCord

Oak Hill, New York
On changes to the course—If I owned a Rembrandt, I don't think I'd go slapping on some reds and yellows just because it was kind of dull.

Raymond Floyd

Oakland Hills, Birmingham, Michigan
The Lord intended this for a golf links.
Donald Ross (1911)

On the 1951 U.S. Open—You have to walk down these fairways single file.
Cary Middlecoff

On the 1951 U.S. Open—I thought I was going to a golf tournament, not on safari.
Sam Snead

On the 1951 U.S. Open—The course is playing the players instead of the players playing the course.
Walter Hagen

On the 1951 U.S. Open—If I had to play this course for a living every week, I'd get into another business.
Ben Hogan

After the 1981 U.S. Senior Open—I don't want to make it a lady's course, but I don't want every hole to play like the last one I'm ever going to play.
Lionel Herbert

FIFTEENTH (455-YARD PAR 4)

On finding the same fairway bunker twice during the 1951 U.S. Open—It was a blind bunker!
Bobby Locke (1951)

[To which Tommy Armour replied: "It's only blind the first time you play it."]

Oakmont Country Club, Pennsylvania
The ideal championship spot.
  Walter Hagen

The final degree in the college of golf.
  Tommy Armour

After winning the 1927 U.S. Open—You had to manipulate
the ball into the hole, not putt it.
  Tommy Armour

After the 1935 U.S. Open—Those were the fastest greens I
have ever seen. It was like putting down a staircase with the
cup on the third step from the bottom.
  Herb Graffis

This is a course where good putters worry about their second
putt before they hit the first one.
  Lew Worsham

Most people seem to have fun here…even when they're lining up their fourth putt.
  Banks Smith

You gotta sneak up on these holes. If you clamber and clank
up on 'em, they're liable to turn round and bite you.
  Sam Snead (1953)

When I saw Jack Nicklaus hit some shots out of the rough
sideways yesterday, I was convinced it was tough.
  Lanny Wadkins (1983)

Olympic Club, San Francisco
The longest comparatively short course I've ever seen.
  Ken Venturi

If Olympic Club were human, it'd be Bela Lugosi. I think it turns into a bat at midnight.

    Jim Murray

Olympic is sneaky quick and sneaky tough. Man, I still love it.

    Johnny Miller

Olympic is just a vulnerable dowager struggling to hide her age, easy pickings for any young purse-snatcher. And then she rips your scorecard to shreds.

    Ron Whitten, Golf Digest *(1998)*

SEVENTEENTH (468-YARD PAR 4)

The worst hole I've ever played in any Open.
    Bernhard Langer

On the steeply sloping fairway—There isn't a green as fast as the seventeenth fairway.

    Jack Nicklaus

EIGHTEENTH (347-YARD PAR 4)

One-putt this green and you get a free game next month.
    Fuzzy Zoeller (1987)

Onion Creek, Austin, Texas
God put it there. All I did was manicure it.
    Jimmy Demaret

Pebble Beach, California

This is a badass course.

Anonymous caddie

As nasty as a cocktail waitress in a dockside café.

Art Spander, San Francisco Examiner *(1983)*

The ultimate architect caused an ocean to carve away land until there stood revealed a golf course fit for Hogan.

Dave Kindred, Golf Digest *(1998)*

If I had one more round of golf to play, I would choose to play it at Pebble Beach. I've loved this course from the first time I saw it. It's possibly the best in the world.

Jack Nicklaus

On the inclement weather—Pebble Beach is the world's leading argument for indoor golf.

Dan Jenkins

They've had rain so many times, they're thinking of holding tournaments indoors. I've often wondered what it was like to play golf inside a ball washer.

Bob Hope

Pebble Beach is Alcatraz with grass.

Bob Hope (1952)

Pebble Beach is a three-hundred-acre unplayable lie.

Jim Murray

I've heard of unplayable lies... but on the tee?

Bob Hope, Confessions of a Hooker *(1985)*

Pebble Beach is so exclusive, even the Samaritans have an unlisted number.

    Peter Dobereiner (1981)

It's like fighting Rocky Marciano. Every time you step onto the course, you're a cinch to take a beating.

    Jackie Burke

Pebble Beach is built right around my game. Unfortunately, it doesn't touch any part of it.

    Mason Rudolph

If you moved Pebble Beach fifty miles inland, no one would have heard of it.

    Jimmy Demaret

On the 1992 U.S. Open—The winds were howling, the greens were like linoleum floors, and the rough felt as if you were walking through a burial ground of sheepdogs.

    Peter Jacobsen

On the extreme playing conditions at the 1992 U.S. Open— There's going to be a lot of extra sales of Chapstick because the USGA officials are smiling so much.

    Johnny Miller

There are a lot of birdies early on the first seven holes, and a lot of bad scores late.

    Tom Watson

SIXTH (516-YARD PAR 5)

This here is the pivotal hole. If you're five over when you hit this tee, it's the best place in the world to commit suicide.

    Lee Trevino (1978)

SIXTH, SEVENTH, EIGHTH, & NINTH

For [the first] five holes, Pebble Beach reveals little of what is in store.... At the sixth, it comes out of its corner, as it were, and delivers four tremendous body blows in succession.
  Henry Longhurst, Round in Sixty-Eight *(1953)*

SEVENTH (107-YARD PAR 3)

I've seen better courses. Number seven, I thought it was a practice hole...and there are too many blind shots.
  Ian Woosnam (1992)

EIGHTH, NINTH, & TENTH

Personal nickname à la Augusta's Amen Corner—Abalone Corner.
  Dan Jenkins

ELEVENTH (384-YARD PAR 4)

Probably the worst hole on the course. Then again, being the worst hole at Pebble Beach is like being the ugliest Miss America.
  Rick Reilly

FOURTEENTH (565-YARD PAR 5)

The only thing gonna stick around that hole is a dart! Yesterday I was on in three, off in four. They oughta put one of them miniature windmills on this thing and charge 50 cents to play it.
  Lee Trevino (1978)

SEVENTEENTH (209-YARD PAR 3)

The seventeenth into prevailing winds looks bleak, barren, and intractable...every other hole is aesthetically pleasing; the nasty, charmless seventeenth is, in the best British sense, hideously ugly. "Take a bogey—if you're lucky—and shut up," it says.

Thomas Boswell

EIGHTEENTH (548-YARD PAR 5)

For those who believe that man came from the sea and faces a deep hidden necessity to return to it someday, there would be no better route than to get a golf club and go to the eighteenth at Pebble Beach.

Dan Jenkins

The eighteenth is better. Better than what? Better than you think it is. Better than its photographs or its reputation. And its reputation is that it's the best finishing hole on earth.

Thomas Boswell (1982)

The green is harder to read than hieroglyphics.

Alan Shipnuck, Sports Illustrated *(1998)*

PGA West, La Quinta, California
TENTH (381-YARD PAR 4)

It's called "Confusion," and that was exactly the state of mind of the architect [Jack Nicklaus] when he built it.

T. R. Reinman

Pinehurst Country Club, Pinehurst, North Carolina

There has never been a better example of the sow's-ear-to-silk-purse metamorphosis than the miracle that James Tuft and Donald Ross wrought in changing a worthless piece of sandy wasteland in North Carolina into Pinehurst.

Robert Trent Jones

The man who doesn't feel emotionally stirred when he golfs at Pinehurst beneath these clear blue skies and with the pine fragrance in his nostrils is one who should be ruled out of golf for life.

Tommy Armour

Pine Valley, Clementon, New Jersey

Here is the ultimate expression of sadomasochistic golf, the supreme example of the penal school of architecture. A Philadelphia businessman, George Crump, conceived the idea, possibly during a nightmare.

Peter Dobereiner, Down the Nineteenth Fairway *(1983)*

Texas with bunkers.

Rex Lardner, Out of the Bunker and into the Trees *(1960)*

Pine Valley has been described as one huge bunker dotted with eighteen greens, eighteen tees, and about that many more target areas.

Mike Bryan, Golf *magazine (1983)*

An examination in golf.

Bernard Darwin

After the 1936 Walker Cup—
We think that we shall never see
A tougher course than Pine Valley.
Trees and traps wherever we go
And clumps of earth flying through the air.
This course was made for you and me
But only God can make a THREE!
    Jack McLean and Charlie Yates (1936)

In all my travels, I do not think I've seen a more beautiful landscape. This is as thrilling as Versailles or Fontainbleau.
    Lowell Thomas

Pine Valley is the shrine of American golf because so many golfers are buried there.
    Ed Sullivan

Though the course is so unremittingly tough and remorselessly unforgiving that even the Light Brigade might have been inclined to retreat, this is no Valley of Death. Pine Valley is beautiful.
    Robert Green, Golf World

The name of Pine Valley is not primarily known because it may be the hardest course in the world to get on. It's because it is the hardest to get round.
    Robert Green, Golf World

You don't make recoveries at Pine Valley, except of course from the sand traps—you merely push your ball into the undergrowth and endeavor to knock your ball out through the bushes to where it ought to have been in the first place.... It has no rough, in the accepted sense of the term, and no semi-rough. Your ball is either on the fairway, in which case it sits invitingly on a flawless carpet of turf, or it is not. If it is not, you play out sideways till it is.
    Henry Longhurst, It Was Good While It Lasted *(1941)*

A desert in the forests of New Jersey—imposes harsh and random penalties on those who fail to find the fairways which rest like stepping-stones in the sand.

Michael McDonnell, The Complete Book of Golf *(1985)*

There is a sense of privilege as well as rare experience in visiting Pine Valley, for it has no parallel anywhere. No course presents more vividly and more severely the basic challenge of golf—the balance between fear and courage. Nowhere is the brave and beautiful shot rewarded so splendidly in comparison to the weak and faltering; nowhere is there such a terrible contrast between reward and punishment, and yet the examination is just.

Pat Ward-Thomas, Masters of Golf *(1961)*

Pine Valley is a weekend in a mental ward.

Charles Price (1983)

FIRST (427-YARD PAR 4)

Foursomes have left the first tee there and have never been seen again. They just find their shoelaces and bags.

Bob Hope

SECOND (327-YARD PAR 4)

Tell me, do you chaps play this hole or just photograph it?

Eustace Storey

Three-putting is considered good form here.

Angus G. Garber III, Golf Legends *(1988)*

Fifth (226-yard par 3)

The fifth is 226 yards, but maybe its length is compensated
by the realization that this is the only short hole where one
can miss the target and still find grass. On the other hand, it
is wiser to heed the old members' saying: "Only God can
make 3 on the fifth."

> *Robert Green,* Golf World

I once did this hole in 2. For several days life had nothing
more to offer.

> *Henry Longhurst*

Eighth (327-yard par 4)

After failing to hole out in single figures—It is all very well to
punish a bad stroke, but the right of eternal punishment
should be reserved for a higher tribunal than a green committee.

> *Bernard Darwin*

The green is only the size of a dinner plate. Actually, that's an
exaggeration—it's more the size of an ashtray.

> *Dan Jenkins,* Fairways and Greens *(1994)*

Poppy Hills, Monterey, California
After the at&t Pro-Am was moved from Cypress Point—It's like
replacing Bo Derek with Roseanne Barr.

> *Johnny Miller*

Portmarnock, Ireland
Fifteenth (170-yard par 3)

One of the best little par 4s in golf.

> *Ben Crenshaw*

[Also quoted as: "the shortest par 5 in the world."]

Royal Portrush, Northern Ireland
SIXTH (193-YARD PAR 3)

A long one-shot hole of a reasonably tame nature; but only one generation from wildness, like a tiger cub born in a zoo. The talons on its green paws know what to do.
Patric Dickinson, A Round of Golf Courses *(1951)*

Prestwick, Scotland
Your first impression as you gaze out on a wasteland surrounded by an old stone fence is that this has to be the biggest practical joke in all of golf. I've got it, you say. You pay your green fee, put down a ball, and aim at the world, take four or five steps and are never heard from again....Without a caddie, it would take you a week and a half to find the third tee.
Dan Jenkins, The Dogged Victims of Inexorable Fate *(1970)*

You would like to gather up several holes from Prestwick and mail them to your top ten enemies.
Dan Jenkins, The Dogged Victims of Inexorable Fate *(1970)*

FIRST (346-YARD PAR 4)

The green was there, all right, as are all the greens at Prestwick, but you never see them until you are on them, which is usually eight or ten strokes after leaving the tee.
Dan Jenkins, The Dogged Victims of Inexorable Fate *(1970)*

Prince's, England
On learning that the course on the English Channel was to be used for bombing practice during World War II—Like throwing darts at a Rembrandt.
Lord Brabazon

Pumpkin Ridge, Witch Hollow Course, Oregon
EIGHTEENTH (545-YARD PAR 5)

The place where dreams go to die.
  Nancy Lopez (1997)

Rancho La Costa, Carlsbad, California
Arnold Palmer had no trouble at all taking a 12 here last year,
although I must say if he played it a little smarter, he could
have made a 9.
  Jim Murray (1968)

Riviera Golf Club, Pacific Palisades, California
Very nice course. But tell me, where do the members play?
  Bobby Jones

It used to be a hustler's paradise.... You could get a bet on
the color of the next dog coming up the fairway.
  Jim Murray (1973)

EIGHTH (368-YARD PAR 4)

Where's the rest of the fairway? Who stole half of your hole?
  Gary Player

St. Andrews, Old Course, Scotland
There are three British Opens: there's the Open in England,
the Open in Scotland, and the Open at St. Andrews.
  Local Scottish saying

St. Andrews is the original masterpiece. Some people say that
God was so preoccupied with the business of Creation that
he devised the Old Course as a practice ground for the Real
Thing.
  Chris Plumridge, The Lure of Golf

Some say God made the Old Course as a kind of practice shot before he addressed the real business of Creation. Others insist that instead of resting on the seventh day, He built the Old Course simply to keep his hand in. Yet others maintain he devised this unique stretch of coastline in nothing more than a fit of absentmindedness.

Raymond Jacobs

If golf has a mother, then without doubt it is St. Andrews, the most famous links in all the world. Sir Winston Churchill is said to have claimed that golf was invented by the Devil, and if this is so, then the famous Old Course must be the Devil's playground.

John Ingham, Guide to Golf Courses *(1992)*

The Holy Land of the Old Course at St. Andrews has hidden bunkers, sort of shell hole depressions in fairways, two fairways crossing each other, parallel fairways and double greens on several levels and with trick contours and areas about the size of Rhode Island; gull feathers and manure in which you can lose a ball, and would drive the Green Committee of a club raving mad, yet is the world's most fascinating golf course.

Herb Graffis, "Esquire's World of Golf" (1966)

One can feel so lonely at St. Andrews missing a putt.

Jack Nicklaus

The mystique of Muirfield lingers on. So does the memory of Carnoustie's foreboding. So does the scenic wonder of Turnberry, and the haunting incredibility of Prestwick, and the pleasant deception of Troon. But put them all together and St. Andrews can play their low ball for atmosphere.

Dan Jenkins

St. Andrews has got a character and features that you find nowhere else. You can play a damned good shot and find the ball in a damned bad place. That is the real game of golf.

    George Duncan

On the sixteen par 4s and 5s, you may hit sixteen 250-yard drives that leave you sixteen perfect lies and sixteen perfectly petrifying second shots.

    George Peper, Golf *magazine (1995)*

It is to the golfer what the Vatican is to the Catholic, what Munich is to the beer drinker, and what Mount Everest is to the climber.

    Hubert Mizell

My most common mistake at St. Andrews is just turning up.

    Mark James

My first impression of St. Andrews was one of strange ambiguousness. I didn't like it, nor, for that matter, did I hate it. I've never been so puzzled after a practice round in my life.

    Tom Watson (1984)

I feel like I'm back visiting an old grandmother. She's crotchety and eccentric, but also elegant, and anyone who doesn't fall in love with her has no imagination.

    Tony Lema (1964)

After a calm day at St. Andrews—We've had it easy. When it blows here, even the seagulls walk.

    Nick Faldo

I don't know whether you have ever played St. Andrews in the wind, but it has been known to make scratch players switch to tennis.

    Charles Price (1964)

How do you get the ball in the hole here? I cannot find the answer.

Paul Tembo (1986)

On his first sight of the Old Course—Say! That looks like an old, abandoned golf course. What did they call it?

Sam Snead (1946)

. . . some acreage that was so raggedy and beat-up that I was surprised to see what looked like a fairway amongst the weeds. Down home we wouldn't plant cow beets on land like that. . . . Until you play it, St. Andrews looks like the sort of real estate you couldn't give away. . . . The only place over there that's holier than St. Andrews is Westminster Abbey.

Sam Snead, The Education of a Golfer *(1962)*

I'm interested in the modern, not the Ancient. . . . There's nothing wrong with the St. Andrews course that one hundred bulldozers couldn't put right. The Old Course needs a dry-clean and a press.

Ed Furgol

At first glance it looks like nothing more than a flat green car park.

Dan Jenkins (1970)

You've got about six acres to aim at.

Fred Boobyer (1984)

The worst piece of mess I've ever played. I think they had some sheep and goats there that died, and they just covered them over.

Scott Hoch (1996)

I hate its arrogant lumps and bumps and the times you must play with one leg up in the air.

    Neil Coles (1984)

The Old Course is an uninteresting stretch of drab linksland. It has so many bunkers that I get the feeling somebody goes out in the dark to dig new ones.

    Fred Daly

First (370-yard par 4)

On driving into the Swilcan Burn in front of the green—I could drive that hole if they put some dirt in front of the green.

    John Daly

On Swilcan Burn—An inglorious little thing…a paltry little streamlet.

    Bernard Darwin

Eleventh (172-yard par 3)

Trouble once begun at this hole may never come to an end till the card is torn into a thousand fragments.

    Bernard Darwin

Thirteenth (398-yard par 4)

It's a great golf hole. It gives you a million options, not one of them worth a damn.

    Tom Kite (1990)

FOURTEENTH (523-YARD PAR 5)

On the best way to get out of "Hell's Bunker"—How about the
9:40 train out of St. Andrews?
   Andrew Kirkaldy

FIFTEENTH (401-YARD PAR 4)

On the tiny Sutherland Bunker—Just small enough for an
angry man and his sand-iron.
   Anonymous

SEVENTEENTH (461-YARD PAR 4) (THE ROAD HOLE)

The reason the Road Hole is the greatest par 4 in the world is
because it's a par 5.
   Ben Crenshaw, Sports Illustrated *(1984)*

*[Also quoted as: "The reason the Road Hole at St. Andrews is the most
difficult par 4 in the world is that it was designed as a par 6." See
Crenshaw's similar comments about the 15th at Portmarnock.]*

The most famous and infamous hole. As a planner and
builder of golf holes worldwide, I have no hesitation in
allowing that if one built such a hole today you would be
sued for incompetence.
   Peter Thomson, Golf Digest *(1984)*

I don't know who designed it, but I hear he's escaped.
   Mark James

I think maybe it is the most difficult hole I ever play, the way they put the flag. I think maybe one day they put the flag on the road instead of the green.

Seve Ballesteros

You walk onto the tee praying you're not going to make 10.

Ronan Rafferty

After taking a 10 in 1960—I should have played that hole in an ambulance.

Arnold Palmer

The seventeenth hole goes against the Rules of Golf. You have to play off a paved road. You don't have to play off a paved road anywhere else I know of, and you don't have to hit over buildings anywhere else, either.

Scott Hoch (1998)

I love the hole. It's an honor to say that I've been eaten alive by it.

Peter Jacobsen

St. Andrews, Eden Course, Scotland
On the "Ladies' Course"—Little more than a succession of putting greens.

Ruth Underhill

The Eden Course, which, in character, is as far a cry from its neighbor as a play by J. B. Priestley is from Shakespeare.

Patric Dickinson, A Round of Golf Courses *(1951)*

Royal St. George's, Sandwich, England

Playing Royal St. George's is like trying to read the mind of a beautiful woman. It can be difficult but never onerous. It is for reading, not bashing. You can be in the soup at St. George's, but it is delicious.

William Deedes

Before the 1993 British Open—It's different. I'd swear the Royal Air Force used a couple of the fairways for bombing runs. Out of the eighteen holes there are eleven that I like very much. The others, I'd rather not play.

Greg Norman

After winning the 1993 British Open—This is the world championship of imagination. And I love it.

Greg Norman

Tongue-in-cheek "short cut" directions to get to the course, sixty miles from London, during the busy Open week—Fly from Heathrow to Paris, take the train to Calais, hovercraft to Ramsgate, and walk down the beach.

Denis Thatcher

St. Melion, England

St. Smelly One.

European PGA Tour nickname

The course is like childbirth . . . a very painful experience. . . . I think the owners were conned. I think that one was designed by Jack Nicklaus's wife.

David Feherty

TPC at Sawgrass (Stadium Course), Ponte Vedra, Florida
On Pete Dye's golf course designed to the PGA Tour's "stadium golf" specifications—The Dyeing Ground.
>   *Anonymous*

PGA Tour Commissioner Deane Beman asked Dye for a golf course that would do for golf what the 200 mph crash did for auto racing.
>   *Thomas Boswell*

Everything here is the dead opposite of Augusta. On purpose, Augusta is pretty pretty. This is mean pretty.
>   *Anonymous*

To play well on this course, you have to be both skillful and lucky, and if you are both skillful and lucky, your name is Jack Nicklaus.
>   *Chi Chi Rodriguez (1983)*

You want controversy. OK, let's have controversy. A lot of guys would like to put a bomb under that thing.
>   *Jack Nicklaus*

The greens here are like car lots. It's a chore to play them.
>   *Tom Watson*

On the sloping greens—Is it against the rule to carry a bull-dozer?
>   *Tom Watson (1982)*

On the sloping greens—I saw Sir Edmund Hillary out there, and he had to walk around the greens.
>   *Tom Weiskopf,* USA Today *(1983)*

The course is 90 percent horse manure and 10 percent luck.
>   *J. C. Snead (1982)*

It's Star Wars golf. The place was designed by Darth Vader.
> *Ben Crenshaw (1982)*

The sorcerer's golf course.
> *Peter Dobereiner,* Golf Digest *(1981)*

If I were condemned to play for the rest of my life on one
course, I would unhesitatingly choose this one and happily
limit my ambitions to breaking 100.
> *Peter Dobereiner,* Golf Digest *(1981)*

It's too early to rate this course. It's like trying to rate girls
when they're born. They get better later.
> *Jerry Pate (1982)*

When I grow up, I want to be like Sawgrass golf course: long
and mean.
> *Leonard Thompson*

If Sawgrass is a major test of golf, I'm the pope.
> *Joe Inman*

SIXTEENTH, SEVENTEENTH, & EIGHTEENTH

Deane Beman's Bad Dream.
> *Dan Jenkins*

SEVENTEENTH (132-YARD PAR 3) (THE ISLAND HOLE)

It's a Dye-abolical hole...a tremulous short iron to an in-
verted skillet. The game's ultimate death-or-glory hole puts a
gulp in every preshot routine, a hitch in every swing, and a
prayer in every follow-through.
> *Ron Whitten,* Golf Digest *(1996)*

The easiest par 5 on the course.
    John Mahaffey (1984)

Every course needs a hole that puckers your rear end.
    Johnny Miller (1984)

The only way to improve it would be to put the green on a barge and have it float around the lagoon.
    Dale Hayes (1984)

Combines a touch of Hollywood and a touch of madness. An island paradise, it is not.
    Angus G. Garber III, Golf Legends *(1988)*

The excitement—and anxiety—of playing the seventeenth actually starts halfway down the par-5 sixteenth, when you clear the tree line and the little island bears itself in full view.
    Peter Morrice, Golf *magazine (1996)*

EIGHTEENTH (440-YARD PAR 4)

If you birdie the eighteenth, do you get a free game?
    John Mahaffey (1982)

Schloss Nippenburg, Germany
On the state of the course used for the German Open—For £500,000, you'd play on a runway.
    Colin Montgomerie (1990)

Seminole G.C., Florida
SIXTH (383-YARD PAR 4)

The finest single hole in the United States.
    Tommy Armour

Shinnecock Hills, Long Island, New York

The Best British Open Course in America.

> Golf *magazine (1995)*

Each hole is different and requires a great amount of skill to play it properly. As I think back, each hole has complete definition. You know exactly where to shoot, and the distance is easy to read. All in all, I think it is one of the finest courses I have ever played.

> *Ben Hogan*

Southern Hills, Tulsa, Oklahoma
FIFTH (614-YARD PAR 5)

This hole is 614 yards.... You don't need a road map for this one; you need a passport.

> *Jay Cronley (1977)*

The Links at Spanish Bay, Pebble Beach, California

Spanish Bay is so much like Scotland, you can almost hear the bagpipes.

> *Tom Watson*

Spyglass Hill, Pebble Beach, California

They ought to hang the man who designed this course. Ray Charles could have done better.

> *Lee Trevino (1985)*

Pebble Beach and Cypress Point make you want to play golf, they're such interesting and enjoyable layouts. Spyglass Hill, now that's different; that makes you want to go fishing.

> *Jack Nicklaus*

If it were human, Spyglass would have a knife in its teeth, a patch on its eye, a ring in its ear, tobacco in its beard, and a blunderbuss in its hand.

> *Jim Murray,* Los Angeles Times

Stone Harbor, New Jersey
FORMER SEVENTH (PAR 3) A.K.A. "JAWS"

I've always held that a golf hole is intrinsically bad if it takes
a local rule to finish playing it.

> *Ron Whitten*

Tralee, Ireland
There are those in the business who say that Arnold Palmer
couldn't build a bonfire even if you gave him the sticks to do
it, but he has done a worthy job here.

> *Jock Howard*

Royal Troon, Scotland
Someone once said that nobody murders Troon. The way I
played the Open, they couldn't even arrest me for second-
degree manslaughter.

> *Lee Trevino (1973)*

Apart from seven Opens and Monty's dad, this is the home
of The Postage Stamp, the ultimate I-could-stand-here-all-
day-hitting-balls-at-that-green-and-not-get-bored hole.

> *Fore! magazine*

Turnberry, Scotland
*Commenting on players' complaints that the 1986 British Open
course was too demanding*—It's not a common entrance exam;
it's an honors degree.

> *Michael Bonallack*

*[Turnberry chairman Alistair Low also gave the following warning:
"If the players thought the rough here was bad, wait until they see
Muirfield next year!"]*

Strangely enough, Turnberry is the only course on the rota of British Open venues—which consist of only links courses—where the ocean actually comes into play.
> *Greg Norman*

To the British, the charm of Turnberry's links lay in the fact that its holes are closer to the sea than those of any of their Open courses. At a Carnoustie, Muirfield, Birkdale, or Lytham, for example, you can't even catch a glimpse of the water from a tee or green. You can see it at St. Andrews, but there is no way to strike a ball into watery oblivion without a hydroplane. Ah, but Turnberry. The water is always there, furnishing a series of backdrops, washing up against a competitor's concentration.
> *Dan Jenkins,* Sports Illustrated

Valderrama, Spain

How do you say "Augusta National" in Spanish? Valderrama!
> *Ron Whitten,* Golf Digest *(1997)*

It was the last act committed by Walt Disney before he died.
> *David Feherty*

It's the best-conditioned golf course in the universe.
> *Ernie Els (1997)*

The greens are so good, you can start celebrating when the ball is six feet away.
> *Bernhard Langer*

SEVENTEENTH (511-YARD PAR 5)

It's a hole that I'm already scared to death of. And I know Seve is, too, and he [re-]designed the dang thing.
> *Tom Kite (1997)*

I know who designed it, and I don't care. He may be the best player who ever lived, but he is no course designer. It makes this course a lottery.

> *Colin Montgomerie (1997)*

With its water in the front and to the left of the green and the intruding rough across the middle of the fairway, [it] has undergone so many face-lifts that it has become known as the "Michael Jackson of golf holes."

> *Dan Jenkins,* Golf Digest *(1997)*

I never much cared for a par 5 where you hit driver, sand wedge, sand wedge.

> *Tom Lehman*

Wentworth, England
That Wentworth is a sonofabitch.

> *Sam Snead*

Wimbledon Common, England
One hole, "Running Deer," is 389 yards long and is so called because that is the longest distance at which you fell a deer with a standard mid-nineteenth-century rifle.

> Fore! *magazine (1998)*

Winged Foot, Mamaroneck, New York
The holes are like men, all rather similar from foot to neck, but with the greens showing the same varying characters as human faces.

> *A. W. Tillinghast [course designer]*

To match par on this course, you've got to be luckier than a dog with two tails.

> *Sam Snead*

The greens are harder than a whore's heart.
>   *Sam Snead*

Winged Foot has the eighteen toughest finishing holes in golf.
>   *Dave Marr (1984)*

During the 1974 U.S. Open—Putting on those greens is like playing miniature golf without the boards.
>   *Hale Irwin*

Putting these greens is like walking on titties.
>   *Homero Blancas (1974)*

FIRST (446-YARD PAR 4)

A motorist attempting to leave the Winged Foot Golf Club takes a wrong turn and accidentally drives across the first tee. He does no damage at all. The green holds up like asphalt.
>   *Dick Schaap*, Massacre at Winged Foot *(1974)*

TENTH (190-YARD PAR 3)

On the house that stands behind the green—Just a three-iron into someone's bedroom.
>   *Ben Hogan*

The slope of the green has been lessened, but it is still more difficult to read than a Joycean novel.
>   *Dick Schaap*, Massacre at Winged Foot *(1974)*

Woburn (Duke's Course), England

The Canterbury Cathedral of golf... the trees are so dramatically ranked on either side [of the thirteenth], it's like driving through the nave of a church.

Fore! *magazine*

FINAL WORDS

Golf's lexicon of colorful words and phrases is
its crowning achievement. For, long after the
urge or the ability to play the game leaves us,
golf's joyful adjectives and modifiers, its splendid superlatives and unequaled accolades, ring
in my ear, the waves of a familiar ocean.
Robert H. K. Browning

FORE!

Golf is a game in which you yell "Fore!", shoot six, and write
down five.
Paul Harvey

The Coarse Golfer is one who shouts "Fore!" when he putts.
Michael Green, The Art of Coarse Golf *(1967)*

Fore!: The first of several four-letter words exchanged
between golfers as one group of players hits balls toward
another in front of them on the course.
Henry Beard, A Duffer's Dictionary *(1987)*

The cry of "Fore!," so feebly and apologetically crooned on English courses, has at St. Andrews its true fiery leonine value; and it has modulations elsewhere unknown.

There is an intonation of Fore! to cover every contingency, and like Touchstone's seven forms of deceit, it has seven shades: there is the Fore courteous, the Fore mock modest, the Fore churlish, the Fore valiant, the Fore quarrelsome, the Fore circumstantial, and the Fore direct.

I have heard them all, the Fore direct being always in unison and terrible as the roaring of a bull.

    Patric Dickinson, A Round of Golf Courses *(1951)*

GOLF CURSES

I golf, therefore I swear.
Anonymous

Golf is a game of expletives not deleted.
    Irving Gladstone

If profanity had any influence on the flight of the ball, the game would be played far better than it is.
    Horace G. Hutchinson

The interesting thing about a Coarse Golfer's language is that to listen to him, one would think that his bad shots came as a surprise.
    Michael Green, The Art of Coarse Golf *(1967)*

I've had words come into my mind while I was digging in a bunker that I never realized I knew... I have never felt better than when I gave up the game.
    Nunnally Johnson

If I were a man, I wouldn't have half a dozen Tom Collinses before going out to play golf, then let profanity substitute for proficiency on the golf course.

Patty Berg (1945)

After carding a 13 at the twelfth during the 1980 Masters—I was afraid to move my lips in front of the TV cameras. The commissioner probably would have fined me just for what I was thinking.

Tom Weiskopf

I tell the lady scorekeepers that if they can hear me cuss, they're standing too close. They've got to realize they're not at a church social.

Dave Hill

NAME DROPPING

**Have you ever noticed what "golf"
spells backwards?**
Al Boliska

According to locker room lore, the name golf arose by default—all the other four-letter words had already been taken.

George Peper

My feeling is that while "Golf" is the name by which we know the game, what we are actually playing should be called "Disappointment."

Chris Plumridge, London Telegraph *(1992)*

On the length of time it takes to sign his autograph—
Sometimes I wish my name was Tom Kite.
> *Ian Baker-Finch (1995)*

On his middle initial—Sometimes it stands for Stupid, sometimes it stands for Smart.
> *Hale S. Irwin*

QUOTES

The hole is more than the sum of the putts.

All is fair in love and golf.
> *Anonymous*

Those who can...golf. Those who can't...golf anyway.
> *Anonymous*

Drive for dough, and pick up putts for dough.
> *Leslie Nielsen,* Bad Golf: My Way *(1996)*

You can lead a horse to water, but you can't make it retrieve your ball.
> *Henry Beard,* Mulligan's Laws *(1993)*

A penny saved is an excellent ball marker.
> *Henry Beard,* Mulligan's Laws *(1993)*

The course of true golf never did run smooth.
> *Henny Youngman*

Golf giveth and golf taketh away, but it taketh away a hell of a lot more than it giveth.
    Simon Hobday

Golf is a good walk soiled.
    Colin M. Jarman (1998)

"FLUFFES"

(FLUFfs & gafFES)

Guesting as tee announcer for the 1929 PGA Championship in Los Angeles—And now on the tee: Walter Hagen...the Opium Champion of the World.
    Fay Wray

He's got to go in for a hernia operation, but when he gets over that, he'll be back in harness again.
    Peter Alliss, BBC TV (1988)

You couldn't really find two more completely different personalities than these two—Tom Watson and Brian Barnes—one the complete golf professional, the other the complete professional golfer.
    Peter Alliss

I can't see, unless the weather changes, the conditions changing dramatically.
    Peter Alliss, BBC TV (1995)

This change of venue will give the Desert Classic golf tournament a much better chance of being as good as it always has.

Labron Harris (1979)

Describing the 1993 Oldsmobile Classic—There are European players here from all over the world.

Mary Bryan

Famous midsouth resorts include Pinehurst and Southern Pines, where it is said that there are more golf curses per square mile than anywhere else in the world.

North Carolina tourist brochure

Winners of the mixed gruesomes at the Strawberry Hill Golf Club were Mrs. M. Steward and N. Ince with 34 points.

Richmond Times *(London)*

He was advised by his local caddie to take a two-iron, settled instead for a tree, and smashed the ball 220 yards straight into the hole.

Bristol Evening Post

After winning a tournament—I'd like to thank all my parents.

Juli Inkster

If it wasn't for golf, I'd be a caddie today.

George Archer (1980)

The par here at Sunningdale is 70, and anything under that will mean a score in the 60s.

Steve Rider, BBC TV

Arnold Palmer, usually a great putter, seems to be having trouble with his long putts. However, he has no trouble dropping his shorts.

U.S. TV commentator

I don't want to beat a dead horse to death.

Lee Trevino

Nick Faldo this afternoon in all blue, with a white shirt.

Tony Adamson

Ninety percent of all putts which finish short of the hole don't go in.

Yogi Berra

If you can't make the putts and can't get the man in from second base in the bottom of the ninth, you're not going to win enough football games in this league, and that's the problem we had today.

Sam Rutigliano

Like a hole in one at golf, a maximum break in snooker can only ever be an aimed-for fluke.

John Spencer (1979)

This game is 80 percent mental, and if you can conquer it mentally, you've got it half licked.

Betty Richardson (1976)

This is the twelfth. The green is like a plateau with the top shaved off.

Renton Laidlaw

I'm not afraid of Jack Nicklaus. If you play better than him, you can beat him.
Tom Weiskopf

Matt Kuchar has the most incredible misdemeanor.
Fulton Allem (1998)

AND FINALLY . . .

May you live long enough to shoot your age.
Traditional English golfing toast

On Fame's triumphant wings his name shall soar
Till Time shall end, or Golfing be no more.
Thomas Mathison, The Goff *(1763)*

INDEX